Cartesian Philosophy and the Flesh

How do you know anything is true? What relation is there between my psyche and your psyche, does one exist? Can we doubt everything or are some things indubitable? What does Jung have to say about body and psyche, body and mind?

Cartesian Philosophy and the Flesh is an analysis and critique of interpretations of Cartesian philosophy in analytical psychology. It focuses on readings of Descartes that have important implications for understanding Jung, and analytical and existential psychology generally. Frances Gray's book raises questions about the 'place' of the body in a theory of the human psyche and about what kind of psyche, if any, is essential to concepts of human being. Gray claims that the debates around Descartes and metaphysical dualism have been oversimplified and that this has had a profound effect on conceptualizing an ongoing relation between psyche and body. The book also explores the relationship between Jung's conception of the phenomenological standpoint and that of Edmund Husserl and Maurice Merleau-Ponty.

Cartesian Philosophy and the Flesh brings together Descartes' idea of self-interrogation and self-reflection and Jung's project in *The Red Book*: the practice of spiritual exercises is the underpinning orientation of both men. It recommends similar practices to anyone interested in the truths of their own living. Gray's book will be of interest to Jung scholars, and those with an interest in Jungian studies, analytical psychologists and philosophers.

Frances Gray is a Philosopher, Mediator and Philosophical Counsellor. She is an Honorary Research Advisor in the School of History, Philosophy, Religion and Classics at the University of Queensland, Australia. She is the author of *Jung, Irigaray, Individuation: Philosophy, Analytical Psychology and the Question of the Feminine* (Routledge, 2008).

Cartesian Philosophy and the Flesh

Reflections on incarnation in analytical psychology

Frances Gray

Routledge
Taylor & Francis Group
LONDON AND NEW YORK

First published 2013
by Routledge
27 Church Road, Hove, East Sussex BN3 2FA

Simultaneously published in the USA and Canada
by Routledge
711 Third Avenue, New York, NY 10017

Routledge is an imprint of the Taylor & Francis Group, an informa business

British Library Cataloguing in Publication Data
A catalogue record for this book is available from the British Library

Library of Congress Cataloging in Publication Data
Gray, Frances, 1949–
Cartesian philosophy and the flesh : reflections on incarnation in analytical psychology / Frances Gray. — 1st dual edition.
pages cm
1. Jungian psychology. 2. Mind and body. 3. Descartes, René, 1596–1650. 4. Jung, C. G. (Carl Gustav), 1875–1961 I. Title.
BF173.J85G73 2013
150.19'54—dc23 2012032392

ISBN: 978–0–415–47936–3 (hbk)
ISBN: 978–0–415–47937–0 (pbk)
ISBN: 978–0–203–08012–2 (ebk)

Typeset in Garamond
by Swales & Willis Ltd, Exeter, Devon

Dedicated with loving appreciation to PC, TP, AGP and MGP

Contents

Preface

This book is a continuation of my interests in the philosophical foundations of C. G. Jung's analytical psychology. I am aware of the multifarious philosophical influences on Jung. However, my work here is quite limited in its scope since its main philosophical focus is the work of the seventeenth-century French thinker, René Descartes, and on the phenomenology of Edmund Husserl. As I read these two thinkers, I doubt that Jung has any direct and conscious intellectual debt to either philosopher. So this is a work of context and situation rather than one exploring immediate, acknowledged influence.

The title, *Cartesian Philosophy and the Flesh: Reflections on Incarnation in Analytical Psychology,* is not so much a reference to the traditions that have developed out of Descartes' philosophy, but to what Descartes himself said. I have deliberately centred my own scholarship on his extant works. And the analytical psychology to which I refer is that of C. G. Jung rather than what has grown out of his work. The notion of incarnation is not theological but rather reflects the complexity of Descartes' and Jung's conception of the human being as a wholeness that is mind and body; and Merleau-Ponty's notion of flesh, of corporeality and human being as consciousness in body.

I did not intend to write this book when I took study leave from the University of New England during 2008. At that stage, I was preparing a manuscript on mysticism, phenomenology and C. G. Jung. As happens from time to time with some authors, the book developed its own identity which I felt I needed to honour. That happened principally because I returned to Descartes' philosophy and began to read it from the perspective of what I think of as a wisdom tradition in philosophy. John Cottingham's work was my inspiration there. I also became aware of Roger Brooke's and Robert Romanyshyn's work of bringing together Jung and phenomenology. Having begun to read Descartes, as I was then doing, I was startled by their anxieties about his philosophy, anxieties that are present in the philosophical debates around Cartesian metaphysics in particular. In many ways, this book is a response to them, and to other detractors of Descartes whose work is represented in analytical psychology and elsewhere.

I would like to thank the University of New England and Cambridge University for their support that has enabled the writing of this book. I would also like to thank Tony Street, Peter Corrigan, Marguerite la Caze, Dominic Hyde, Michelle Boulous Walker and Lesley Gardner for their insight and helpful discussions with me about various topics in this book.

I would also like to thank Kate Hawes and Camilla Barnard at Routledge for their patience and support. Thank you, also, to Colin Morgan, Richard Willis and their staff at Swales & Willis Ltd for their most excellent editorial help.

Reflection

Here we are, an invisible presence in a small, snug place, quite isolated, observing. And here we have a man, quite alone, oblivious to our presence, sitting by the fire, in his winter dressing gown. It's an important detail that he is by the fire, wearing his winter dressing gown, and that he is alone. He needs solitude, and he seems to need comfort in that solitude. That tells us, or should alert us to the fact, that he has some minimal concern with his body. 'By the fire, in a winter dressing gown' suggests acknowledgement of the season, of coldness and its effect on him, of perhaps a need to be warm to think clearly, and to be undisturbed by physical perturbations. He is going to do something he has wanted to do for who knows how long: he has set himself up so that he can follow a train of thinking, undisturbed, a train of thinking that he hopes will reveal some truth to him. 'Truth' is important to our man: he says (for he speaks out loud from time to time, muttering to himself) that he has been struck by the number of falsehoods that he accepted as true in his childhood, that he has based a whole edifice on them, and that he needs to start again, from the foundations, to produce some enduring knowledge. He tells himself that he has to demolish everything: strong language that. 'Demolish everything' and he confesses to himself that this is a huge enterprise. We know it is, too, and we wonder, perhaps with a smirk on our faces, if what he is proposing is possible. We know, don't we, that we are all products of our pasts, of our histories in the social world as women and men, and we are not going to be seduced by the possibility that we can stand aside from those pasts, from those histories. Our man is kidding himself if he thinks that he can demolish everything. But, no, he can see that for himself. For now he pauses in his thinking: demolish everything? No, that is not possible, he concludes, it will be sufficient for him to find some reason to doubt the uncertain and indubitable together with the patently false.

'Where will he start?' we wonder. The answer comes quickly. And we are shocked: isn't he now saying that he will begin with the senses, for what he has held to be true has come to him through his sense and yet his senses have sometimes deceived him? Come on, we urge, you're a fool: begin with the senses? Firstly you say you're going to doubt everything, then you modify that as you realise you can't, and now you're going to doubt your senses because you've made mistakes in the past because of your senses?

Your senses, we muse. What is it about the senses that is so compelling to pick on? Ah, yes, he's saying that they're unreliable. And he's making a division between his mind and his body? Well, maybe we all do that, make a division between our minds and our bodies. Is this simply an intellectual exercise for him? Is he experiencing this, or thinking this, a cognitive apprehension?

We wonder . . .

Descartes is credited with being the father of modern psychology. To Descartes can be traced the initiation of the major concepts which have framed psychological thinking during the last three hundred years. He advanced the notion, later to be substantiated by the neuroanatomists and the neurophysiologists, that the brain is the organ of the mind. He projected the pattern of the basic mechanism in neurophysiology – that of the reflex action. The greater portion of the energies of the neurologists and physiologists, ever since the time of Descartes, have been devoted to the elaboration of both these notions and to the revelations of their structural and functional equivalents. He, to a no lesser degree, shaped and affected the thought of the following centuries in what is called philosophical psychology.

(Galdston 1944: 125–126)

He who does not doubt does not bear himself. Such a one is doubtful; he does not grow and hence he does not live. Doubt is the sign of the strongest and the weakest. The strong have doubt, but doubt has the weak. Therefore the weakest is close to the strongest, and if he can say to his doubt, 'I have you,' then he is the strongest. But no one can say yes to his doubt, unless he endures wide-open chaos. Because there are so many among us who can talk about anything, pay heed to what they live. What someone says can be very much or very little. Thus examine his life.

(Jung 2009: 301)

Introduction

Reading analytical psychology philosophically

> I can hardly draw a veil over the fact that we psychotherapists ought really to be philosophers or philosophic doctors – or rather we already are so, though we are unwilling to admit it because of the glaring contrast between our work and what passes for philosophy in universities
>
> (Jung 1954: 181)

> L'honnête homme n'a pas besoin d'avoir lu tous les livres, ni d'avoir appris soigneusement tout ce qu'on enseigne dans les écoles . . . Mais il vient ignorant dans le monde, et comme les connoissances de ses premières années ne reposent que sur la foiblesse des sens ou l'autorité des maîtres, il peut à peine se faire que son imagination ne soit remplie d'un nombre infini d'idées fausses, avant que sa raison ait pu prendre l'empire sur elle; en sorte que par la suite il a besoin d'un bon naturel ou des leçons fréquentes d'un homme sage, tant pour secouer les fausses doctrines dont son esprit est prévenu, que pour jeter les premiers fondements d'une science solide, et découvrir tous les moyens par lesquels il peut porter ses connoissances au plus haut point qu'elles puissent atteindre.
>
> (Descartes 1701)

It is generally acknowledged that Descartes has had a profound influence on the development of modern thinking since the Enlightenment. Some of that acknowledgement includes scathing analyses of his metaphysical dispositions towards dualism and the difficulties that ensue, especially in relation to his concept of the relation between body and mind, his notion of material body, and his arguments for the existence of God. Some acknowledgement points towards the intellectual gratitude we need feel towards the man who transformed, in many ways, philosophical method and its relation to modern science and mathematics. Either way, Descartes' work is astonishing in its breadth, and in its capacity to engender debate, and deep thought. His influence is not confined to philosophy alone, however, as is also well known.

Yet that the importance of Descartes' philosophy to Jung's analytical psychology is underestimated is a principal claim which I spell out in some detail in the pages of this book. I argue that readings of Descartes' work that we can find in various post-Jungian commentaries do not take into account recent scholarship and that those readings fail to do justice to the treasures that are there for unearthing in Descartes. I argue that the impact of Descartes' philosophy has not been all negative, and that, indeed, the development of phenomenology as method owes much to Descartes' own understanding of his novel philosophical method.

Roger Brooke's 1991 reading of the relationship between Jung and phenomenology was a landmark in Jungian scholarship. Brooke took on the task of showing that Jung's analytical psychology could be reframed within the phenomenological tradition, especially from the perspective of Maurice Merleau-Ponty and from the perspective of Martin Heidegger's existential psychology. In the process, Brooke identified a number of philosophical views that he felt had influenced both Edmund Husserl and Jung; in particular, what he seems to have seen as an incipient Cartesianism that is in evidence in their work. Brooke's sympathies are not Cartesian, so he rejects, in particular, aspects of Jung's work that demonstrate that incipience. And he re-reads Jung in what he considers to be a more enlightened way.

In this book, I explore some of Brooke's arguments, and those of Robert Romanyshyn, which read Descartes and phenomenology in what I think of as fairly orthodox, and negative, ways. I re-read those arguments in the light of recent Cartesian scholarship. I suggest that we need to take cognisance of this scholarship in our assessment of Jung's work. I propose that, far from rejecting Descartes outright, Husserl and Merleau-Ponty are open about their intellectual debt to him. In view of this, I reassess Brooke's and Romanyshyn's readings of both Jung and phenomenology.

I argue to the conclusion that Jung's apparent Cartesian assumptions can be positively read within a revised phenomenological framework. In order to do this work, I read philosophically, and I need you, the reader, to do the same thing. What does it mean to read philosophically? This is an important question to ask at the beginning of this book. As I understand it, to read philosophically, we need to be prepared to read carefully, to dismantle ideas and their assumptions, to exercise patience and charity and to be open to the text that unravels itself before our eyes, and to put into suspension or to parenthesise some of our own assumptions as we need. This requires the practice of patience. Michelle Boulous Walker talks about reading philosophy as 'the patient work of thought' and of 'sitting with' the world and of taking time to so read (Walker 2011: 265). I take, and I ask you to take, this seriously, even though you may not be a philosopher.

For me, however, this is an important question because I am a philosopher, and, unlike Sigmund Freud, Jung has not held much sway in philosophical thinking, for example in postmodernism and in feminist theory, as I have argued elsewhere (Gray 2008). As an aside, Jung's presence in the academy, his predominance or absence, does not matter so much in itself; it seems a bit ingenuous to read or not read someone because they are popular or influential.

Of course *why* they are popular or influential, or not so, might count as a reason for reading or not reading them. Perhaps their ideas are compelling, new, different or apt for a moment in the history of philosophy; or racist, sexist, elitist and thus outmoded. In either case, one might assume that reading a particular text or set of texts is worthwhile.

The former is just what I assume about Jung's texts. And because I am a philosopher, I read him philosophically in the sense just indicated. That means, not that I read Jung *as if* he were a philosopher, because he was not, and he made that very plain; nor do I read Jung because of his use of sophisticated and nuanced use of philosophical language, because that is mostly absent from his work. However, Jung did use philosophical concepts and ideas that bear remarking upon; he did think philosophically because he thought about existential meaning and about metaphysics: being human, reality, life and death, symbolism. And he very often framed his thinking within the philosophical tradition. We find him, for example, using or referring to Plato (Jung 1968, 1971), Aristotle (Jung 1954), Origen, Abelard, Kant and Schiller (Jung 1971). That by no means represents all of his deployment of the philosophical tradition, but in these few references, there is enough to show the scope of his reading and scholarship.

So here we have three dimensions of Jung's work that are interesting from a philosophical perspective:

1. thinking philosophically
2. use of philosophical concepts and ideas
3. philosophical context and tradition.

Similar points may be made about almost any other academic tradition and disciplinary approaches to almost any field. Considering these three orientations of Jung's work, there is material ripe for philosophical investigation, critique and comment. When I say that Jung thought philosophically, in that he asked questions and thought about existential meanings and metaphysics, I would also make the point that he makes many philosophical assumptions that are worth uncovering and exploring. In this book, I deal with some of those assumptions by exploring his place in the philosophical tradition handed to us from René Descartes. And I do this as a philosopher.

In this book, I defend the inner/outer trope as an important existential orientation towards the world. I also examine in detail the concept of dualism. As a preliminary, l ask you to think along with me, very broadly, about distinctions and why we might make them.

The distinction, a preliminary

Consider a world where no distinctions are made, where everything that is encountered is seen through the same cognitive eyes, the same perceptual framework, the same psychological, moral and aesthetic orientations, where the same glumpy boundaries are attributed to everything. In such a world, it is imaginable that none of us would know where we begin or end: I would not know if I were thinking this thought and writing this book, or if you were. Indeed, there would be no distinction between you and me, or any distinction *possible* between you and me. Given the nature of this imaginary situation, the fine tuning done by the mind and reason, the subtlety of our tastes and the nuanced way we engage with ourselves and others and with the world generally, would be absent. Thus if we could not or did not make any distinctions, there would no way of determining what is good and bad: everything would go along in its glumpiness: without restraint, people could kill and eat people, could masturbate in public, have sex with whomever, wherever and whenever they wanted regardless of consent considerations, kill their families, wear what they like, eat what they like, live where and how they like, say what they like, in general, *do anything* that they liked. One wonders if there would be people at all: what would societies look like? How would they function? One wonders if such a world could ever be productive, encouraging of life and growth. My hunch is that such a world would implode: it would be the rule of chaos, the rule of amorality, the rule of death and destruction.

The obvious point that I am making here is that we need to make distinctions in order to survive as individuals and as groups. Not only do we *need* to do that, though, our psychological and mental makeup is such that this is what we do, as human beings. There is both a genetic and a social component involved in our making of distinctions (we sense danger, our hearts race, we take off in the fight or flight response) so that we are disposed to behave in discriminating ways as we encounter our worlds. That said, it is obvious that the making of distinctions, the use of our discriminatory powers, is old, very old, beyond that fight or flight instinct, as any quick look at the remainders of ancient civilisations will show. Groups survived as cultures because they built and manufactured places to live and tools to use, because they became aware of the importance of clean water sources, because they developed trade routes and complex belief systems and recorded what they knew for their generations to come. The making of distinctions, then, is not simply a matter of choice, but of survival. From a theoretical perspective in the Western intellectual tradition, different ways of conceiving the fundamental matter of being and moral codes were developed and contested, as was also the case in the East where sophisticated systems of thinking produced metaphysical and ethical orientations towards the world.[1]

As we have developed into newer, and differently complex forms of life and culture, our thinking and explorations have grown beyond immersion in a world where we have little control and where we remain enclosed within a maternal matrix (Bordo 1986: 38). Now, for better or worse, we have the technology, beyond the hearth, so to speak, that can make us warm on cold days, the technology to make us cool on hot days, the technology to fly from one side of the world to the other in a matter of hours, find out the genetic structure of life, cure diseases, change our gender profile virtually or in fact, and get information from deep space using the latest technology. These technological developments are based in choices we have made around our figuring out how things work, and then utilising what we have discovered to improve how we live.

You may be wondering why I am telling you what you probably already know. Well, the reason is this. As I see it, some academic commentators and theorists have focused not so much on *not* making distinctions *at all*, but on making distinctions of a certain kind (Plumwood 1993: 47). Overwhelmed by the weight of history and ideology that highlights rampant racism, sexism, slavery, colonialism and Western ideological expansionism, commentators have argued that specific sets of distinctions, namely those expressed in terms of dualistic structuring, have permeated Western thinking to the detriment of humanity, and to nature (Plumwood 1993; Abram 1996; Shusterman 2008). And a common complaint about both René Descartes and Carl Jung is that they share in the dualistic traditions of European thought, and carry with them the prejudices embedded in those dualisms. Further, some analytical psychologists in the tradition of Jung have assumed that there is a link between the way in which Descartes mobilises dualism and Jung's conception of mind and psyche, linking Descartes and Jung as if they are rather naughty distant relatives in cahoots with one another (Brooke 2000; Mook 2000; Romanyshyn 2000). This is without considered and reflective analysis of Descartes' work, and without placing Descartes, and subsequently Jung, within the philosophical milieux in which they were writing, or, and this may be more important, attending to more than quotes and arguments taken out of context. That dualism is bad, bad, bad, seems to have developed as recent orthodoxy, one that has dominated much social ontology and epistemology at the end of the twentieth century. Yet there are various ways in which dualism can be construed, there is scholarship rereading Descartes, and there are reasons to have an open mind about what dualism entails that may give us pause to consider just what all the commotion is about.

It is not my job here to settle the arguments about dualism. Whether we are talking about dualistic structuring (an aspect of which is 'value dualism', as we shall see), that is to say the relationship between paired terms where one of the terms is considered superior to the other, or about the nature of the mind (metaphysical dualism) – is the mind material or non-material? – is not the principal concern of my book. The vast literature on the mind–body problem, for example, is testament to the complexity and the seriousness of the issues surrounding dualism. Eliminating the mind as a non-material object or aspect of a human being does not result in value-free enquiry, even though some would argue that it does. I raise it as an example of some philosophers' apparent commitment to value-free enquiry. As Deborah Brown points out, 'attempts to ground the mind or self in the objective, publicly observable properties of the body or behaviour have not proved terribly successful either' (Brown 2006: 3).

In Chapter 3, I examine how dualism has been characterised, and trace the elements of what I see as some of the most important arguments around the topic. Let me say that my examination is rather truncated and deliberately so, since the range and impact of the debates around dualism require judiciousness in selecting material that is pertinent to the themes of this book. An important context of my discussion of dualism is that I argue for recognition of philosophy as spiritual practice. By extension, I claim that this is fundamental to phenomenology and to some interpretations of analytical psychology. Here is part of that context.

Meditation, philosophy and wisdom

> By the time of the Platonic dialogues, Socrates was called *atopos*, that is, 'unclassifiable.' What makes him *atopos* is precisely the fact that he is a 'philo-sopher' in the etymological sense of the word; that is, he is in love with wisdom. For wisdom, says Diotima in Plato's *Symposium*, is not a human state, it is a state of perfection of being and knowledge that can only be divine. It is the love of wisdom, which is foreign to the world, that makes a philosopher a stranger in it.
>
> (Hadot 1995: 57)

Pierre Hadot argues that '(e)veryone is free to define philosophy as he likes, to choose whatever philosophy he wishes, or to invent – if he can – whatever philosophy he may think valid'. Descartes and Spinoza still remain faithful to the ancient definition: for them, philosophy was 'the practice of wisdom' (Hadot 1995: 272). Throughout this book, I accept this assessment by Hadot of Descartes' philosophy as the practice of wisdom. I argue that, for Descartes, one of the fundamental aspects of the practice of wisdom is the use of meditation such as we find it in his *Meditations*. I compare Descartes' method as meditation with some of the meditational practices that are recommended in Buddhist scriptures, and in the yoga sutras. I pay particular attention to *vipassana* and to hatha yoga. I also explore the relation between meditation and scholarly work in terms of therapeutic practice. I note now that Hadot's view that philosophers are strangers in the world exemplifies the insight that the love of wisdom remains as foreign today as it ever has been.

Central to this discussion is the senses, their place in developing truth as insight to the nature of reality, and the knowledge that might come from this development. I argue that Descartes' search for indubitable truths cannot happen without the senses, a position he gestures towards in *Meditation VI* and in the *Passions of the Soul*. I argue that the *vipassana* focus on the senses enters territory which was not possible for Descartes because of his theological commitments and the limitations of transcendental subjectivity.

Descartes argues that the senses have deceived him and that you cannot trust what has deceived you at least once. According to Descartes, there are 'three kinds of primitive ideas or notions, each of which is known in its own proper manner and not by comparison with any of the others: the notions we have of the soul, of body and of the union between the soul and the body'. Knowledge of the union of body and soul is governed by the senses rather than by the intellect (Descartes 1991: 226, 227). Certainty, in his view, cannot come from the senses, but from the intellect and from thought alone. Certainty and knowledge are matters of intellection; but at the same time, Descartes also argues that the:

> use of my senses had come first, while the use of my reason came only later; and I saw that the ideas which I formed myself were less vivid than those which I perceived with the senses and were, for the most part, made up of elements of sensory ideas. In this way, I convinced myself that I had nothing at all in the intellect which I had not previously had in sensation.
> (Descartes 1984: 52)

Descartes asserts here that he once held that anything that comes before the mind has its origins in sensation, and he comes to doubt that because he has been deceived by his senses. So the body, in its sensation, he held, is the *a priori* condition of his thinking. Descartes later reaffirms the critical role the body plays in his being human.

As a contrast, in the Buddhist practice of *vipassana*, thinking is discouraged and one is asked to focus on sensations in the body. Truth will be realised by focusing on sensations and not on thinking. Descartes focuses on thinking to realise truth. So, in Descartes' case, the focus is on thinking; and in the case of *vipassana* or insight meditation, the focus is on sensation. Ultimately, however, in *vipassana* one also notices that sensations rise and fall away. There is intellection required here as one realises impermanence, the insertion of self-reflective awareness. In both thinking and sensing, the subject is engaged, and bracketing or suspension of previous beliefs and opinions paves the way for insight and illumination, and the basis of indubitable belief in the case of Descartes. This is what matters. This is why this phenomenological account, that takes into consideration different meditational traditions, is highly instructive, and it is part of what informs my discussions in this book.

Phenomenological dimensions

In his *Second Meditation*, René Descartes raises and responds to these now, surely infamous, questions:

> But what shall I now say that I am when supposing that there is some supremely powerful and, if it is permissible to say so, malicious deceiver who is deliberately trying to trick me in every way he can? Can I now assert that I possess even the most insignificant of all the attributes which I have

> said belong to the nature of a body? I scrutinize them, think about them, go over them again, but nothing suggests itself . . . But what about the attributes I assigned to the soul? Nutrition or movement? Since now I do not have a body, these are mere fabrications. Sense-perceptions? This surely does not occur without a body, and besides, when asleep, I have appeared to perceive through the sense many things which I afterwards realized I did not perceive through the senses at all. Thinking? At last I have discovered it – thought; this alone is inseparable from me. I am, I exist – that is certain. *But for how long? For as long as I am thinking. For it could be that were I totally to cease from thinking, I should totally cease to exist.*
>
> (Descartes 1984: 18; my italics)

We might note that for Descartes it is not sufficient that I think, *simpliciter*: I have to be *aware* of my thinking. For it is not clear that the temporal condition implied by 'totally' entails permanence. That is to say, perhaps Descartes is entertaining the possibility that he might stop thinking for a short period and that that would amount to total cessation of thought, but that he might then recover himself and begin thinking once more. And indeed in the text that follows this is evidence that that might be the case, because he speaks of sleeping and not thinking when he is asleep. So that is what I am interested in here. If Descartes' thinking is his essence, then is it possible to continue to exist, even momentarily, without one's essence and what would such an existence amount to?

Descartes' list of what counts as thought is also found in *Meditation II*. 'But what am I then? A thing that thinks. What is that? A thing that doubts, understands, affirms, denies, is willing, is unwilling, and also imagines and has sensory perceptions' (Descartes 1984: 19). In this book I conclude that other ways of looking at the mind and consciousness suggest that the end of thinking is not the end of mind, but instead, that the end of thinking as a deliberate act of will opens up the possibility of a different phenomenological presentation of oneself to oneself.

Thus my interest in this text is not, as is often the case, in the malicious deceiver. Rather, I am drawn by the phenomenological aspects of the italicised text, what I call Descartes' subjective temporality of existence proposal: that I exist only so long as I am thinking and that it *could be* that if I totally cease from thinking then I should totally cease to exist. The modal nature of the latter leaves open the possibility that I may *not* cease to exist if I were to cease thinking. And that is what I am going to explore in this section, the idea that I might exist even when I am not thinking.

God ends up guaranteeing Descartes' existence, but this is not a phenomenologically based experience of the Divine, rather it is an article of faith. Reason always lingers in the background or strongly makes its presence felt throughout Descartes' work. The same is the case for the phenomenologists we encounter, as it is for Jung. We should not underestimate either the power or the importance of reason; we need it as a guiding hand to preserve our integrity and our sense of being in the world. My book in a sense is also a plea for reason.

I argue that Descartes' notion of mind as a substance, the principal attribute of which is thought, and which is, therefore, non-material, is incomplete as an account of the human *psyche*. Yet his conception of human *being* is clearly in excess of the incompleteness of his mind hypothesis. I argue that the human *body* is the *a priori* condition for the possibility of any certainty, that the senses provide the evidence of the latter claim, and that the subjective temporality of existence proposal, in its incompleteness, falls short of accounting for imagination and sensation. Finally I propose a way of understanding the relation between flesh, corporeal experience, intersubjectivity and transcendental subjectivity which does, nonetheless, depend on a Cartesian-like mind.

Reading phenomenology

In his discussion of idealism in Husserl's phenomenology, Dan Zahavi remarks:

> [l]et me at the outset confess that I don't think it is really possible to propose an interpretation that accords with everything Husserl had to say on the topic . . . he at various times defended different views on the matter . . . my interpretation does justice to core components of his proposal.
>
> (Zahavi 2010: 285–286)

Echoing Zahavi, I acknowledge both the vastness (and, in my case, the difficulty of coming to terms with) Husserl's work. I hope to do justice to what I see as some fundamentals in Husserl's phenomenology. That means I need to work across several texts but, since this is not a book about Husserl, I limit my comments to the concerns of this book.

I shall be working through the details of some arguments around Descartes' philosophy and Jung's analytical psychology more carefully in Chapter 1. I use that work to bring into focus one of the key categories of Jungian thought, the imagination. Further, its connection to the body and the senses means that the imagination, the body and its senses form a triad that situates and contextualises the body in the world, and the world in the body. If we can give an account of these, then we can establish a case for treating Descartes sympathetically as we read Jung. For Descartes, imagination and wonder are central to his philosophy; the imaginative play of phantasy is important to Husserl, and I connect with this importance as I develop a way of reading Jung that returns to the subtleties of Descartes' thought.

In figuring out Jung's approach to onto-epistemology, I develop what I think of as his Fog Argument in terms of direct knowledge of the psyche. I propose that his conceptualisation of mind and body depends on a notion of the imagination which we can glean from Descartes' Real Distinction argument. In support of the arguments of Descartes' *Meditations* I shall also draw on the arguments of his final treatise, *Passions of the Soul*, which looks much more closely at the question of the senses and the imagination. If it is the case that that Descartes' argument in *Meditations* is making an epistemological rather than an ontological point, as I believe it is, then the importance of the imagination as corporeally locatable comes to the fore.

In turn, the elements of this argument rely on the notion of the intentionality or directedness of the mind which is central to phenomenology. Indeed, the role of metaphor, imagination and intentionality in phenomenology, such as we find in Brooke (2000), can be seen as a kind of bridge between Descartes and Jung. This will be the topic of discussion in Chapters 4 and 5, where I examine the phenomenology of Husserl, Merleau-Ponty and Heidegger and their relationship to Descartes before exploring the further relationship between Jung and phenomenology. The body and corporeal experience are the focus of this exploration, a point I initially make in my discussion of spiritual practice.

Descartes argues that material bodies have a principal property, extension, and that the mind has a principal property, thinking. He argues that one cannot attribute thought to material bodies and that one cannot attribute extension to the mind. Thus there is a real distinction between the two substances and their properties which I deploy in my examination of dualism. He allows, however, that the two substances can causally interact, or at least influence each other. This raises issues about their integrity as substances because if they are causally connected, then they must have something in common.

In the *Sixth Meditation*, Descartes argues that the human being is a third kind of substance and this brings together the mind and the body.

He is right about thoughts not having extension: we cannot say what size and shape thoughts are, and we can even only vaguely locate them. Even if we had the technology that could map brain processes, there is no way of telling what particular thought (say of a spotted dog) is going on in someone's head: we would have to ask the person to identify the content of the thought. That means that from a phenomenological perspective, first-person accounts are primary.

For now, let me say that we shall look more closely at the body and mind problem in Chapter 2. As Susan Blackmore remarks, the debates in philosophy about Cartesian and other forms of dualism have been, and remain, long and vigorous. This is the case even in non-religious cultures (Blackmore 2005: 3). If the mind and body are separate, then what does that mean? Separate what? They seem to influence each other, but does the mind influence the body or the body influence the mind? What kind of account can we give of 'influence'? Would we say that the body causes the mind or that the mind causes the body? Do the mind and body interact or are they separate parallel systems? Are the body and mind the very same thing experienced under different guises? What very same thing are they: material or non-material? How can we know this? Can we have direct experience of the body and of the world and what would that amount to? Is that an epistemological or an ontological question? Many of these questions are germane to analytical as well as other sorts of psychology and I shall be exploring those that I think are central to this book.

In Chapters 6 and 7, I explore focus on the body in both 'Western' and 'Eastern' thinking: in Western philosophy, and in hatha yoga, and *vipassana* or direct-insight meditation. In the case of the latter, I argue that these practices are spiritual practices in the sense articulated by Hadot and that they exemplify 'spiritual exercise' in a similar way to Descartes' *Meditations*. I also argue that, as is the case with *Meditations*, both yoga and *vipassana* are predicated, ultimately, on a phenomenological reduction, as articulated by Husserl. Lastly, I argue that one of the fundaments of Jung's conception of individuation is as spiritual exercise.

An approach to the mind/body distinction such as we find in Rozemond's reading of Descartes is extremely helpful here, where the imagination is central to the notion of 'spiritual exercise'. All of these thinkers and their ideas come together in a refiguring of the body as a lived body and as, to use Merleau-Ponty's later term, flesh. My final chapter examines how a reading of flesh is consistent with Descartes' notion of the body as a machine, and with Jung's, and phenomenological, accounts of human being as phenomenological, autonomous being. And for this, paradoxically, we need a robust notion of dualism and of the interior/exterior trope.

I am not a German speaker or reader. Throughout this book, I rely on the English translations in Jung's *Collected Works*. Sonu Shamdasani is very critical of these translations, as we see in his work on the identity of Jung (Shamdasani 2005). In my view, it would be also so much better to see a presentation of Jung's work in chronological order. That is not the case. I feel a sense of frustration at both my language ignorance and at my reliance on translation that does not pick up philosophical subtlety or innuendo.

In his introduction to *The Red Book,* Shamdasani remarks that there are three stylistic registers in the *Red Book.* 'One of them faithfully reports the fantasies and inner dialogues of Jung's imaginal encounters, while a second remains firmly and disconcertingly conceptual. Still a third writes in a mantic and prophetic, or Romantic and dithyrambic style' (Jung 2009: 222). From the perspective of the argument in this book, Shamdasani's remark casts some light on the possibilities of the psyche to display and to fashion itself. It shows the psyche's capacity to move about within itself, to reflect both its immanent obedience to itself and to its transcendent propensities.

The psyche, as our human psyche, an enfleshed personal psyche echoes in Merleau-Ponty's notion of flesh as elemental. While we might be able to think ourselves dualistically, the conceptually informed activities of our minds do not necessarily reflect the basic fact of our fleshiness that he so beautifully captures. We might see Jung's work as well as Descartes' and Jung's as attempts to understand this complexity that is human being, and beyond. Indeed, the prospect of posthuman being is entertained in my final chapter.

So let us see how we get there, to that prospect.

Chapter 1

Analytical psychologists read the philosophy of René Descartes

René Descartes' radical interrogation of his fundamental assumptions that we find in his 1641 work, *Meditations on First Philosophy*, is well known for its controversial arguments about the *cogito* and the distinction between body and mind. Descartes' arguments, which also include the ontological argument (for the existence of God) and an argument for the existence of material bodies, have been the subject of intense philosophical debate that continues to this day.

We find the *cogito* and the beginnings of the mind and body distinction arguments highlighted in *Meditation II*, on which much debate has centred. The *cogito* involved his concluding that his thinking is his essence. This more than controversial claim has captured the anglophone philosophical imagination for three and a half centuries. If his thinking is his essence, then without thinking, Descartes cannot exist. And if we extrapolate that to ourselves, for surely this is a kind of phenomenological insight that Descartes has had, will we too, conclude that our thinking is our essence? What, then, is the status of Descartes' body and also of my body? Isn't it the case that I cannot exist without my body? After all, my body goes with me wherever I go; it's there when I wake up in the morning, when I go to sleep at night; am I not, in some sense, my body? These are obvious rejoinders to Descartes. Yet there is also a sense in which my thinking, of which I am conscious, *is* me. My thinking, and more generally, my conscious life, and the life of my psyche do indeed make me into who, and what, I am. Without my very own consciousness that delivers to me awareness of my bodily sensations, an awareness of my body itself located in space and time, and that brings the world to me in awareness and me to the world, I would surely be no more than a rock or a drop of rain. My corporeal sentience, and my consciousness, co-operate in producing me.

Further, I seem also to have a life of the psyche that is not exactly conscious: I dream, I say things I didn't intend to say, I create images and phantasies from who knows where. Is this merely my memory at work, or is there an unconscious domain that is an aspect of myself? In any case, my memory is not always before me: I raise things up from my memory, I forget, I remember that in a right-angled triangle, the square on the hypotenuse is equal to the sum of the square of the other two sides; I recall my youth; and when my children were born and what their tiny mouths looked like when they said 'moon' as I pointed it out to them in the night sky; my memory functions as an aid to my conscious life, and gives to me a sense of personal history, the history of others, a living, chronology with past, present and future.

Debates about the mind and body and their constitutive role in human identity focus on the nature of the mind and of the body and their relation to each other. In the case of Descartes, the debates can resolve into issues around the notion of there being two distinct substances: material body substance, the principal attribute of which is extension, and thinking substance. Descartes does not give a principal attribute to thinking substance, although we do know he believed it to be unextended.

It is not until Franz Brentano, in the nineteenth century, highlighted the Aristotelian-inspired Scholastic notion of the intentional inexistence of mental objects, that the mental – and here I mean this, quite deliberately to cover all manifestations of psychic being – came to be identified as having specific, unique properties. This idea, which we now conceive of as intentionality, finds a home in the development of phenomenology, as we shall see later on in this book. For the moment, I invoke Hegel's use of the term phenomenology as 'the science of knowing in the sphere of appearances' (Hegel 1977: 493). Adapting his conception, I use the term 'phenomenology' to refer to various theories that give primary attention to the conscious phenomena of which we are aware in our everyday lives. While I conceive of phenomenology as principally having arisen from the work of Edmund Husserl and his predecessors who focused on the activities and functions of mind and consciousness (for example, Descartes, Hume, Kant and Hegel), I acknowledge its more extensive use external to philosophical debates, for example in psychology. I discuss the idea more fully in concert with the discussion of intentionality. So let us begin with Descartes.

Descartes' views on mind and body and their relationship are very clearly articulated in *Meditations.* Outside the philosophical community what is less well realised, or at least not acknowledged sufficiently, is that when Descartes published *Meditations on First Philosophy*, he also published, in the very same volume, a set of six *Objections* sourced from leading philosophers and theologians of his day, and his own *Replies*.[1] This was followed by the publication in 1642 of a further set of *Objections* (making seven sets of *Objections* in all) plus a *Letter to Dinet* (1642). Descartes had already published *Rules for the Direction of the Mind (Regulae ad Directionem Ingenii)* in 1628, and *Discourse on the Method*,[2] *Optics*, *Meteorology* and *Geometry* in 1637. The *Meditations* were followed by *Principles of Philosophy* (1644), *Comments on a Certain Broadsheet* (1647) and *The Passions of the Soul* (1649). The dialogue *The Search for Truth* (date uncertain) was published after Descartes' death.

Many of the issues raised across the *Meditations* are also explored, elaborated and given context in these other works, where we also see progression and change in Descartes' thought (Machamer and McGuire 2009). The *Objections* and *Replies* to the *Meditations* pose questions to Descartes, followed by his responses. He variously takes the questions seriously, ignores some, fudges his responses to others, and generally defends and explains the positions he arrives at in the *Meditations.*

So why would this matter to any scholar other than someone who is an expert in Descartes' philosophy? Why do we find these comments at the beginning of a work on C. G. Jung and analytical psychology when he was not a philosopher, and as we know, psychology is psychology, not philosophy? Well, one reason is that if you are going to use someone's work as the scholarly basis of your own, you will undoubtedly want to check your sources, check what it is that the writer says, at least as far as it is possible to do so.

As I noted in my introduction, there are translation difficulties that present some enormous challenges to us all when we do not read in the language in which the relevant texts have been written. But there are other issues to consider as well. Intellectual rigour is something we need to demand of ourselves, so far as it is humanly possible, if we are to be reputable researchers and scholars. Those of us who are teachers advise our students to go to original sources rather than using secondary literature, to keep up with current thinking, and to be as thorough as they can be in their reading of important works; and rightly so. In other words, it is good scholarly practice. Getting an overview of someone's work is sometimes possible and, at others, not so possible. Theorists who are very productive and live a long life, for example, can change their minds, developing positions that are inconsistent with each other. A central problem that grips someone's imagination throughout that person's lifetime can be differently approached and differently conceived, resulting in quite different solutions that may even then be viewed as provisional.

What Descartes actually said across the whole range of his *oeuvre*, why he said it and how he came to have a particular view is one thing. Then the modifications of, and changes to, his views indicate the thoughtfulness and agility of his intellect, and suggest to his readers that a comprehensive overview is desirable. How he is interpreted and presented is another. Obviously the two are related. In a rigorous presentation of his views, evidence for those views needs to come from his own writings rather than from secondary sources, so that there is, as much as possible, some agreement between the work and its interpretation.

Descartes' arguments are often difficult to follow; and he uses a vocabulary with which many of us are no longer familiar, the language of Scholastic philosophy. Such textual correspondence and teasing-out of the fabric of his language result in a more robust and grounded presentation and interpretation. If particular arguments extend beyond specific works and into others, and if they are, even, in the same work but in different places in that work, we need to recognise this in our own work.

And within this context, we need also to be aware that philosophy is a cantankerous discipline. There are many interpretations proposed by many different philosophers with respect to a specific philosopher and his/her work (apart from Descartes, we can think of, for example, Plato and Aristotle, and David Hume and Immanuel Kant and Franz Brentano and Maurice Merleau-Ponty and Martin Heidegger, Simone de Beauvoir, Luce Irigaray and Martha Nussbaum, among others). There is often limited agreement over the same philosopher or philosophical concept. Some of this has to do with a philosopher's intellectual development and abandoned views, some has to do with inconsistencies, some has to do with revision of previously held views or to do with a change of mind about an issue. Some has to do with limited attention to the primary works, their complexity, and the evolution of thinking exhibited by a specific philosopher or philosophical notion.

Not only do we need to check for correspondence between our views and our sources, and for the scholarly scope of specific arguments, their context and place in a thinker's work, we need also to think about the validity of 'accepted' or 'orthodox' interpretations of the primary texts or basic sources. If we check our sources and read 'accepted' interpretations against those sources, we may decide that 'accepted' interpretations are lacking. It is quite likely that a lack of this kind will devalue the work that we ourselves are doing.

So let us imagine that we are, for example, attempting to construct some position or other that Jung might or might not have held (which is perhaps, itself, an 'accepted' position). A good example here is the idea that we have minds that are internal to us, and that there is a world outside our minds. Now we might invoke an 'orthodox' interpretation of Descartes to help us in that work of construction. An interpretation that does not refer directly to his writing, nor place Descartes in his philosophical context, will, inevitably, lead to an interpretation of Jung that, in principle, could be seen as quite misguided. I am not arguing that one should *never* use secondary sources. Far from it. I am merely saying that there are different uses and abuses of ideas, and that it is very useful, and desirable, to check them out before proceeding with detailed critique and commentary. As we proceed, we identify further instances of what I am talking about here.

We begin this chapter by mentioning, very briefly, Descartes' intellectual development, a detailed account of which is found in Stephen Gaukroger's scholarly and insightful biographical study of Descartes that is instructive for us all.

Gaukroger remarks that:

> The neglect of philosophers' intellectual development in Anglophone philosophy is peculiarly selective: no one would run together early and late Plato, and most would distinguish early and late Aristotle after the pioneering work of Jaeger; and no one would run together early and late Wittgenstein or even early or late Russell. But in the case of seventeenth- and eighteenth-century philosophy, very little care is taken to understand the development of and changes in doctrine in the work of individual

> philosophers. Commentators on Descartes in the twentieth century, especially (but by no means exclusively) in Anglophone philosophy, have not taken much notice of Descartes' intellectual development, assuming that *Discours de la méthode* (1637), the *Meditationes* (1641) and the *Passions de l'âme* (1649) somehow capture and sum up the whole of his thought . . . this homogenization of his thought has resulted in many misconceptions about what Descartes was trying to achieve and why he employed the means he did, as well as in a neglect of significant changes in his doctrines.
>
> (Gaukroger 1995: 11)

Gaukroger goes on to list three instances where Descartes' doctrines are mischaracterised because Descartes' earlier material is read through his later material. He argues that Descartes' scepticism, his physical doctrines and Descartes' conception of natural philosophy and its attendant mechanism theory are so construed as 'to obscure the rather specific conditions under which the latter doctrine is formulated, thereby completely missing the point of the exercise in the first two cases and misunderstanding how the exercise was designed to be carried out in the third' (Gaukroger 1995: 11–14). I shall not repeat Gaukroger's arguments here, but some of these points turn up later in the arguments around Jung's allegedly unfortunate Cartesian influences found, so it is asserted, in his conception of the mind, and of the world, and which have far-reaching implications for Jungian thought.

That said, it is salutary to wonder if we have done a similar thing with Jung's work, homogenising his thought as if he had little intellectual development beyond his confrontation with the unconscious after his relationship with Freud came to an end. Jung's written *corpus* is vast, so vast indeed that it would seem to be important to take intellectual chronology into consideration as we read and reflect on his work.[3] Noting the centrality of the *Red Book* to understanding Jung's later work, Sonu Shamdasani argues, for example, that unless Jung's 'confrontation with the unconscious is placed in proper perspective', one is in 'no place to understand Jung's intellectual development from 1913 onwards and not only that, but his life as well' (Shamdasani 2005: 103). Shamdasani also argues that the decision to publish the *Collected Works* organised thematically rather than chronologically does not represent the evolving nature of Jung's thinking because he changed and edited his material in an ongoing way. Hence there are different, later versions of essays that reflect different thinking (Shamdasani 2005: 54).

Descartes' writings are not as extensive as Jung's, but limited reading of his extant work has produced some well-defined intellectual prejudices. For instance, a widely held belief about his philosophy is that Descartes 'invented' psychological internalism, the idea that the mind is internal to the body and as such, is the principal source of ideas (Lau and Deutsch 2010). Relatedly, the idea that 'science of the mind' resembles 'nineteenth-century introspectionism, a study of the conscious mind based on direct inner awareness' is attributed to Descartes.

Deborah Brown points out that this view is based on the real distinction between mind and body which assumes a 'disintegration' of the two. However, she argues, this reading of Descartes overlooks the original unity of mind and body to which Descartes subscribed. She says that 'although it is true that the Cartesian mind is not defined by its relation to matter, it is created conjoined to matter with which it forms a system of coordinated functions, and with which it causally interacts' (Brown 2006: 3). Attached to these beliefs are the related ideas that Descartes 'invented' the subject/object distinction and that it is almost entirely due to his philosophy that the world has become an object which we look at as if we are spectators to something in which we do not take part (Bordo 1986; Abram 1996; Romanyshyn 2000).

I shall be discussing some of these views in greater detail, but I want to point out here that they are, generally speaking, caricatures of Descartes' ideas rather than considered accounts of his work. Recent scholarship on Descartes and the passions, together with work on the history and philosophy of science, either directly or indirectly, has done much to address some of these issues (Gaukroger 1995, 2006; Rozemond 1998; Brown 2006; Machamer and McGuire 2009; Daston and Galison 2010).

An issue around which much of the work in this book revolves concerns the status of the psyche in relation to the world. We *might* take some liberties, and lump together a whole bunch of terms that have almost been strung together as if they are interchangeable (Martin and Barresi 2008; Gay 2009). 'Soul', 'spirit', 'psyche', 'mind', 'consciousness' are cognate terms but what their referents are, or even if they have referents, is a tricky question. Debates around personal identity such as we see beginning in Hume's and Locke's work, and then the interrogation of the relationship between mind and brain, in the work of mind/body and consciousness studies theorists in the past fifty years or so, tend to opt for language less religiously loaded than 'soul' and 'spirit'. A history of such concepts and their uses is way beyond the scope of this current project. Distinctions made by Descartes, Jung, Husserl and others point to clear differences as well as to some similarities between their usage, in both emphasis and meaning. The 'ego' of Jung, for example, is different from the 'ego' of Husserl, yet we can understand what each is talking about when we consider the English equivalent 'I'. In either case, the ego connotes an idea of a centre of consciousness that has various functions, one of which might be seen as a psychic unifier.

In Western metaphysics, deliberations about the soul are very old: the soul's existence or non-existence, its relation to the body and if, indeed, body and soul are one and what that could mean; whether or not the soul is reborn upon corporeal death; whether or not the soul is the form of the body are all issues that have been debated over the centuries. Some of the debates date back to the pre-Socratics. Those discussions had developed and continued in one form or another among philosophers until Descartes and beyond him, albeit in a transformed manner, as Martin and Barresi point out. In other words, not just the definitional question, but the status of any of these phenomena pre- and post-date Descartes, and they do not really look like getting sorted out in the foreseeable future.

What the soul is like has also been the subject of much debate, with scholarly argument about 'its' various 'parts' and 'faculties'; if 'it' were immaterial, whether or not 'it' could have parts or faculties; and how the soul relates to the body, to the senses and to reason. We need to be aware that Descartes talks about the mind as well as the soul. He argues that the soul is indivisible, and he identifies various functions or activities in which the soul engages. In *Passions of the Soul* he argues against the separation of the sensitive soul and the rational soul such as are found in Scholastic philosophy.

> All the conflicts that are usually supposed to occur between the lower part of the soul, which we call 'sensitive', and the higher or 'rational' part of the soul – or between the natural appetites and the will –consists simply in the opposition between the movements which the body (by means of its spirits) and the soul (by means of its will) tend to produce at the same time in the gland.[4] For there is within us but one soul, and this soul has within it no diversity of parts: it is at once sensitive and rational too and all of its appetites are volitions.
>
> (Descartes 1985: 345–346)

The model against which Descartes is railing in this quotation can be found in various forms in Western philosophy from the pre-Socratics onwards. It is well articulated by Plato, and then carried into Scholastic thinking. 'Rational soul' as 'mind' is evident in Plato's works in both *Phaedo and The Republic.* Plato's tripartite soul includes the reigning principle, the intellect. This conception of mind, as we see above, is retained to some extent by Descartes, importantly without the notion of parts or partitions, but rather as a function of a single unified soul. It appears, however, that Descartes' notion of mind and soul are distinct, yet related. As Brown points out, Descartes argued to Regius that he believed the soul is the form of the body. His correspondence with Regius in 1641, which predates *Passions of the Soul,* is interesting in light of Brown's discussion.

By the time of the *Passions,* Descartes was arguing for the existence of an indivisible soul. In this earlier material, he also argues for the existence of 'only one soul', 'the *rational soul* ' in human beings. He claims that 'no actions can be reckoned human unless they depend on reason'. He goes on to argue that the vegetative and sensory aspects of soul that are found in plants and animals are also found in human beings but 'in the case of human beings they should not be called *souls*, because they are not the first principle of their actions, and belong to a totally different genus from the *rational soul'.* A little further on,

Descartes clearly identifies *mind* with *rational soul* (Descartes 1991: 182). In this account, only humans have rational souls. Descartes is indicating the advisedly cautious use of the term 'soul'. Apart from the substantive issues involved, we can see here an instance of development and modification of Descartes' views. What is particularly noteworthy for our purposes is Brown's reminder about the conjoining of mind and body; and also Descartes' insistence on the simplicity of the soul. These are both issues I take up in succeeding chapters.

We turn now to the subject/object distinction, what has come to be the bane of many theorists in recent years. The subject/object distinction was important to Aristotle, to his logic and to logic since; and debates about subject terms and their referents and thus to substance and essence and predication were seriously engaged in by scholastic philosophers. It has been argued that the idea that the categories of inner and outer, observed and observer, were not as clearly defined as they subsequently became with the Cartesian interiorisation of thought (Bordo 1986). Indeed, Susan Bordo mounts a case for the extremity of such a split having begun with the 'discovery' of perspective in the visual arts (Bordo 1987). 'Objectivity' (I-subject-here and you/it-object-there) becomes almost a dirty word, with the separation of mind from nature seen as a schism that has caused untold harm. As an object, the world or nature or you, and I, are estranged from each other. I make of the object something that I can manipulate, instrumentalise, control, even destroy. I as subject have dominance over the world, nature or you, as object. I am primary, you are secondary. I exist before you exist. Given my existence, the world exists.

While it is arguable that the *cogito* provides a philosophical context for this view, as I see it, it is neither true of the *cogito* nor is it a view that is sustainable. Its ethico-moral dimensions, expressed in the language of harm to oneself and to world that we shall shortly encounter, is not a view that is tenable when we take on board the historical dimensions of objectivity through a scientific perspective (Daston and Galison 2010).[5] Lorraine Daston and Peter Galison argue, for example, that the notion of objectivity underpins scientific practice and that objectivity was considered to be an epistemic virtue. According to them, epistemic virtues in science are preached and practised in order 'to know the world and not the self' (Daston and Galison 2010: 39). Epistemic virtue, the idea that the moral character of a researcher is integral to practice, relocates the focus, in the case of science, away from knowledge of oneself to knowledge of the world. Yet both the character of the scientist and the object of her/his investigation remain closely intertwined.

They speak of the 'tone of exhortation and admonition that permeates the literature of scientific instruction, biography and autobiography from the seventeenth century to the present' as being 'frankly religious'. They indicate that this language has a religious sensibility of humility and wonder, and of 'discipline and sacrifice'. They argue that epistemic virtues 'are norms that are internalized and enforced by appeal to ethical values, as well as to pragmatic efficacy in securing knowledge' (Daston and Galison 2010: 39–41). From their analysis, we can glean that the forced separation of self and science is something of a fiction. Self and science remain together through the glue of epistemic virtue which remains, albeit differently formulated, to this day. As I see it, objectivity, considered as an epistemic virtue, aims at the truth of nature and the world characterisable as a genuine other.

Furthermore, Daston and Galison argue that epistemic virtue, as a scientific desideratum, aims to stem the tide of epistemic anxiety, that is to say, fears about obstacles to knowledge. They maintain that objectivity is connected with a development of the scientific self that has involved a realism captured in terms of truth-to-nature, trained judgement, mechanical objectivity and structural objectivity. Their work helps to pinpoint some of the issues that emerge in reflections on both Descartes and Jung. For example, a number of critiques suggest that Descartes affected a radical split between subject and object that has damaged human/nature relations because of the resulting anthropocentrism. Such critiques seem to imply that a return to a more unified conception of human/nature relations will somehow restore that almost uterine state that obtained prior to the devastating severance from a benign mother nature. I shall argue shortly that, paradoxically, criticisms of the subject/object distinction fail to measure up to an ethico-morality which is respectful of either the uterus or the mother whose uterus is at stake. Without a robust sense of subject and object, we can have no robust sense of alterity with its attendant notions of respect and integrity.

If the *cogito* does result in a solipsistic, totally disconnected world (of one isolated, lonely being), then it is because of a failure to understand its fundamental methodological importance in its ultimate grounding of the subject/object distinction. The point is that such a being cannot actually be a subject to itself without this distinction. Descartes' rudimentary recognition of his own subjectivity through his thinking process, articulated as doubt, foreshadows the later development of Brentano's theory of intentional objects which we explore in later chapters of this book. Indeed, Bordo argues that Descartes 'provides the first real phenomenology of the mind' (Bordo 1986: 443). The subject/object distinction is critical to the development, and subsequent elucidations, of various phenomenological perspectives, as we shall see. And the *cogito* is not the sum of Descartes' work, as I have already noted.

Undoubtedly Descartes' specific argument for a radical substantial and thus real distinction between mind and body, and the multiple interpretations it has engendered, has fashioned many of the debates that have arisen. Likewise, his articulation of the *cogito* has had a profound impact on the development of metaphysics in the anglophone, francophone and germanophone philosophical cultures. The *cogito* has been particularly influential in the work of Edmund Husserl and Maurice Merleau-Ponty, key figures in the development of phenomenology and whose work, in turn, has been the subject of great interest to some analytical psychologists and post-Jungians, for example, Roger Brooke, Robert Romanyshyn and Lionel Corbett. These post-Jungians are of special interest to my project here, since they have explored Jung's place amongst phenomenologists. The theoretical connections between Descartes, the phenomenologists, Jung, and post-Jungians are often hastily judged in that, for instance, Brooke, Romanyshyn and Corbett have taken on board what I see as accepted or orthodox interpretations of Descartes' philosophy. What have they said and why is it important?

Analytical psychologist reading Descartes

I am often surprised when I read analytical psychologists' interpretations of philosophy. It seems that some analytical psychologists take philosophical positions as having 'had their day', that philosophical ideas have a finite life. What is not realised in this reading of philosophy is that, while there are most definitely philosophical fashions (for example, the idealism of F. H. Bradley, or the verificationism of Rudolph Carnap and the logical positivists), philosophers consistently mine their own archive. Philosophers develop new and different ways of reading philosophical problems through interpretation and reinterpretation of that archive. The archive is always open and always in need of evaluation and re-evaluation. What can be rejected by one generation of philosophers will be embraced by another and subsequently dismissed or rethought. The recent revival of Aristotelian and virtue ethics is testament to this. Thus we do need to think of philosophy as a living tradition.

That said, we also need to remind ourselves that phenomenology had its origins in philosophy: philosophical phenomenology was one of its first manifestations. Bordo's comment that Descartes provided the first real phenomenology of the mind highlights this point: and after him came Hume, Kant, Hegel and Brentano, all of whom took seriously the idea that conscious life was worthy of philosophical attention. Indeed, not only worthy, but fundamental to our conceptions of who we all are as human beings. The richness of the Western philosophical tradition provides some wonderful contexts from which to engage with, and develop, our own thinking and approaches to issues that come up when phenomenological approaches to various disciplinary areas are under the spotlight.

Within this frame, it is rather startling to find Roger Brooke claiming that:

> [p]henomenology is primarily a method, but it must immediately be said that phenomenologists, even amongst Husserl's closest colleagues and pioneers, did not follow the method that Husserl described. For many, the three prongs of Husserl's method have all undergone change, or, as in the case of the transcendental reduction, have been utterly rejected. The transcendental reduction has been seen by most phenomenologists (perhaps

> unfairly?) as an unfortunate and ultimately futile return to the idealism of Kant and Descartes, in which self and world have once again been severed.
> (Brooke 2000: 3)

Brooke's parenthesised 'perhaps unfairly?' suggests a potentially sympathetic reading of Husserl. However, in my view, that is not the case. Brooke's comment that the 'three prongs of Husserl's method have all undergone changes' and that the transcendental reduction has been utterly rejected by phenomenologists needs careful consideration. Husserl was not founding a church with a *credo* from which there could be no deviation. The nature of philosophy is such that conversation, criticism and exchange of views are part of the process of philosophising.

The controversial nature of many of the claims Brooke makes here is supported by a close reading of those very colleagues and pioneers. Both Heidegger and Merleau-Ponty, for example, relied quite heavily on Husserl's expositions of phenomenology. I say 'expositions' because, like Descartes and Jung, Husserl himself was a prolific writer who reflected on and redeveloped and rejected and modified his views over many years. What he wrote in 1907 was not necessarily a position he held in 1913 or 1931.

From a philosophical perspective, discussions of, for example, the *epochē* or phenomenological reduction, an idea that is central to Husserlian phenomenology, continues to excite philosophical interest with differing interpretations suggesting its importance to philosophical method and theory (Merleau-Ponty 1962, 1968; Mohanty 1995; Zahavi 2003; Zahavi *et al.* 2003; Moran 2005; Beyer 2011). Given this, we might note that the diverse nature of philosophy is such that it would be rare to find a case in which all philosophers unanimously agreed on every detail of even one position. Philosophers argue about the features and implications of any one interpretation and will attempt to persuade their colleagues that their interpretation, and not a contrary position, is more plausible than any other.[6] Some philosophers will modify and will even reject aspects of their own position if they can see that they have been mistaken or misguided in some way. At the other end of the spectrum, there are rarely cases in which a particular position is 'utterly rejected'. Many philosophers are advocates of various aspects of the philosophies of both Kant and Descartes; just as many would debate the idea that Husserl or Descartes are idealists; and equally many would argue that Descartes' and Kant's philosophies do not promote the severance of self and world. The point that I am making here is that differences of opinion, development and modification of philosophers' ideas, the waning and waxing of different concepts and interpretations, are *de rigueur* for philosophy. Brooke's comment then, reflects not so much on Husserl's failure as an early phenomenologist, but suggests Brooke's lack of familiarity with the history of philosophy, its methods and techniques, and the idea that philosophy is a living tradition. The fact that so much philosophy is written in the present tense ('Plato argues . . .' 'Descartes says that . . .') is testament to that living tradition. So that, rather than Husserl's influence, being a thing of the past, current scholarship actually reflects the ongoing importance of Husserl to philosophy.

Brooke's apparent acceptance of the view that Descartes' (and Kant's) philosophies promote, or are instances of, the severance of self and world assumes a reading of Descartes of which we are given glimpses in other of Brooke's texts (Brooke 1991). Similar assumptions can be seen operating in various works by Romanyshyn and Corbett and others. The first assumption is that the body and the mind are radically separate, so radically separate that there is no legitimate connection between them.

Descartes' belief that the mind is thinking substance and the body is material substance, a machine, without contextualising his argument, seem to be the unspoken culprits of this de-legitimating. The upshot of this is that the mind is seen as 'interior' or internal to a body which encounters a world (including the body) 'exterior' or external to a mind. 'The Cartesian dualism of an interior, subjective knowing mind sealed off from an exterior, objective world to be known and exploited repeats itself in the European movements of expansion into the New World', argues Romanyshyn (2000). He does not mention any previous expansion by Greek and Roman, Norse and Norman, or of the Christian Crusades, all of which brought slavery, death and exploitation.

European expansion during and post Descartes imitated its own history as much as it imitated Cartesian metaphysics, if indeed it did the latter. To place at the feet of Descartes a kind of responsibility for exploitative expansion into the New World, which is what Romanyshyn implies, is at the very least, illustrative of an acute historical naivety. Since Jung attaches great importance to the history of ideas and to the genealogy of symbols, those in Jung's footsteps need to bear in mind that considered and informed historical awareness is significant for interpretations of the psyche. Jung himself appears to have been open to the historical exigencies of human being, revealed especially in his development of ideas around the collective unconscious. Even if one does not subscribe to the latter concept, the point remains: the psyche has developed over centuries and centuries. Knowledge of its history, which entails knowledge of world histories, is critical.

The interior/exterior trope attributed to Descartes posits the mind as privileged over the body in such a way as to downplay radically the role of the body in human experience. I shall be examining this contention in greater detail in later chapters, but for now let it be said that one of Descartes' central concerns was precisely to figure out the relation between mind and body. He most certainly postulated a metaphysical difference between mind and body, but, as some commentators argue, that does not entail an inevitable collapse into the view that the body either does not matter at all or that its role is minimal in individual human experience (Brown 2006). Descartes' affirmation of the union of mind and body in *Meditation VI*, which we shall be looking at later, is often overlooked by those anxious to point the finger at his unredeemable dualism. Unfortunately, Brooke and Romanyshyn seem to have fallen into that camp as well.

We also need to note that the interior/exterior trope expressed by the language of severance and the sealed-off nature of the Cartesian subject do not take account of the methodological considerations that frame Descartes' *Meditations* if that, indeed, is what Brooke and Romanyshyn have in mind. They seem to be arguing that separation is somehow fundamentally mistaken, a bad alternative to the world view it replaced. This 'drama of parturition', as Bordo calls it, intersects with the kind of epistemic anxiety we saw spoken about above (Bordo 1987: 59ff). As I read their work, the drama continues, the epistemic anxiety remains. For Brooke and Romanyshyn Descartes' philosophy is couched in terms of separation and loss: an age of innocence, a uterine existence in maternal benevolence and eventually 'recollected' by Jung, is seen as a pure, original state of being from which succeeding generations have strayed, to their detriment. In this view, humans are immersed in a life world that somehow encapsulates a truth that is timeless and universal.

Brooke maintains that the:

> historical drama of western consciousness . . . repeats a process according to which the ensouled presence of the medieval world receded behind the veil of Judeo-Christian iconoclasm and Galilean science. This world, God-forsaken, became merely a set of mathematical co-ordinates upon a geometric grid. Instead of trusting the presentational quiddity of our experience, we are heirs to a representational reality, a world as illusory as a dream.
>
> (Brooke 2000: 13–14)

Such is his interpretation of the metaphysical inheritance of Jung and Galileo; such is Descartes', Copernicus' and Galileo's interpretation of their own lives and the world as they saw it. Clearly, they got it wrong, or someone did after them, so powerful was their unchallengeable insight! The radical nature of any of this early work in modern science, its benefits to us and the advantages that we have inherited as part of the legacy are ignored entirely.

There is no acknowledgement that this mediaeval world view is itself a product of interpretation, nor that the phase of Jung's life which Brooke is discussing is also in part, an effect of interpretation. If we are to take the interpretational thesis[7] seriously, then we need to acknowledge that the 'truths' that we perceive at moments of heightened engagement and/or openness to our worlds and our own lived experiences are largely artifacts of that experience, and our history, at a particular moment. While we might remember them very clearly, we could be mistaken in clinging to them as if they were the bearers of timeless truths, to which we always long to return.

According to Romanyshyn, the 'worlds' (the 'world' of the mind and the 'world' of the body) Descartes articulates are abandoned, by the divine being. Descartes 'places God at the beginning of his philosophy as a watchmaker who, having set the mechanism of the universe in motion, is no longer needed, except for an occasional repair, otherwise called a miracle' (Romanyshyn 2000: 12). The trope of separation and loss is also seen operating here: we are separated from the divine creator and the soul that we inherit as a result of our divine origins. It is clear that Descartes did not hold this view: a perusal of *Principles of Philosophy* or *Passions of the Soul* shows Descartes' acknowledgement of an immanent God.[8] And what does Descartes say as he thinks about God at the end of *Meditation III*?

> I should like to pause here and spend some time in contemplation of God: to reflect on his attributes and to gaze with wonder and adoration on the beauty of this immense light, so far as the eye of my darkened intellect can bear it. For just as we believe through faith that the supreme happiness of the next life consists solely in contemplation of the divine majesty, so experience tells us that this same contemplation, albeit much less perfect, enables us to know the greatest joy of which we are capable in this life.
> (Descartes 1984: 36)

Descartes' humility in the face of his divine creator is extraordinarily touching. He does not sound like a man contemplating a watchmaker who has abandoned him, not at all. The gratitude and wonder expressed by Descartes suggest his belief in an immanent divine being, the 'immense light' contrasted so beautifully with his 'darkened intellect'. Perhaps Romanyshyn is taking poetic licence with his description of what he holds to be Descartes' metaphysics. Yet Descartes himself is in no doubt about the magnificence of the divine being, and of his place with the Divinity through eternity. The watchmaker description seems especially inept read in the context of Descartes' profound confession of contemplative wonder.

In Brooke's and Romanyshyn's assumptions about Descartes' philosophy, we can see that his complex thinking and the struggle that he had in seizing upon the few certainties with which he eventually settled are enormously underestimated. Little attention is paid to Descartes' arguments: we have no sense of the breadth or development of his ideas. We can detect an almost cavalier attitude to Descartes' philosophy which diminishes its importance to Western thinking and, in particular, to phenomenology as it developed in the twentieth century. His work is reduced, it seems to me, to one or two clichés that do not capture the seriousness of his work, its historical context or the methodological innovativeness of the *Meditations* in particular.

Descartes was a radical figure: the new (Cartesian) philosophy taught by Descartes' disciple Regius was condemned by the Utrecht Magistrates at Voetius' instigation in 1642.[9] As we shall see, Descartes' method departed from standard philosophical practices; his appeal to his own experience, its errors and the problematic nature of its truths, and then to reason, authorises his own subjectivity as a source of knowledge and understanding. From this germinates the possibility of the centrality of one's own experience and the application of one's own reason, as a basis of philosophy. Given this, the turn to psychology at the end of the nineteenth century may owe more to Descartes than many of us have been prepared to admit. The authority of the subject is also seen flourishing in phenomenology, something that is overlooked by both Brooke and Romanyshyn, who are more concerned with what they see as the worrisome nature of the spectator created by Descartes' philosophy. Where do we witness this?

In the 'Introduction' to Brooke's *Jung and Phenomenology*, Romanyshyn remarks that '[p]henomenology and the depth psychology of Freud and Jung were called into being by the cultural-historical psychology of the spectator consciousness, which, in abandoning the world, lost touch with the world' (Romanyshyn in Brooke 1991: xiv). Bordo's work on the effect of the discovery of perspective in the Italian Renaissance might provide some fodder for a claim that a spectator consciousness had developed prior to Freud and Jung (Bordo 1987). Within the historical context, the framework of phenomenology could well be articulated as a development of a spectator consciousness. But one might wonder what counts as a spectator consciousness and what does not? How are we to think of 'spectator consciousness'? Presumably if one is a spectator, then one looks at (something), an object, say: spectatorship is intentional. Do we go through our lives as if we were watching a cricket or football match or as if we were at a concert or attending the theatre?

One of the premises operating here is undoubtedly that it is possible to view the world as an object, to functionalise somehow the world as if it were 'there' for *our* use, beyond us, and as if no interdependence were manifest in the resultant relationship. Inescapably, one remains in relationship with the world, even in this negative spectatorship of an abandoned world. The unmentioned difficulty is the profound anthropocentrism to which such a view might give birth. In this view the world, conceived of as a nature *there* for human plundering, does become an object of utility, with the devastation of forests, waterways and the destruction of wildlife and its habitat. I do not doubt that this may well have happened (and is continuing to do so). What I do doubt is that it is Descartes' fault. The interpretation of his philosophy by successive generations can be true to his spirit of truth-seeking and faith; or it can disregard the overall intent of his *oeuvre* bound by its own concerns and projects.

Thus, assuming that such a spectator consciousness had developed, one wonders if its development is attributable to Descartes himself (and not to readings that interpret and postdate him). One also wonders if the development of spectator consciousness entailed that the world would be abandoned and what that would mean, anyway. Maybe it means precisely that.[10] Descartes' contemplative disposition and then his further work, including *The Passions of the Soul*, suggest otherwise.

The alleged radical split between subject and object in which the object – in this case, the world – is ultimately abandoned is not an automatic consequence of that split. Let us ask ourselves: what is the nature of that radical split, and what purpose does it serve? For example, Hegel's master/slave dialectic, in which reflexivity is a logical constituent of both subject and object, requires quite a radical separation of subject and object which, however, remain in relationship.[11] Nor does Hegel's master/slave dialectic privilege either subject or object: it cannot, given the logical precondition of the constitution of both (Hegel 1977). The dependence of the master on the slave, and then its consequences (and later highlighted by Karl Marx) suggests the vulnerability of both subject and object: and also points to the conceptual difficulties implicit in the notions of either absolute subjecthood or absolute objecthood. Brentano's intentionality thesis, which we encounter in later chapters, and the phenomenology which grew out of it, retains a healthy, although difficult, notion of objecthood that is deeply intertwined with intentionality, inter-relationality and intersubjectivity.

This discussion suggests that it is not, however, just a matter of going on to acknowledge Descartes' complex thinking, and then all issues will be resolved. That Descartes did think complexly is not the issue: complexity of thinking is no guarantee of rightness or wrongness, of high or low quality of argument or of the persuasiveness of an argument. Acknowledgement might, in fact, impel us to consider the philosophical arguments and discussions that permeate Cartesian scholarship. In my view this will lead to a better reading of Jung's work – his philosophical foundations are strong and do need to be taken into consideration in assessing and critiquing analytical psychology. Hence what does matter is the way in which Descartes is read selectively and in such a manner so as to obscure elements of his philosophy that already anticipate some of the objections raised by Brooke, Romanyshyn *et al.* Furthermore, a more detailed reading of Descartes would show that some of the assumptions in the 'accepted' dogma on Descartes, what I referred to as caricatures of his work, are problematic.

Undoubtedly there are problems with the ways in which we conceive of, and inhabit, our worlds. Conception and habitation are closely connected. Very clearly some readings of Descartes have seen his work as part of the origin of those problems. I have been attempting to show that such readings are ill informed and inaccurate. We need, though, to explore why this matters to readings of Jung and to analytical psychology. Without anticipating too much what comes in the next chapters, let us remind ourselves that Descartes did return to himself in a ground-breaking phenomenological encounter with his own thinking.

Finally, in this chapter, I want to raise a question about epistemic virtue, to borrow Daston's and Galison's term, that relates to the much-maligned subject/object distinction. We can detect in Brooke's and Romanyshyn's work a latent desire to collapse the subject and object distinction. As we shall see later, this is reflected in, and central to, their problematising of the inner and outer trope. What seems to be at stake here is the issue of respect for the other: if we objectify the world, that is to say, make it into an object in some of the ways I have been suggesting, we fail, it would seem, to respect the integrity and value of the world, especially the world of nature. They seem to be thinking that only by dissolving the separation can we come to terms with our own reliance on, and interdependence with, the natural world. In other words, our sociality, and our embeddedness in nature, can be fully recognised only on the condition that we see ourselves as part of, not separate from, the world which gives us birth. Inter-relatedness and intersubjectivity are to be privileged, reflecting, as they do, the way things really are, for us, as human beings. On their views, the subject/object distinction is anathema to such a conception. However, I think that the opposite is the case, as we shall see.

In the next chapter, I begin an exploration of the issue by examining some of the phenomenological dimensions of Descartes' *Meditations.* I take a different approach to the subject/object distinction by looking at some methodological considerations that affect how we understand the processes involved in scrutinising our own beliefs. I argue that the *Meditations* can be read as a spiritual practice in the tradition of Stoic and Epicurean philosophy.

Taking this discussion on board, I suggest that Jung's work, in particular his meditative stance in *The Red Book*, can be likewise conceived as spiritual practice, albeit of a different order. Begun as it was with Jung's confrontation with the unconscious, *The Red Book* exhibits a similar existential radical self-examination as Descartes' *Meditations* does epistemologically. However, I argue, the *Meditations* are not limited to settling purely epistemological questions around doubt. Personal transformation is effected through the processes in which Descartes engages. Thus existential and epistemological concerns meet in the *Meditations.*

Through spiritual practice considered in terms of a therapeutics of the soul, the threat of severance and separation that we have seen mooted by Brooke and Romanyshyn is challenged and, perhaps, dissipated, as Descartes becomes anchored in his being and brought back to himself and his world. Jung's return is also marked by such transformation, I claim. Later, a similar process is undergone by Edmund Husserl in his efforts to establish phenomenology as a science. In these ways, Descartes, Jung and Husserl are kindred spirits. Let us see how this works.

Chapter 2

Spiritual exercises and Descartes' *Meditations*

> The power of memory is prodigious, my God. It is a vast, immeasurable sanctuary. Who can plumb its depths? And yet it is a faculty of my soul. Although it is a part of my nature, I cannot understand all that I am. That means, then, that the mind is too narrow to contain itself entirely. But where is the part of it which it does not itself contain? Is it somewhere outside and not within it? How then, can it be part of it, when it is not contained in it? I am lost in wonder when I consider this problem. It bewilders me. Yet men go out and gaze in astonishment at high mountains, the huge waves of the sea, the broad reaches of rivers, the oceans that encircle the world or the stars in their courses. But they pay no attention to themselves.
>
> (Augustine 1961: 216)

> First Annotation. The first Annotation is that by this name of Spiritual Exercises is meant every way of examining one's conscience, of meditating, of contemplating, of praying vocally and mentally, and of performing other spiritual actions, as will be said later. For as strolling, walking and running are bodily exercises, so every way of preparing and disposing the soul to rid itself of all the disordered tendencies, and, after it is rid, to seek and find the Divine Will as to the management of one's life for the salvation of the soul, is called a Spiritual Exercise.
>
> (Ignatius of Loyola 1522–1523 (1914))

I focus, initially, in this chapter, on Descartes' *Meditations on First Philosophy* (hereafter '*Meditations*') as an exercise in practical philosophy, specifically as the practice of spiritual exercises. I use the term 'practical' advisedly, and emphasise the methodological, experiential and phenomenological grounding of the *Meditations*. I place the *Meditations* within the tradition of spiritual practice as it had developed in Western culture from the time of Greco-Roman antiquity. Epistemic virtue, which we saw highlighted in the work of Daston and Galison in Chapter 1, fits within this same tradition. As we shall see, the double focus on the subjective and on the objective, alluded to by Daston and Galison, is evident in Descartes' and Jung's work.

The spiritual tradition, in the sense in which I shall shortly outline it, is fundamental to various forms of phenomenology, specifically in relation to the methodological turn of Edmund Husserl's *epochē* and to the idea of being in the present moment or *prosoche.* I maintain that Jung's work in analytical psychology can also be placed in that tradition. I also hold that Descartes and Jung were doubly oriented towards the cognitive aspects of mental life, an orientation which does not result simply in epistemic transformation; psychological or affective transformation, as a therapeutic aspect of spiritual practice figures in their orientation towards their own selves and the world. Both the method and content of their epistemic pursuits, together with their philosophical orientations, belong in a tradition of wisdom and ethical practice (Jung 1966: 121; Descartes 1985: Dedicatory Letter to Elizabeth 191).

In my view, Descartes and Jung, to varying degrees, use the techniques of spiritual exercises, developed as cognitive practice, to effect fundamental *psychological* transformation. Their texts, considered in part as therapeutic discourses aimed at mastery of the passions, overcoming ignorance, self-improvement, cognitive clarity and a focus on truth, open up methodological possibilities to us as readers in our own quests for epistemic enlightenment. As John Cottingham points out, the general aim of mastery of the passions towards which spiritual practice aimed was 'not merely intellectual enlightenment, or the imparting of abstract theory, but a transformation of the whole person, including our patterns of emotional response' (Cottingham 2005: 5). In my view, such a transformation can result either in disaffection from the everyday world, such as we might see in the practices of the Desert Fathers or any ascetics who live solitary lives, or it can ground a greater sense of the ontological integrity of otherness with, perhaps, an attendant ethic of alterity. Descartes and Jung belong in the latter rather than the former camp.

They were both familiar with Western spiritual practice and that familiarity founds remarkable, and novel, changes to our understanding of the role of the mind in our apprehension of the world. The separation of mind and body, and the split between inner and outer 'reality', are certainly seen in both cases. I argue that both the separation and the inner and outer trope and its cognates (interior/exterior, for example) are important existential and phenomenological distinctions framing our understanding of human being. I shall be arguing that, in spite of their drawbacks, the spatial orientations to our worlds and ourselves implicit in this trope positively dispose us to recognition of the other, mechanical or sentient.

Meditation and philosophy

My focus in this section will be on the *Meditations* as an exercise in *cognitive* meditation and in phenomenology; it will also open up the possibility of regarding Jung's work as part of the meditative tradition in which Descartes' *Meditations* is to be located.

In *Philosophy as a Way of Life*, Pierre Hadot argues that philosophy, prior to Descartes, had developed as exegesis.

> Insofar as philosophy was considered exegesis, the search for truth, throughout this period was confounded with the search for the meaning of 'authentic' texts; that is of those texts considered authoritative. Truth was contained within those texts; it was the property of their authors, as it was the property of those groups who recognized the authority of these authors, and who were consequently 'heirs' of this original truth.
>
> (Hadot 1995: 73)

Reading Descartes within this context is very illuminating for the modern reader, especially when we note that Hadot goes on to use the term 'spiritual exercise'. He notes the disconsternation the contemporary reader might feel at the use of the term 'spiritual', but maintains that:

> It is nevertheless necessary to use this term, I believe, because none of the other adjectives we could use – 'psychic,' 'moral,' 'ethical,' 'intellectual,' 'of thought,' 'of the soul,' – covers all the aspects of reality we want to describe. Since, in these exercises, it is thought which, as it were, takes itself as its own subject-matter, and seeks to modify itself, it would be possible for us to speak in terms of 'thought exercises.' Yet 'thought' does not indicate clearly enough that imagination and sensibility play a very important role in these exercises . . . these exercises in fact correspond to a transformation of our vision of the world, and to a metamorphosis of our personality. The word 'spiritual' is quite apt to make us understand that these exercises are the result, not merely of thought, but of the individual's entire psychism.
>
> (Hadot 1995: 82)

Hadot's decision to use the term is interesting, then, when we turn to Descartes' *Meditations* and consider their place in the philosophical canon.

As is commonly known, Descartes was educated by Ignatius of Loyola's counter-Reformation religious organization, the Jesuits. Stephen Gaukroger gives a very full description of the Jesuit educational system that would have been in place at La Flèche, which included the thirty-day spiritual retreat (Stohrer 1979: 11; Gaukroger 1995). Thus Ignatius' *Exercitia Spiritualia* is a text with which, undoubtedly, Descartes was familiar. Walter Stohrer argues that the

> case for a textually grounded convergence of emphasis and congruence of concern can be made with some confidence. Regarding the preliminary attitudinal and dispositional components of solitude and objectivity, as well as methodological refinements of self-activity, reflective concentra-

> tion, continuity, and repetition, the textual evidence for such a linkage is compelling.
>
> (Stohrer 1979: 26)

Assuming that Stohrer is correct, Ignatius' influence on Descartes is significant, and important for our understanding of Descartes' work.

Hadot argues that Ignatius' text is 'nothing but a Christian version of a Greco-Roman tradition . . . both the idea and the terminology of *exercitium spirituale* are attested in early Latin Christianity, well before Ignatius of Loyola, and they correspond to the Greek Christian term *askesis*.' He argues that *askesis* is not to be understood as asceticism, but as 'the practice of spiritual exercises' (Hadot 1995: 82, 126–144). Consequently, the asceticism of Loyola's exercises is more descriptive of their nature than of any intrinsic asceticism, as we today understand and associate with the term.

Hadot argues that the Greco-Roman understanding of *askesis* has important implications for construing the place of spiritual exercises in ancient thought and in philosophy more generally. He reminds us that the Hellenistic and Roman spiritual traditions sought principally to come to terms with the passions, the cause of all suffering. The Stoics and the Epicureans developed different ways of dealing with the passions. Hadot argues that the task of philosophy is to educate people 'so that they seek only the goods they are able to obtain, and try to avoid only those evils which it is possible to avoid'. The Stoics distinguished between what is dependent on humans and what is not. They held that *moral* good and evil, circumscribed by our free will, is the limit of our sphere of influence. According to Hadot, the Stoics held that everything else beyond moral good and evil does not depend on us; it is outside our freedom, particularly 'the necessary linkage between cause and effect . . . It must be indifferent to us: that is, we must not introduce any differences into it, but accept it in its entirety, as willed by fate. This is the domain of nature.' Hadot remarks that here we have a reversal of our usual way of seeing things, and that the transformation of vision that came with this reversal (from 'human' to 'natural' vision) is not easy to achieve. Spiritual exercises aided that transformation and were practised daily within the various philosophy schools (Hadot 1995: 83). Hadot cites Philo Judaeus of Alexandria's two lists of spiritual practices, and from them, we get the idea of the richness and practicality – moral and psychological – of spiritual exercises:

1.

- research (*zetesis*)
- thorough investigation (*skepsis*)
- reading (*anagnosis*)
- listening (*akroasis*)
- attention (*prosoche*)
- self-mastery (*enkrateia*)
- indifference to indifferent things

2.

- reading
- meditations (*meletai*)
- therapies of the passions
- remembrance of good things
- self-mastery (*enkrateia*)
- accomplishment of good things.

Hadot emphasises the utmost importance to the Stoics of *prosoche*. He describes it in terms of

> continuous vigilance and presence of mind, self consciousness which never sleeps, and a constant tension of the spirit. Thanks to this attitude, the philosopher is fully aware of what he does at each instant and he *wills* his actions fully. Thanks to his spiritual vigilance, the Stoic always has 'at hand' (*procheiron*) the fundamental rule of life: that is the distinction between what depends on us and what does not . . . Attention to the present moment is, in a sense, the key to spiritual exercises.
>
> (Hadot 1995: 84)

This intense regimen embodies the philosophical life – as Hadot says, for the Stoic 'doing philosophy meant practising how to "live": that is how to live freely and consciously'. Liberating ourselves from our own individuality through spiritual practices, we are able to understand that we are part of a 'reason-animated *cosmos*' and also to give up desire for what does not depend on us, and concentrate on what does, the moral good (Hadot 1995: 86). Note that meditation is one aspect of spiritual exercises.

It is intriguing that the Epicureans also went in for very disciplined spiritual exercises that cultivated healing, a 'therapeutics' of the soul. Hadot describes this as 'bringing one's soul back from the worries of life to the simple joy of existing'. The Epicureans, Hadot argues, held that people are unhappy because they spend their time worrying about things that are beyond their control: people fear and desire unjustifiably, at the expense of what is there before them – the 'pleasure of existing' which is framed by desires that are natural and necessary (for example, not to be hungry, thirsty or cold). Focusing on philosophy as therapeutics, the Epicureans saw that spiritual practices 'are required to heal the soul' (Hadot 1995: 87). Although there are some very detailed accounts of Epicurean spiritual exercises, including material for meditation and the study of physics, and with a strong emphasis on *prosoche*, Hadot points out that healing the soul is paramount for the Epicureans. For the Stoics, *prosoche* 'means metal tension and constant wakefulness of the moral conscience'. For the Epicureans *prosoche* is 'an invitation to relaxation and serenity' (Hadot 1995: 88).

At this point, we might ask how well either Descartes or Jung fits into this description of philosophy as spiritual exercise, that is to say, philosophy as the practice of self-knowledge through learning to live as better individuals, above all, when Jung is not even a philosopher. From what we have seen in the work of Hadot, and if we take it at face value, we can say that Descartes, through his education with the Jesuits, had probably been exposed, implicitly if not explicitly, to a way of doing philosophy that certainly had gone out of fashion by his time. Engagement with words, and not engagement with life, was the legacy that was bequeathed to him through scholastic philosophy. The exegetical tradition had come to dominate, as it most likely still does.[1] How aware of this Descartes was, we cannot say. Yet we do find him, in *Meditation I*, saying (famously) that he had been struck by the 'large number of falsehoods that I had accepted as true in my childhood, and by the highly doubtful nature of the whole edifice that I had subsequently based on them' (Descartes 1984: 14).

It looks as though the exegetical tradition was a tradition he found profoundly unattractive as the basis of his search for true belief. Descartes' decision to retreat into himself in order to purge himself of his previously held opinions has elements of spiritual exercises – *skepsis, prosoche, enkrateia, meletai.* His apparent embracing of his own mind as the site of philosophical practice – a turn inward – is thus quite instructive given the Stoic and Epicurean emphasis on spiritual exercises. Deborah Brown points out that Descartes' ministrations to Elizabeth helped to foster their discussion of the relationship between 'happiness (contentment of mind) and fortune'. Descartes' remedies – psychotherapeutic techniques which involved disengagement from her senses and imagination – are distinctly Stoic (Brown 2006: 18–19).

Hadot's claim that Ignatius' exercises are a Christianised version of a Greco-Roman tradition might seem then, in Descartes' philosophy, a secularised return to philosophy as practice, indeed philosophy as a way of life. However, his sensibility remains distinctly theological, if not confessional.

John Cottingham argues that another very important influence on Descartes is the philosophy of Thomas Aquinas which 'offered an integrated vision in which the pursuit of virtue and the cultivation of knowledge are closely linked' (Cottingham 2006: 196). Cottingham quotes from *Summa Theologica*:

> it belongs to wisdom, as a gift, not only to contemplate Divine things, but also to regulate human acts. Now the first thing, to be effected in this direction of human acts is the removal of evils opposed to wisdom: wherefore fear is said to be 'the beginning of wisdom,' because it makes us shun evil, while the last thing is like an end, whereby all things are reduced to their right order; and it is this that constitutes peace.
>
> (Aquinas 1947, 2:45 article 6)

We have seen that Descartes was capable of profound wonder at the Divine being. His proof for the existence of God in *Meditation III* is an intellectual exercise, designed to cultivate knowledge, which, convincing or not, is grounded in, and accentuates, the contemplative mood of the *Meditations*. The kind of knowledge cultivated by Descartes aims at indubitable belief, and his belief in God is an aspect of that belief.

Turning our gaze away from Descartes, we come to Jung, whose psychological work, we can see immediately, is a therapeutics in the Epicurean sense of healing the soul. We cannot conclude from this, however, that Jung's psychology is an instance of spiritual exercises. Even so, methodologically, *prosoche*, *akroasis*, *enkrateia*, *meletai* are evident in Jungian practice. Jung's prolific writings demonstrate *skepsis* and *anagnosis*, each of which contributes to the therapies he develops with his patients. In my view, it is precisely a transformation of vision, together with a metamorphosis of the whole personality, and involving a patient's whole psychism, that is effected through analytical psychology, and this seems consonant with the spiritual practices Hadot outlines. Jung is very clear that the task of psychotherapy is to deal with the whole of the psyche (which includes the unconscious). He argues that:

> the principal aim of psychotherapy is not to transport the patient to an impossible state of happiness, but to help him acquire steadfastness and philosophic patience in the face of suffering. Life demands for its completion and fulfillment a balance between joy and sorrow.
>
> (Jung 1954: 185)

In these comments, we might construe Jung to be talking about the passions and self-mastery as symptom and 'cure'. Assuming a patient is gripped by some psychological upheaval, and thus in the throes of passion, the answer is not to send her/him in the other direction – the impossible state of happiness. Rather it is to achieve a kind of balance and acceptance that will restore her/him to equanimity. Jung seems to be echoing some of the sentiments expressed by the Stoics.

A contextual link between Jung and Descartes is indicated by Jung's interests in Ignatius' *Exercitia Spiritualia*, on which he gave some lectures between June 1939 and March 1940. His lectures, which are available as a compilation of student notes in English, raise questions about their authenticity and meaning beyond the usual scope of a manuscript written by the hand of the author. As with other works, such as the much-disputed *Memories, Dreams, Reflections*, they seem to sit within the Jungian *corpus*. Jung's own notes do not illuminate all that much since they are 'neither extensive nor clearly structured nor detailed' (Becker 2001: 55). Jung's analysis of Christian imagery, predictably perhaps, focuses on the psychological – archetypal and psychogenic – expressions of Christian faith with mixed results. According to Kenneth L. Becker, Jung's interpretation of Ignatius' writings misrepresents the Christian Gospel and the soul. When we take these issues into consideration, we can clearly see that Jung had an acquaintance with the *Spiritual Exercises*.

It is not surprising that Jung's interpretation of the *Exercises* is unorthodox. Becker argues that Jung's approach to Christianity, emphasising, as it does, the psychological and psychodynamic aspects of Christian imagery 'excludes in principle the perspective of the Gospel message and of genuine Christian religious experience'. But, maintains Becker, Jung's approach is actually 'congruent' with the Christian message because it 'recognizes our woundedness, and the healing, life-giving message and reality of love Jesus reveals' (Becker 2001: 322). We see several years later that Jung's unorthodox approach to Christ, for example, is no more apparent than in his letter to Victor White in 1953:

> Forget for once your dogmatics and listen to what psychology has to say concerning your problem: *Christ as a symbol is far from being invalid,* although he is one side of the self and the devil the other . . . From the psychological standpoint the experience of God the creator is the perception of an overpowering impulse issuing from the sphere of the unconscious.
>
> (Jung 1976: 133)

What might appear to us now as a typical expression of Jung's belief framework, to some eyes and ears at the time of his writing, would have been quite radical. Dealing with the problem of evil by evoking a twin-natured self, and an experience of the divine as an impulse of the unconscious, gives to ethics, theology and spirituality a startlingly anthropocentric dimension.

An examination in detail of Jung's lectures on Ignatius' *Exercitia Spiritualia* is far beyond the scope of my present concerns.[2] However, it is important to note that Becker's elucidation of the lectures is fascinating as it uses Jung's other writings extensively, and in so doing 'corrects' what Becker considers to be inferior translations in the *Collected Works*. Given Shamdasani's criticisms of translations of the *Collected Works* that I noted in my introduction, it is very refreshing to come across alternative translations and amendments that attend to omitted words and phrases.[3] Becker's end note 5 at Chapter 14 is of special interest to us:

> Note that the CW translation has distorted the text, especially by emphasizing or absolutizing the self at the cost of the individual. Jung didn't write that self-recollection is a gathering of self, but that self-reflection ('*Selbstbesinnung*': 'being mindful of oneself'; Jung repeats the same term here, and in the whole paragraph) means collecting oneself ('*Sich-selber-Sammeln*'). Also, the German text does not carry the hint of the individual's dissolution seemingly implied in 'our existence as separate beings'; there is no plural here. In the whole text Jung is not talking about what happens to several of us as separate beings, but about the process in any particular individual. So this statement rather means that the special existence and identity the ego insists on (with its egoistic, narrow and projective stance ['*Ichhaftigkeit*'] over against the unconscious and the outer world) is '*aufgehoben,*' i.e. annulled, experientially invalidated, as the psyche is transformed and lives with a new more comprehensive consciousness.
>
> (Becker 2001: 295–296 note 5)

Becker's translation brings with it a different emphasis, and a different meaning. That 'self-reflection means collecting oneself' has quite different connotations from 'self-recollection is a gathering of oneself'. 'Self-reflection' implies that one thinks about or contemplates one's self in one's entirety; 'self-recollection' implies some form of temporality, perhaps in the operation of memory, for 'to recollect', as it is commonly used, means 'to remember' and, less commonly, 'to gather together again'. Either way, temporal considerations intrude through memory or repetition ('again').

There is a sense in which Descartes is also concerned with self-reflection in his interrogation of what he is. He is not *remembering* who he is, not gathering together the pieces of himself spread around and decentred. Nor is Jung's concern, for example, in the *Red Book: Liber Primus* to remember who he is: his confrontation with the collective unconscious delivers to him a sense of himself not previously known or realised. Assuming that there is a relation between meditation and reflection, that meditation can take the form of reflection, for example, we can intuit the importance of reflection, and of self-reflection, as they emerge to reveal the radical potential of spiritual exercises.

These brief comments serve to indicate that Descartes and Jung share a common intellectual tradition, stretching back to antiquity. They do not assume that Descartes exerted any direct influence, methodologically speaking, on Jung. What they do, however, is to suggest ways in which Ignatius' spiritual exercises influence the development of their respective methods. The attention to detail that we find in the practices they develop, and exhibited through their writing, is reminiscent of Stoic, and Epicurean, spiritual practices. In his view, these practices were then revamped by Ignatius, who himself is in the tradition of Christianising pagan spiritual exercises and philosophy as theology. Let me now turn to Descartes' *Meditations* in the hope of gaining a fuller appreciation of their spiritual exercise qualities.

Descartes' *Meditations*

I begin by acknowledging that there are numerous excellent papers on Descartes' *Meditations on First Philosophy* (hereafter '*Meditations*') *as* meditations (Rorty 1983; Hatfield 1986; Lang 1988; Vendler 1989; Rubidge 1990; Lavery 2007). I do not plan to summarise them in this chapter; however, Gary Hatfield's excellent reading of the relationship between Descartes and the meditative traditions of Ignatius and Augustine is the springboard for entering into my discussion of the *Meditations*. Secondly, assuming that Descartes would have been familiar with Ignatius' *Exercitia Spiritualia*, that they undoubtedly have had an influence on Descartes' *Meditations* and noting that they are written in the first person, let us consider who the meditator might be.

The Ignatian spiritual exercises are *given to* a meditator under the guidance of a spiritual director. In the *Exercitia Spiritualia* the subheading to the 'Annotations' that precede the instructions for the first week is addressed to the instructor, and to the meditator: 'To Give Some Understanding Of The Spiritual Exercises Which Follow, And To Enable Him Who Is To Give And Him Who Is To Receive Them To Help Themselves'. In the Second Annotation we read that:

> the person who gives to another the way and order in which to meditate or contemplate, ought to relate faithfully the events of such Contemplation or Meditation, going over the Points with only a short or summary development. For, if the person who is making the Contemplation, takes the true groundwork of the narrative, and, discussing and considering for himself, finds something which makes the events a little clearer or brings them a little more home to him – whether this comes through his own reasoning, or because his intellect is enlightened by the Divine power – he will get more spiritual relish and fruit, than if he who is giving the Exercises had much explained and amplified the meaning of the events. For it is not knowing much, but realising and relishing things interiorly, that contents and satisfies the soul.
>
> (Ignatius of Loyola 1522–1523 (1914))

Very clearly, the instruction to the spiritual director is to be succinct and not to get too carried away; his or her role is circumscribed by the experience of the meditator who will get a whole lot more out of the spiritual exercises if s/he works it out for her/himself. Thus a degree of initiative and self-reliance is demanded of the meditator regarding where s/he goes with the meditational material. The exercises themselves aim to 'conquer oneself and regulate one's life without determining oneself through any tendency that is disordered'. The conquering and regulating of oneself are reminiscent of the conquering of the passions which we earlier noted was the aim of Stoic and Epicurean spiritual practices.

Gary Hatfield (1986), John Carriero (2009) and John Cottingham (2006) use the expression 'Descartes' meditator' or 'the meditator' (that is to say, in the third person). Indeed, it is commonplace amongst Descartes' commentators to use this expression. Their use of the third person seems to invoke the Ignatian spiritual director/meditator dyad that would cast Descartes in the role of the spiritual director. On this view, Descartes is leading a meditator through the process of doubt and resolution, to a form of 'spiritual' and, in this case, cognitive enlightenment.

Yet from Descartes' first-person description of the meditational process, we might conclude that he is the meditator. In this scenario, we might conceive of him as someone who is meditating and then carefully recording what is happening to himself with the result that he progresses to the same place as the third-person meditator. There is no spiritual director (except perhaps for divine inspiration), and Descartes is going it alone, as it were.

Alternatively, we might understand him as a spiritual director, but as someone who is directing us, the readers. This would preserve the Ignatian dyadic quality of the *Exercitia Spiritualia* and cast Descartes as both spiritual director and meditator. On this view, we are co-meditators with Descartes who is simultaneously directing our efforts but not disclosing all that he might disclose. Presumably the light of our own natural reason will have a role to play in our transformation. *Our* role here, as meditating readers, is to be taken along with him, as he invites us to experience what he experiences in his quest for cognitive enlightenment. Hopefully, we will likewise be enlightened. If we ourselves have to do some work to 'get more relish and fruit' then, as a spiritual director, Descartes only 'ought to relate faithfully the events of such Contemplation or Meditation, going over the Points with only a short or summary development'. As he admits of himself in Rule Ten of the *Regulae*, 'the natural bent of my mind, I confess, is such that the greatest pleasure I have taken in my studies has always come from not accepting the argument of others but from discovering arguments by my own efforts' (Descartes 1985: 35). We might be similarly inspired to use his work as a challenge to our own intellectual questing as we go through the *Meditations*.

Since one of my aims in this book is to highlight the phenomenological dimensions of the *Meditations*, I remain within the first-person usage, and I take the last of these three options. I assume that Descartes is telling us what it is like to be a meditator going through the process of doubt, evaluation and reconstruction of opinions and beliefs. And we are along for the ride but it is a profoundly serious trip with important consequences for us.

In view of this, it is good to bear in mind that Descartes is well aware of the impact the *Meditations* might have in method and in substance. In his 'Preface to the Reader', Descartes tells us that he has already sent the *Meditations* to learned men 'for scrutiny before they went to press' and also asks that his readers suspend their judgement until 'they have been kind enough to read through all these objections and my replies to them' (Descartes 1984: 8). Predominantly, learned men engaged with the substantive issues of the *Meditations.*

Mersenne, however, remarked to Descartes, and Descartes himself admitted, that the *Meditations* come as a result of training and their subject matter is complex, demanding time and reflection (Descartes 1984: Second Set of Objections 87; Second Set of Replies 94). In my view, our understanding is enhanced if we attempt to practise what Descartes himself is doing: that is, to put aside our own preconceived opinions and beliefs for the time we are reading. Difficult though that might be, it helps to get the gist of both the substantive and phenomenological orientations of the *Meditations.* Indeed, Descartes had told Elizabeth that 'it is very necessary to have properly understood once in a lifetime, the principles of metaphysics, since they are what gives us the knowledge of God and our soul'. There is a cautionary message with this, though, as Descartes also comments that it would be 'very harmful to occupy one's intellect frequently in meditating upon them since this would impede it from devoting itself to the functions of the imagination and the senses' (Descartes 1991: Letter to Elizabeth 228).

The first-person narrative of the *Meditations* conveys almost a sense of relief at Descartes' finally making the time to do what for years he had wanted, that is, to get back to the foundations of his opinions and beliefs. His meditational focus on his process of doubt sets the stage for a phenomenology that involves a reduction, or a bracketing, of his opinions. Descartes' six *Meditations* take us on a journey from his initial doubt to his affirming that he has established the grounds for indubitable belief. As I understand it, it is best to read the *Meditations* as a whole work, and to read them several times; and not to get too caught up in the details of each argument as it comes up on our initial reading.

That said, one might be forgiven for overlooking the narrative at the beginning of Descartes' *First Meditation*: preamble might seem inconsequential in terms of the larger project. This narrative I hold, however, undercuts or dislodges some of the 'accepted' views and assumptions about Descartes' philosophy. His short description of his life and of his finding time to set himself up for the meditative reflection in which he subsequently engages is what orients us to his overall project in the *Meditations*. It is there, in that narrative, that Descartes tells us that he has decided that if he is to be certain of anything, then he needs to doubt everything that he has ever been taught. It is there that Descartes tells us that he has been deceived by his senses, and that one cannot totally trust those who have deceived us at least once. And it is there that we see that Descartes is not interested in dismissing the body *tout court* or in banishing the body forever from his philosophy or in postulating a permanent and final severance between body and mind. What Descartes *is* doing is admitting to the possibility that the body, through the senses, can deceive. And he is making the logical point that it is possible to conceive of the mind independently of the body. There is no logical contradiction in this possible conception. But this logical point arises from an existential state of affairs that Descartes deliberately constructs through his process of radical doubt that is the focus of his meditation.

Read in conjunction with other of Descartes' writings, one can also appreciate that the discussions in the *Meditations* often mirror or reflect related ideas and investigations that he developed and reflected upon throughout his professional life. The *Regulae*, the *Principles of Philosophy* and the *Discourse on Method* all bear testament to this. Thus the centrality of the *Meditations* to Descartes' life and work should not be underestimated; yet they should not be taken as a final, definitive statement of his philosophy without bearing in mind the rest of his work, and the 'Objections and Replies' to the *Meditations* themselves.

Thus the *Meditations* operate at several levels: methodological, ruminative, existential, deliberative, introspective, meditational and logical. His scepticism about the body and the world in which he exists is not irrevocable and absolute, but is, instead, a critical and essential aspect of the process that he inaugurates as a philosophical method.

I have been developing the idea of spiritual exercises as the foundation for philosophical practice evident in the Stoics and the Epicureans, and I have been emphasising that we need to understand the *Meditations* as a particular approach to philosophy. Why bother? Why think of philosophy in this way? Does it matter, and does it make any difference? 'Meditation', we saw, is one form of spiritual exercise, and is a focus of Ignatius' exercises. That approach, I hold, highlights philosophy as practice. Hence my answer to this question lies in a turn-away from our everyday, living worlds, the bustle and concerns of everydayness. Time for reflection, which is what meditation entails – in any religious tradition, at least – brings us to ourselves in a way many of us experience infrequently in our lives. We saw that Descartes had longed for this as the context for his own epistemological investigations.

When we look at how Descartes is proceeding in his intellectual quest, we can see that he is not a disinterested observer, attempting only to come to scholarly grips with a text before him. Indeed, it would be fair to say of Descartes that the text he is *very* interestedly engaged *in*, rather than observer *of*, is the text of his mind. In my view, for example, he does not simply notice that he is thinking. He is bound up in, indistinguishable from, his thinking, and that is the nature of the *cogito*. 'So that after considering everything very thoroughly, I must finally conclude that this proposition, *I am, I exist,* is necessarily true whenever it is put forward by me or conceived by my mind' (Descartes 1984: 17).

We saw above that Descartes argues that he had come to see the number of false opinions he had accepted as true and that, since then, the principles he had established were so badly formed that they could only be dubitable and uncertain. So he had decided that for once in his life, he would 'unpack' (French: *défaire*) all of the received opinions that he had accepted until then. He wanted to establish something firm and constant in knowledge (*les sciences*).[4] Hadot remarks that anyone can make up any philosophy they like:

> Descartes and Spinoza still remained faithful to the ancient definition': for them philosophy is 'the practice of wisdom . . . It invites us to concentrate on each instant of life, to become aware of the infinite value of each present moment, once we have placed it within the perspective of the cosmos. The exercise of wisdom entails a cosmic dimension.
>
> (Hadot 1995: 272–273)

Descartes' desire to establish something firm and constant in knowledge might seem to be inconsistent with Hadot's claim about philosophical wisdom and cosmic dimensions. Yet, and I think this is really interesting, Descartes' meditational *method* (and not only the method of doubt) is precisely what makes possible the scientific enterprise.

If we map Descartes' scepticism on to the meditational technique he uses, we can, as Hatfield points out, see that Descartes was closely following standard religious technique in religious meditation. And here is an important distinction: Descartes' is a religious technique concerned both with secular, philosophical certitude and, ultimately, with religious revelation involving certitude of his belief in God, and the ensuing wonder that accompanies that certitude. His *Meditations* are to do with cognition, *and* illumination of the soul. Overall, however, Descartes aims to establish the grounds for indubitable belief, and his reliance on solitary reflection with the focus on his own cognitive life is a phenomenological turn. What comes before him is not a world of objects, but the world of his own mind where thinking is the centrepiece, and a preliminary guarantor of his own existence. External to him is the existence of God, the ultimate guarantor of all existence. This God, having left his imprint on Descartes' soul, is identified in the ontological argument where Descartes, taking the cue from both Augustine and Anselm, argues that his idea of a being no greater than which he can imagine, is an innate idea. It is 'the mark of a craftsman stamped on his work . . . I am somehow made in his image and likeness' (Descartes 1984: 35).

Now whether or not we do, as a matter of fact, attain indubitable opinions or beliefs, is open to question: Descartes argued that indubitable belief for him came in the form of a reflexive process in which his doubting proved that he was thinking and thus existing, and what did the thinking was an immaterial soul. This metaphysical revelation rested on what, for Descartes, was equally indubitable, that God exists. The existence of an immaterial soul whose essence is thinking is a matter to which I shall return later; I do not plan to examine his arguments around the existence of God. Yet one might conclude that the existence of God provides the cosmic dimension about which Hadot speaks above. For now, I want to suggest that these two pillars of indubitable belief – the *cogito* and the existence of God – can be seen as an *attainment* in so far as Descartes clearly initiates a process of reasoning that led to their discovery. Of itself, such an attainment is not of interest to me. What is of interest, though, is the *process* of reasoning by which Descartes was able to attain the beliefs he came to regard as indubitable. Again, this is not in terms of the logical steps of the argument – that is extensively covered in the literature on Descartes. That process of reasoning relies, I hold, on not the suspension of judgement, but on the suspension of opinion, which, as we shall see, is a turning point for Western philosophy.

We become aware as we read that Descartes' *prosoche* and *enkrateia* are embedded in his meditational technique. This echoes the careful, methodical structure of Ignatius' spiritual exercises. It also opens the door to Jung's work in the *Red Book* which, as we shall see, I hold is a meditational text vastly different from, but in the same tradition as, Descartes' *Meditations*, as I have so far outlined that tradition.

Meditation and doubt

As I have been arguing, when we explore the *Meditations*, we need to acknowledge that they *are* meditations, and that they contain argument, which, from the perspective of philosophical process, offers some insights into how we might attain indubitable opinions or beliefs. Hatfield argues Descartes' *Meditations* draw on two meditational traditions, the Ignatian and the Augustinian, that reflect 'differing accounts of the cognitive basis of meditative experience implicit or explicit in various writers' such as Aristotle (Ignatius) and neo-Platonic (Eustace of St Paul in the Augustinian tradition) (Hatfield 1986: 48). Hatfield identifies two trinitarian doctrines, 'the three powers and the three ways', which, he argues, are typified, respectively, in the Ignatian and the Augustinian traditions.

> The 'three powers' refers to three powers of the soul – memory, understanding, and will – and enjoins that meditation should engage each of these . . . (t)he second doctrine parallels the first by introducing three 'ways' or stages through which the meditator should pass. In the first of these, the purgative, the body is mortified, so that one may turn away from sin, the senses and sensuality. This prepares the soul for the illuminative way, in which one endeavours to achieve a positive exercise of the Christian virtues, by becoming aware of the moral power of the soul through the example of Christ or by other divine illumination. Souls that have achieved illumination may then enter the unitive way, seeking union with God through joining of their own wills with the divine will.
>
> (Hatfield 1986: 49)

Hatfield maintains that there are obvious similarities between the three ways, the three powers, and Descartes' *Meditations*. He cites the latter's purging of the senses and 'even the perception of simple mathematical truths (First Meditation)', and suggests that Descartes 'is illuminated by the *cogito* and by the knowledge of God (Second and Third Meditation), and seeks to direct his will in the manner intended by God (Fourth Meditation)' as instances of the correspondence with the three ways. Hatfield also notes that the three powers are exemplified in Descartes' recalling that he has been deceived by the senses, by dreams and by his notion that there is a God who can do everything. Descartes' understanding of memory leads him to 'draw various conclusions about the deceptiveness of the senses, and the possibility of delusion, even about mathematics'. His will is strengthened by his focus on his grounds for doubt and his positing of the evil genius as aids in resisting 'his old, possibly erring opinions' (Hatfield 1986: 49). Hatfield's analysis makes the distinction between religious and cognitive meditation, and thus introduces us to another way of thinking about meditative practice in a secular context. That secular context is a novel use of meditational practice, not only because Descartes draws on the Augustinian mode, emphasising method over the powers of the soul, but also because we are led to see that introspection can transform our own understanding of epistemological beginnings.

Hatfield contends that, as well as argument, the *Meditations* also contain exemplification, another aspect of meditational practice not seen in either of the trinitarian doctrines. 'Exemplification' is seen in bringing various matters 'directly before the mind, as a direct vision of God or as Christian virtue is exemplified in a contemplation of the life of Christ' (Hatfield 1986: 49). This is important for reading the *Meditations* in a broader context than philosophical argument. At times, as anyone who does read the *Meditations* would be aware, argument from Descartes is thin on the ground. Hatfield argues that the vital step of abstracting the mind from the senses is the groundwork for the deriving of *sum* from *cogito*. He argues that this is an instance of 'direct apprehension of the meditator's own thinking.' This is supported by Descartes' admission that 'When someone says, 'I am thinking therefore I exist', he does not deduce existence from thought by means of a syllogism, but recognizes it as something self-evident by a simple intuition of the mind' (Descartes 1984: Second Set of Replies 100).[5] I say 'supported' because there has been much philosophical discussion devoted to the *cogito*, including some about the nature of the move from *cogito* to *sum* (Hintikka 1962; Bordo 1987; Markie 1992; Johansson 2003; Bardon 2005; Tomhave 2010). I shall be returning later to the *cogito* when I discuss the interior/exterior trope. For now, we need to recognise that Descartes' *Meditations* rupture older Aristotelian-inspired European thinking about philosophical issues and how they might be approached, while simultaneously drawing on forms of philosophical practice seen, notably, in Augustine's *Confessions* (Augustine 1961; Hatfield 1986).

Hatfield's exploration of the relationship between Descartes and the various forms of meditation available to him suggests the character of Descartes' doubt. Hatfield's plotting of the two forms of meditation on to Descartes' systematic doubt shows us just how intimately connected meditational technique and doubt are. From what we have just seen, though, it is easy to overlook the novelty of Descartes' sceptical stance, and thus, in my view, the importance of his meditational technique. As I understand it, we see here a marriage of sceptical stance and meditational technique that ground the beginning of phenomenological philosophy. I would not want to say that scepticism always accompanies phenomenological philosophy, but in the case of Descartes, doubt functions to nudge him towards reflection on what is going on in his mind, then, there at that moment.

Stephen Gaukroger argues that Descartes' is different from previous philosophical scepticism that had been framed principally in terms of Pyrrhonism. The Pyrrhonian sceptics were concerned with peace of mind and they argued that we are unable to choose between different sets of beliefs because we always end up in contradiction. Sextus Empiricus puts it like this:

> Scepticism is an ability to set out oppositions amongst things which appear and are thought of in any way at all, an ability by which, because of equipollence in the opposed objects and accounts, we come first to suspension of judgment and afterwards to tranquility.
>
> (Annas and Barnes 2000: [8] 4)

But, as Gaukroger points out, Descartes' scepticism, rather than Pyrrhonian, was *hyperbolic* or 'that form of doubt which questions things that you can be (and may remain) certain about' (Gaukroger 1995: 310). Descartes' immediate focus was on the querulous nature of his own belief, and as a consequence of this, peace of mind would emerge to relieve him of the dissatisfaction commonly held opinions had caused in him (Cottingham 2006). Hence he was interested in the *grounds* for his opinions and whether or not they rested on an indubitable basis. Justification, then, was fundamental to Descartes' idea of indubitability, and indubitability was the solid rock on which he could found true opinions. And the *method* involved in both the doubting and then the justification of his opinions is critical to our understanding of what he was on about.

This hyperbolic doubt, encompassing as it does his very ordinary assumptions about the world – that he has arms, that the paper is real, for example – is a means for testing his opinions. Methodologically, Descartes' phenomenological reduction in which 'accepted views' are set aside, is a fundamental departure from Pyrrhonism. He focuses on his conscious thought processes while simultaneously setting aside his sensuous experience of the world, which, as we have seen, he thought could be a source of error. This is, in my view, a two-tiered process: withdrawal from the world and withdrawal from senses are related, but not identical, processes. The latter is fraught with difficulty, as we shall see later when we discuss both hatha yoga and vipasssana, the unwavering focus of the mind being central to successful suspension of the senses and cognition of the world. Descartes does not go into detail about *how* he encouraged his own suspension. We do know, though, that solitude is, for him, a prerequisite for meditation. On this note, we saw Hatfield arguing that this sets the stage for the *cogito.* Descartes concludes, though, in *Meditation VI* that his senses are more often right than wrong, so he, in effect reinstates the body as a conveyor of truth (Descartes 1984: 61). But the actual process of bracketing the body has been seen as an incursion into a disembodied world of mind only that traps Descartes and prevents his return to the everyday. I do not agree with this view, which, in effect, overlooks the phenomenological orientation of the *Meditations*.

A key point here rests on the legitimacy of claiming that Descartes was engaged in bracketing the body. As I shall argue later, there can be a strong relationship between bracketing the body and denying its existence, but the latter is not a direct result of the former. Hyperbolic doubt of the form we see in Descartes' work, I shall argue, can and does entail bracketing. Note that Gaukroger framed such doubt in terms of questioning things 'that you *can* be (and may remain) certain about'. Descartes' convincing himself that there 'is absolutely nothing in the world, no sky, no earth, no minds, no bodies' and then asking the question, 'Does it follow too, that I do not exist?' and responding, 'No: if I convinced myself of something then I certainly existed'

(Descartes 1984: 16–17) leads, as we have seen, to the *cogito*. The point here that cannot be stressed enough is that the *cogito* is illumination and, as such, it is an immediate intuition. Gaukroger makes the point that intuition has 'two distinctive features: it is an instantaneous act, and it consists in a clear and distinct grasp of an idea' (Gaukroger 1995: 118). Further, Gaukroger stresses that '*intuitus* is a paradigm form of inference' (Gaukroger 1995: 341).[6]

I have been arguing that there is a connection between the *Meditations* and phenomenology. In my view, the first *Meditation* marks the beginning of an original phenomenological orientation of thinking in which Descartes' methodological scepticism renders the body as the principal victim of the doubting process. Descartes' sceptical method centres on his decorporealising his experience – as we saw above, Hatfield holds that this is a necessary step in his intuiting the *cogito*. Perhaps a reason we might find this strange is that we do not *consciously* 'forget' our bodies. Yet we decorporealise our experience in perhaps hundreds of ways every day, as we focus on the activities necessary to live, and thus we forget about our bodies. We get in the zone, as it were, and are lost in writing, talking, reading, the cyber world, making dinner, driving our cars. We might find it equally strange if we actually focus very directly on our bodies, on our twinges and niggles and twitches and itches, and nothing else (as happens in various stages of yoga and *vipassana*, as we shall see later). Furthermore, to embrace scepticism, and to think about how we are and have been in the world, and then to admit that we really are or have been actually mistaken, sometimes, might also seem a bit strange. In any case, the key issue is both mental *and* sensory attention, and the role they play in our experience and our epistemic practice and belief.

Descartes deliberately decorporealises his experience as he argues that his senses have deceived him, and that they are not ongoingly reliable. His drawing our attention to the fickleness of the senses amounts to saying that our bodies, as the site of sensory experience, are not to be trusted. We do, though, on an everyday basis, actually trust our bodies, that they, on the whole will work effectively, and that they will be, and are, reliable. Descartes is enunciating a relationship between senses and body here, a relationship we tend to take for granted. And this is where the point I was making above is pertinent. We do take our bodies for granted, so to stop and say, 'Hey, you can't even be sure that you *have* a body', might seem overwhelmingly confronting. Descartes moves from making the point about the wisdom of always trusting something that has deceived him once to involve himself very deeply in his hyperbolic doubt. He doubts his own sanity, even:

> Again, how could it be denied that these hands or this whole body are mine? Unless perhaps I were to liken myself to madmen, whose brains are so damaged by the persistent vapours of melancholia, that they firmly maintain they are kings when they are paupers, or say they are dressed in

purple when they are naked, or that their heads are made of earthenware, or that they are pumpkins or made of glass.

(Descartes 1984: 13)

The very detailed account that Descartes gives in *Meditation I*, and then in the five subsequent meditations, of what he is thinking, and thus what reasoning process he is going through, might be flawed as a logical, sequenced argument. Yet if we take on board Hatfield's notion of exemplification in terms of its role and its correlation with mental intuition, we can see the technical importance of direct apprehension as a philosophical tool.

Questions to do with phenomenology, and with exemplification and direct intuition, cannot be far from the mind of anyone who takes Jung's work seriously. Why? Recall that Hatfield regards 'exemplification' as bringing various matters 'directly before the mind, as a direct vision of God or as Christian virtue is exemplified in a contemplation of the life of Christ'. In Jung's *Red Book: Liber Novus*, the visual and literary material indicates that Jung encountered psychological phenomena of a highly sophisticated nature. That he gives his full attention to these phenomena is unquestionable: the detail in the illustrations and text is quite astonishing. That Jung had any kind of direct intuition is open to question: but it is arguable that his theory of mind, as we explore later, rests on a notion of direct intuition. Let us briefly turn to the *Red Book* to see what I mean.

The *Red Book: Liber Novus*

Jung's *Red Book: Liber Novus* is a visual instantiation of the elements of Philo's spiritual exercises. Its magnificent presentation of both text and illustration is awe-inspiring: here we have an exploration of unconsciousness vastly different from what we have seen in Descartes' *Meditations*, yet central to understanding Jung, just as the *Meditations* are central to understanding Descartes. The contrast is heightened if we consider that Descartes' is always a *conscious* set of rational deliberations aimed at certitude while Jung's is a work of explorative imagination, baroque in its sensibilities. Any adornment in Descartes' *Meditations* is a consequence of his thinking process – his turn of phrase, his allusion to his contemplating in wonder the divine being – necessarily minimalised in his transient sceptical stance.

Sonu Shamdasani, who edited and introduces *Liber Novus*, describes it as an 'extended process of self-experimentation . . . a work of psychology in a literary form' (Jung 2009: 194). There is no room in my current work to undertake a wide-ranging exploration of this psychological self-experimentation. I make some very general remarks about it, as the work of psychology that it is, but also as an important meditative record, a disclosure of a duality immanent in psychic life. That is to say, in his immersion in the unconscious and its manifestations of various archetypes through the images we find in the *Red Book,* Jung figures the psyche in both personal and suprapersonal or collective dimensions. Jung's notebooks, *Black Books,* where Jung records the experiments he undertakes with himself, are the basis of *Liber Novus* into which those records are subsequently transcribed.

The *Red Book* is a direct contrast to Descartes' *Meditations.* While Descartes' method secures his consciousness during the *Meditations,* Jung's exploration exceeds the boundaries of the discursive, and establishes the importance of phantasy and an awareness of his situatedeness in a psychic historical continuity. It does not aim to uncover indubitable foundations for belief. Yet it does have an epistemic function. Shamdasani notes that in the *Protocols* for *Memories, Dreams, Reflections* Jung 'recalled that his scientific question was to see what took place when he switched off consciousness'.[7]

According to Shamdasani, the deeply personal process of self-experimentation and exploration embarked on by Jung is based on Ludwig Staudenmaier's self-experimentation around automatic writing from which emerged 'a series of characters' with whom he could have dialogue. Staudenmaier experienced 'auditory and visual hallucinations'. The seriousness of the enterprise turns on Staudenmaier's aim, which was to use self-experimentation 'to provide a scientific explanation of magic'. Shamdasani also cites Swedenborg and Silberer as similarly interested in allowing the eruption of spontaneous imagery through writing and hypnosis (Jung 2009: 200). Jung's aim, then, can be framed within a rationale that has scientific knowledge as its *telos*. Its epistemic value, though, is not a product of rational thinking. Rather, it rests in its profoundly imaginative sensibility.

We saw earlier that Jung had given lectures on Ignatius' *Spiritual Exercises.* A key technique in the *Exercises* is to use the five senses in constructing images on which one might meditate. For example, in the Second Week Ignatius instructs the exercitant in this way:

> After the Preparatory Prayer and the three Preludes, it is helpful to pass the five senses of the imagination through the first and second Contemplation, in the following way:
>
> > **First Point**. The first Point is to see the persons with the sight of the imagination, meditating and contemplating in particular the details about them and drawing some profit from the sight.
> >
> > **Second Point**. The second, to hear with the hearing what they are, or might be, talking about and, reflecting on oneself, to draw some profit from it.
> >
> > **Third Point**. The third, to smell and to taste with the smell and the taste the infinite fragrance and sweetness of the Divinity, of the soul, and of its virtues, and of all, according to the person who is being contemplated; reflecting on oneself and drawing profit from it.

> **Fourth Point**. The fourth, to touch with the touch, as for instance, to embrace and kiss the places where such persons put their feet and sit, always seeing to my drawing profit from it.
>
> (Ignatius of Loyola 1522–1523 (1914): 39)

I doubt that it can be claimed that Jung's use of imagination is directly attributable to Ignatius' *Exercises.* That is not the point I would want to make. Rather, it is to help situate Jung within a tradition of deployment of the imagination for epistemic gain. Descartes, we saw earlier, had cautioned Elizabeth about ignoring the functions of the imagination and the senses by too frequently meditating on metaphysical principles. Jung's more immediate context provided imaginative sources through Goethe and Nietzsche; and his obvious interest in art (Jung 2009: 196, 203–204) would undoubtedly have fuelled his inquisitiveness about the boundaries of rational consciousness.[8]

Jung's *Red Book* reproduces an almost epic commentary and visual display, depicting aspects of a journey of a soul. In the style of Augustine's *Confessions* and *Soliloquies*, and Nietzsche's *Zarathustra*, the text is dialogical in one form or another, through the use of personification in which either the other speaks in the first person, or speaks in the first person through reported speech (Augustine 1961, 2000; Nietzsche 1999). The text is highly imagistic and follows its own conversational logic. It reports encounters with divine and evil beings. Sometimes it is commentary on the pictures which often take the form of a mandala. The pictures and text are passionate: urgency, despair, hope, wonder, joy, emerge as the self-exploration continues. There is no resolution . . . Yet Jung concludes the handwritten draft with '*Finis,*' surrounded by a box.

Jung's words before '*Finis*' gesture towards the importance of the Middle Ages, and he says that he 'must catch up with a piece of the Middle Ages – within myself'. A long process of self-discovery and explorative confrontation with the collective unconscious has resulted in this declaration to himself. Its meaning is uncertain. His work on types, which relies heavily on classical and mediaeval philosophy, was begun in 1913 (Jung 1971). Perhaps this work had helped to focus his interest in the imagery of that period; Jung's influences are so complex that it is difficult to tease out all of the threads, so who knows? What I want to stress, though, is that the penultimate words of *Liber Primus* are, 'The touchstone is being alone with oneself. This is the way' (Jung 2009: 330).

In my view, we have encapsulated in these two sentences a living endorsement of the importance of solitude to the directionality of spiritual practice. We see that in Descartes, and we see it now in Jung. Certainly, there is a major teleological difference between Jung and Descartes – the conscious/unconscious 'divide' would be a sterling example of this. But the notion of solitude gives us a clue to working through what I see as the puzzle of twoness; the puzzle relating to the group of tropes that burden Brooke and Romanyshyn: subject/object, interiority/exteriority, for example. Another 'pair' that might be added in here is imagination and reason: yet in Descartes they are not competitors for the epistemic or emotional limelight: they work together, and I think the same is true of Jung, if not quite so explicitly. A question which can be raised is, 'What is the opposite of solitude – is there one?' If we insist on a 'mend' in the tear between human consciousness and world, where does this leave any distinctions at all? I explore this in the next chapter.

Importantly for now, there is a major teleological difference in the two approaches to, and uses of, spiritual exercises, and meditation. We can think of this in terms of *existential appropriateness* to the intended outcome of spiritual practice. While Descartes includes imagination in his list of what thinking is, it is a silent aspect in his phenomenological deduction which is itself an imaginative mental act. Yet it is not a silent, but a very prominent, and noisy (to carry on with the auditory metaphor) aspect of Jung's spiritual exercise of being led by his unconscious.

Consider, for example, that through the use of the imagination, Jung arrives at what I think he would claim is a demonstration of the objectivity of the psyche. Descartes abdicates from what he has accepted as true and in a sense he is committed to an austere minimalism of image. The thinking thing he finds himself to be appears to be minimally conscious of its own self in its different manifestations of thinking, particularly in doubt. It is uncertain that Jung engages in a similar abdication; yet he pushes past the extremities of the conscious by permitting a dissolution of its constraints. As a scientific concern, Jung aimed to find out what would happen if he 'switched off consciousness' and undertook 'frequent exercises in the emptying of consciousness' (Jung 2009: 200). To be open in this way demands courage. Some of the aspects of spiritual practice that we saw in Philo's list are most certainly evident in the legacy of Jung's experience. If nothing else, attention, self-mastery and meditation are manifest in his intensely figured prose. And we should, also, consider that the *Red Book* exemplifies, in the sense of spiritual exemplification, Jung's spiritual commitment and insight together with his belief in the possibility of a therapeutics of the soul.

I take up some of the issues raised here later on, but many, if not all, of the critiques of the inner and outer trope rely on some notion of subjectivity and objectivity, which they, it seems to me, simultaneously disavow. The dualistic structure in which these tropes sit now becomes the topic of the next chapter.

Chapter 3

Descartes and the making of distinctions

What are the difficulties with the subject/object and inner/outer distinctions? How can we imagine those difficulties when 'inner' and 'outer' with respect to ourselves and not-ourselves seem so much part of the furniture of our worlds? One way to do this is to conceive of them as instances of a wider notion, that of dualism, which has been part of the conceptual framework of philosophy since its beginnings.

Dualism takes on many faces: metaphysical, moral, aesthetic, psychological. Often there is implicit value judgement contained in its use; often it is meant to indicate separation of different orientations. 'Day and night' can be, for example, seen as a dualistic structure that either describes my psychological disposition, with the further pairing of 'day' and 'sunny' as desirable and 'night' and 'darkness' as undesirable; or it may simply be a description or a naming of time in a twenty-four-hour period. This mix of common usage and metaphor inflected with value might well be part of the problem, so let us look at some of the structures of dualism, assuming we can identify such, and see how it works. Overall, we can locate dualism within a broader categorisation of distinction making, so we begin there.

We can never know what were the original distinctions, or how and why they arose, but we might assume that, as humans, our ancestors' survival motivated acting on dangers and opportunities they discerned in their environments. Further, just as we do, they undoubtedly lived in and through change: diurnal, annual, climatic, illness and health, plenty and scarcity, birth and death. This anthropological observation is about everydayness to some extent and about practicality and survival: it suggests that a basic separation of the world into two different, and opposite, kinds has its origins in human existence and perception. What it also suggests is that the history of human action, and human recorded thinking, is the history of dualism, of making distinctions and thinking in opposites: day/night, safety/danger, cold/hot, dead/alive, poisonous/beneficial.[1]

'Dualism' is not something new, invented as a result of the scientific revolution of the sixteenth and seventeenth centuries, a departure from a wholistic feminine world that saw a seamless continuity between humans and where they found themselves.[2] We find, across cultures, gods and demons, good and evil, heroes and villains, god and humans, humans and animals, body and soul, in which a preference is accorded to one pair of the conjunction. Such preferencing effected a change in understanding: from conjunction to disjunction: either god or demon, good or evil, hero or villain, and so on. A vision of what the relevant world *should* be like, and how that *should* be brought about meant that customs, rituals, wars, and hierarchies that favoured some groups, concepts and belief systems over others were devised to implement and sustain that vision. So what is apparent is that disjunctive preferencing already includes some idea of value, so that the axiological dimensions of dualism have had a pervasive presence for a long time in human history.

That, however, is not the whole story, as the current and various understandings of dualism indicate. Howard Robinson says that:

> [t]he term 'dualism' has a variety of uses in the history of thought. In general, the idea is that, for some particular domain, there are two fundamental kinds or categories of things or principles. In theology, for example a 'dualist' is someone who believes that Good and Evil – or God and the Devil – are independent and more or less equal forces in the world . . . Because common sense tells us that there are physical bodies, and because there is intellectual pressure towards producing a unified view of the world, one could say that materialist monism is the 'default option'. Discussion about dualism, therefore, tends to start from the assumption of the reality of the physical world, and then to consider arguments for why the mind cannot be treated as simply part of that world.
>
> (Robinson 2009)

It is wise for us to bear in mind the various uses of 'dualism', and especially Robinson's suggestion about the 'default option', materialist monism. Materialist monist views represent a turn in thinking about not only fundamental reality, but also in what is to be preferred from an explanatory perspective. In this view of the world, there is only one kind of 'stuff' – material or physical – that comes into being and goes out, has causal efficacy and occupies space and time. 'God' is explicable in terms of the human psyche; and unnatural occurrences such as miracles can be explained by the laws of nature.

We can see the various uses of dualism reflected in the rather contentiously debated politics of metaphysics and ontology that contributed another dimension to philosophical discourses at the end of the twentieth century. We can also see its predominance in feminist and gender debates, in postmodern deconstructionist antitheory, and in cultural and postcolonial studies. Analyses of dualism have often revolved around questions of essence and social construction, and nature and nurture.

Robinson's own understanding of dualism is embedded in a now long-standing debate over metaphysical dualism that has its origins in pre-Socratic philosophy. However, his general description of dualism as a domain-specific pairing of terms ('kinds or categories of things or principles') can be thought of as a thumbnail sketch that is both very brief and very informative. Robinson's characterisation takes a neutral view with respect to the relationships between the pairs of terms constituting the relevant dualism. Indeed, Robinson's example from theology tells us that the paired terms, Good and Evil, or God and the Devil, 'are more or less equal forces in the world'. He does not allude to a hierarchy or value ladenness around the pair, that, for example, one should be preferred to the other, or that one is superior to the other from a moral perspective, for instance. Their being equal forces in the world suggests, instead, that questions as to which should be higher in any proposed hierarchy, are void.

As a matter of fact, Descartes holds that 'it is quite clear that sensations in the soul are a direct function of what happens in the body, and in particular, in the central nervous system' (Brown 2006: 69; Descartes 1984: 56–61). If that is the case, then there is an interdependence of mind/soul and body that seems to imply there is some causal *necessity* intrinsic to that relationship – you can't have one without the other. Thus Descartes' discussion of the relation between mind and body is salient for our purposes, dealing as it does with some of the problems of metaphysical dualism that have allegedly beset not only his own philosophy, but subsequent theories of mind and body, and influenced – but not determined – the generations that have followed (including Jung).

Value dualism

Recent analyses of dualism have argued for an explicit value ladenness of hierarchically ordered paired terms. The trend to rethink the body after Freud and Foucault, and specific critiques of dualism by feminist, environmental, cultural and political theorists have meant that dualistic paradigms have come under very close scrutiny (Merchant 1989; Heyes 2007; Shusterman 2008). For example, in Val Plumwood's view:

> [d]ualism is a relation of separation inscribed and naturalized in culture and characterized by radical exclusion, distancing and opposition between orders constructed as systematically higher and lower, as inferior and superior, as ruler and ruled which treats the division as part of the beings construed not merely as different but as belonging to radically different orders or kinds, and hence as not open to change.
>
> (Plumwood 1993: 47–48)

Plumwood argues that the resulting oppression that is the outcome of particular figurings of gender, environment, race and colonisation has unacceptable implications for women, for nature and for ecology, indeed for all 'inferiorised others'.

Plumwood methodically demonstrates that her view of dualism is evident in Descartes' philosophy, that is to say, as she understands his work. She sees his as a development of earlier Aristotelian thinking about the rationality of nature that paralleled Aristotle's view of human rationality. Aristotelian thinking was 'organised around hierarchy' (Plumwood 1993: 105), and Cartesian philosophy, she holds, develops and expands the rationalist tradition. Ultimately, though, rationality is stripped from nature, and centred on the human, and human reason, and thus the mind.

Plumwood identifies five features that she maintains constitute the logical structure of dualism:

1. backgrounding or denial
2. radical exclusion or hyperseparation
3. incorporation or relational definition
4. instrumentalism
5. homogenisation or stereotyping (Plumwood 1993: 48–55).

These logical features are evident in the case of Cartesian dualism, she asserts, the mind being superior to the body in a hierarchy constructed around reason, with the human (in virtue of its possession of reason) being superior to nature. The alignment of reason with the human renders the body and nature as polarised others, devoid of mind and intentionality, and seen in terms of mechanism. She argues that in 'dualistic structure, as in hierarchy, the qualities (actual or supposed), the culture, the values, and the areas of life associated with the dualised other are systematically and pervasively constructed and depicted as inferior' (Plumwood 1993: 47).

Plumwood argues that Descartes' dualism is not simply a matter of a distinction between mind and body, as some commentators assert. Rather, it is a distinction embedded in a hierarchy, the elements of which are just those points 1–5, above. The value ladenness of Descartes' dualism is illustrated in his use of 'radical exclusion, through relational definition (defining nature as lack), and through instrumentalism and homogenisation' (Plumwood 1993: 112).

Plumwood's account brilliantly analyses 'the dominant conception of reason' that 'gives rise to a dualised structure of otherness and negation' that 'corresponds to that of classical propositional logic' (Plumwood 1993: 42). Far from there being *naturally* present in the world relations of domination, on this account, those relations are constructed around how humans, male humans in particular, have thought about the world. Subsequently male privilege has been construed in terms of categories of exclusion, denial, and othering, that relegate nature, and women, to an inferiorised alterity, subordinate to male hierarchies of value.

Plumwood's is one account of the value ladenness of dualism that endorses a view, found elsewhere, of Descartes' culpability in the current eco-crisis (Abram 1996; Brooke 2000; Romanyshyn 2000). She remarks that:

> [o]n Descartes' account, mind, the inner mechanism which explains the operations of the mechanically conceived human body, also divides humans utterly from the rest of nature from which mind is totally absent . . . [s]ubject/object dualism is another legacy of the Cartesian denial of mindlike features of the world which underlies western scientific accounts of objectivity.
>
> (Plumwood 1993: 113, 123)

Undoubtedly the view that the radical separation of mind and body, humans and nature, and objectivity and subjectivity has dominated scientific and cultural practice since the scientific revolution is convincing. My worry though is that the tendency to 'blame' Descartes unfairly describes his projects, and takes his work out of a context in which it is best understood. More on this in a moment.

An important consideration here is Plumwood's acknowledging that it is not just a matter of distinctions being made, that we come up with categories, or classes, or two-term distinctions: it is what is *done* with the distinction that creates the problems. One might say that the coming up with a distinction, and doing whatever we do with that distinction, are separate but connected processes. So any distinction that involves paired opposites is potentially dualistic on this reading. What might seem to be a relatively harmless distinction becomes a dualism when we attribute a greater value to a quality, or category, or prefer it over its opposite partner in some systematic way. This is relevant to arguments about Descartes, especially in relation to the *cogito*, where there seems to be a very heavy bias towards the mind over the body. As we shall see, however, this is orthodoxy about Descartes, rather than either his intention or what he argued, full stop.

For now, let me say that Plumwood's account of dualism is very different from the apparently value-free analysis offered by Robinson and others. Consider the following. According to John Foster, '[d]ualism is a doctrine about the mental and the physical realms and the relationship between them'. We can, he says, identify five claims that conjoin to produce the doctrine.

1. There is a mental realm.
2. The mental realm is fundamental.
3. There is a physical realm.
4. The physical realm is fundamental.
5. The two realms are ontologically separate (Foster 1991: 1).

Foster is talking about *what there is and the nature of what there is, and the relationships between propositions.* In short, how are the mind and body related? Are 'they' separate, the very same thing under different descriptions, or one thing with ontologically different properties? His account of mind/body dualism does not deal with the question of value through an extrapolation of hierarchies. For him, mind/body dualism is a metaphysical problem that cannot be solved by appeal to values. Rather, it is the terms and intricacies of argument that dictate the acceptability and soundness of views around the mind/body question. One might even eliminate the mind as a category altogether, as materialists have asserted one should.

Foster identifies weaker and stronger materialists, the former who claim that 'all concrete entities, at least all that figure in the fundamental reality, are physical'; and the latter who claim that 'concrete reality is, at least at the fundamental level, purely physical – that every contingent fact, or state of affairs, is either physical or physically constituted' (Foster 1991: 17). Foster maintains that materialists are concerned to 'adjust' dualists' views of the mental, in a move that he sees as running counter to 'common sense'. The common-sense view, he claims, accepts the irreducibility of mental phenomena: mental phenomena retain their identity as mental phenomena because they are of a different non-material order from material or physical phenomena. He proposes that materialists adjust dualist views in one of two ways:

1. by showing that mental phenomena '*are* amenable to a materialist treatment' or
2. by rejecting the existence of minds and mental phenomena (mental nihilism or eliminativism).

Such adjustment deals interestingly with the mental in terms of Plumwood's account of dualism. In Foster's case, the givenness of categories (mind or consciousness, for example) is up for grabs: the material world is seen as ontologically basic, and the mind is cast as ontologically dubious. On this view, a materialist account of the mind is inevitably reductive, even if it does not entail eliminativism. Once a materialist account is settled, the possibility of collapsing public and private with respect to mental contents is available.

In theory, this would mean that second- and third-party access to my thoughts or to your thoughts becomes potential, as our minds, now material entities, would inhabit the domain of the publicly observable. Doubt might be cast on notions like freedom of the will as a 'convenient fiction': what used to be our private minds would now be seen as public, material entities subject to the same forces and necessities as any other public, material entity. Observation of our behaviour and of our brains would amount to observation of our selves. Along with this, the role of prediction in relation to people's behaviour might take on a whole new face: given our own behaviour in the past, and given similar behaviour by our fellow humans, we might be slotted into categories of inevitability in which the past dictates the future in strong deterministic patterns.[3]

It is plausible to assume that if there is any value dualism, meaning that there are instances of two-term distinction making, which either implicitly or explicitly privileges one member of the pair over the other operating here, it is that the material hierarchically dominates the mental (or spiritual). If mental language were retained, it would be recoded to mean not what we currently take it to be, but as an alternative to its *real meaning*, namely that it signifies a different set of materialist assumptions. On this view, Plumwood's notion of hyperseparation is at work, and this is where it gets interesting: it is the *mind*, and not the material, that is excluded. In other words, matter, in this case, is privileged over mind.

While Foster's defence of dualism, in which the mental retains a metaphysical integrity of its own, is an attempt to repudiate the claims of materialists, eliminativism, for example, favours the precedence of the material over the mental. One eliminates what one does not want, or is no longer useful, or is unsatisfactory from an explanatory and evidential perspective. As we saw, Plumwood argues that backgrounding or denial, radical exclusion or hyperseparation, incorporation or relational definition and instrumentalism are features of dualism, and now, here they are appearing in materialist accounts. In the materialist view, issues around the mental as an ontological category can be relatively easily dealt with if its existence is denied, and supplanted by an account that is more understandable, has the science to back it up, and is theoretically reliable. I say 'relatively easily' but this is difficult to achieve. And that is just what might be claimed by proponents of materialism, that *their* accounts capture the truth of the matter, are more relevant and in touch with modern science. Far from accepting the terms of a dualist debate (that there are two substances or two sets of properties, for example, one mental and the other physical), adjustment by materialists seeks to identify what is *really* the case. On this view, the mental is explicable in terms of the material and we do not *need* the language of the mental.

Amongst the questions we might raise is whether or not Descartes' distinction between mind and body is dualistic in the sense outlined by Plumwood. While her analysis raises issues about how we are to think about dualism, we seem to have two different conceptions, one value-free, the other value-laden. The trouble is that for many traditionally conceived dualisms, Plumwood would seem to be right about the hierarchically embedded nature of our thinking about oppositional categories: sex/gender and class systems, and the Pythagorean Table of Opposites illustrate this very nicely (Aristotle 1991: Book 1 986a). And, from a moral perspective, our conceptions of good and bad are completely value-laden, even in the making of the fundamental distinctions we make (thou shalt not kill, lie, commit adultery, steal, drive too fast).

In relation to Descartes, it is overly simplistic to argue that his mind and body distinction was embedded in a hierarchy that had all of the features of Plumwood's dualism. Descartes' account of the union of mind and body, for example, could suggest that he conceived of that union as basic, so that mind is not privileged over body. Rather, mind as consciousness is the instrument of awareness of embodiment and could not operate without body. This is a significant modification of what many of us have come to believe about Descartes' dualism, and it reflects Jung's own position on mind and body.

The critics of Jung, who see his work as a reiteration of Descartes' dualistic metaphysics, seem to be unaware that Descartes fruitfully, although controversially, employs the notion of a real distinction between mind and body, that his dualism is, in part, procedural, and thirdly, they seem, even if unwittingly, to buy into the populist idea that his metaphysics exemplifies Plumwood's analysis of dualism. Before moving on to explore this more, let me indicate where we are in our argument.

As I see it, there are three points to take from this discussion:

1. The relationship between the paired terms in the metaphysical debate has been seen to be value-laden.
2. The existence of at least one of the terms in the metaphysical dualist debate is highly contentious.
3. Value dualism argues not that there are ontological categories or properties or substances, but that there are hierarchical relations between paired terms, explicable in the logical structure argued for by Plumwood.

Commentators who raise objections to Jung seem to be oblivious to the above discussions and distinctions. They seem also to be unaware that making distinctions that are *not* dualistic, making distinctions that *are* dualistic, and acknowledging that such distinctions can serve us all well, existentially and in our theory making, are part of the cognitive apparatus of theoretical and practical life. In defending the earth, or the soul, or suggesting that inside/outside distinctions accept and exaggerate the subject/object distinction, they take on board an acritical view of dualism which does not reflect the complexity of debates around dualism. Nor does such acritical simplification do justice to either Descartes or Jung. As Deborah Brown points out, there are some very difficult issues to be contended with in Descartes' dualism. In particular, the relationship between mind and body is not straightforward:

> The sense in which the mind 'in-forms' the body is the sense in which, at any given time, a parcel of matter through its relation to a mind becomes a human body, matter being otherwise undifferentiated . . . The Cartesian mind does not in-form the body in the way the soul does on Scholastic account, that is, in the sense of determining all the functions of the body. But by its relationship to a mind, matter is promoted to a special status and subject to new modes of explanation. . . . The human body cannot properly be understood apart from the mind to which it stands in a non-accidental relationship and with which it comprises a functional unity.
>
> (Brown 2006: 6)

The idea that there is a rational soul, the mind that acts indifferently in relation to the body and the world, is challenged by the above considerations. Furthermore, the role of the passions is critical to our understanding of the mind/body relationship, and to Descartes' meditational method and its aims. I return to this important point later in the chapter.

Thus, it seems almost undeniable that such dualism is present in our thinking. To pre-empt my discussion of the natural attitude, value dualism might be seen as just the kind of judgement that needs to be suspended in the phenomenological *epochē*.

The construction of paired terms that are opposites might be a part of what we have come to see as natural orientations towards the world and ourselves. Many of us subscribe to the notion of free will and to the possibility that we, as agents, can make genuine choices. If we are entirely physical matter and if all physical matter is subject to causal laws, then free will and the possibility of making genuine choices would turn out to be a fiction. There are pragmatic reasons, of course, for going along with these fictions, if that is what they are, since our legal systems, for example, are built on ideas of free will, agency, culpability and moral responsibility. The resolution of the metaphysical issues in which mind/body dualism are embedded will some day, no doubt, give us some clarity. If we did turn out to be totally physical matter systems and thus subject to causal laws, one wonders if we would still continue *as if* we have free will and are agents. These matters are far beyond my concerns in this book, however.

One lesson we might draw from such considerations is that some dualistic notions can be very useful to us. In the above examples, it seems as if dualistic structures might be seen as pragmatic: notions of good and evil, legal and illegal, decisions about whether or not to eat meat, and if so, tofu or lentils, or lamb or chicken, form part of the way our societies operate. We accept that, and it works.

An extension of this pragmatic characterisation of dualism is to do with method. Descartes' *Meditations*, aimed as they are at discovering indubitable belief, might be seen as invoking the radical distinction between mind and body as a methodological move. That is to say, he engages in a procedure or method that will lead to a resolution of the doubts he is entertaining. Such a method, let us call it methodological dualism, is part of a philosophical process of thinking and explanation, integral to an overall argument that results not in a definitive metaphysical and/or value dualism, but in a different mode of conceiving problems engendered by these dualisms.

A concept tied to methodological dualism is the teleological notion of existential appropriateness: one goes about achieving one's ends by describing them in such and such a way, and then enacts that description through a particular procedure or method. In Descartes' case, he firstly describes his doubt (that he has taken as true things that turn out to be false), then describes what his ends are (indubitable beliefs), then describes how he will achieve those ends (by being alone, and doubting everything). An effect of that 'how' is that Descartes comes to the conclusion that he cannot doubt that he is thinking (even though he can doubt the existence of his own body). The dualistic separation that occurs here – the distinction between mind and body – then becomes central to his *reconstruction* of the world from first principles (Gaukroger 1995: 344). Descartes' return to the body and mind as a unity in *Meditation VI* comes, on this reading, as a reinstatement of what he has always held to be the case, but put in suspension for the sake of certainty.

Very clearly, Jung is not engaged in a teleological process such as this. His encounter with the unconscious, for example, as we saw in the *Red Book,* came about because of his desire to see what would happen if he switched off consciousness. Methodologically, what he does, and what Descartes does, are quite differently motivated. From the perspective of existential appropriateness, the descriptions of what they do and why are quite different. Jung does, however, insist on the unity of mind and body, yet he focuses very often on the psyche *as if* the psyche, considered as distinct from the body, is privileged. Let us see where Jung does this.

Setting the problem

Both Roger Brooke and Robert Romanyshyn highlight some problems in the same piece of text in volume 8 of Jung's *Collected Works*. This is the text which I shall refer to as the Fog Argument:

> It is my mind, with its store of images, that gives the world colour and sound; and that supremely real and rational certainty which I call 'experience' is, in its most simple form, an exceedingly complicated structure of mental images. There is, in a certain sense, nothing that is directly experienced except the mind itself . . . So thick and deceptive is this fog about us that we had to invent the exact sciences in order to catch at least a glimmer of the so-called 'real' nature of things.
>
> (Jung 1972: 623)

Although, Brooke claims, Carl Jung does not discuss Descartes at all, his 'failure to conduct an adequate phenomenological epoche' (*sic*) means that Jung 'is often submerged in Cartesian philosophy – and with it, Galilean science'. Brooke argues that Jung saw psychological life 'encapsulated within the head' where 'the world drained of human habitation is reduced to the *res extensa* of Descartes that is, the realm of mathematical and physical co-ordinates (Brooke 2000: 20–21). Likewise, Romanyshyn finds the text quoted above very worrisome, claiming that 'it clearly illustrates that his psychology is haunted by a dualism of inside and outside, leaving soul without world and world without soul' (Romanyshyn 2000: 31). The above is a source of Brooke's complaint about Jung, in which, yes, Jung *is* speaking about the mediating effect of the mind in relation to the world and 'its colour and sound'. It is not to be so straightforwardly understood however.

Jung's comments about the mind are made while he is attending to the mind/body question, specifically while he is discussing the nature of spirit.

Thus, in my view, he is deploying what I referred to above as methodological dualism. He begins his discussion by arguing for a nuanced understanding of 'spirit' in virtue of the ambiguity surrounding its use. He argues that when he utters 'the word "spirit," no matter how accurately I may define the meaning I intend it to convey, the aura of its many other meanings cannot be wholly excluded' (Jung 1972: 602). In part, this illustrates Jung's awareness of the complexity of terms and concepts.

Follow his discussion through to the problematic quote, and even if one can critique his findings, it cannot be maintained that he had a habit of conflating various semantic contexts. Indeed, his awareness of the difficulties he attempts to express and discover with and through language is a feature of his writing.[4] His remarks about the mind/body relation emerge in his reflections on other sets of relations, those between spirit and life, life and living body, spirit and psychic factors (Jung 1972: 604).

He sees his approach as essentially empirical rather than philosophical and is careful to allude to the possibility that he might be seen as taking the opportunity to 'indulge' in talk about mind and body. His point, though, is that he is seeking clarification of the term 'spirit' in relation to life, and the living body and, for him, this does raise questions about the relation between mind and body. Here, he is identifying what I consider to be his existentially appropriate context.

Jung maintains that talking about the living body is an easier task than talking about the more general concept 'life' because the body is a 'visible and tangible reality'. He takes a systemic and functional view of the body and notes that the body 'is a phenomenon of the living being apprehended by our senses . . . a purposive arrangement of matter that makes a living being possible'. We need to note that he distinguishes between the body *per se*, and its living system, noting that he will not defend or criticise the separation of the body and the living being. As we shall see later, this is entirely in keeping a distinction made also by Husserl and Merleau-Ponty. Jung's awareness that he is dealing with a dualistic conception of body and psychic factor finds him postulating an apparently causal relation between body and psyche: the body makes life possible, and the psyche is necessary for the life of the body (Jung 1972: 605). Here we see a reiteration of the position that Descartes holds.

Jung identifies different approaches to thinking of the relation between psyche and body. He raises the question of the 'ancient duality of mind and body' as a possible way of understanding the notion of living being, asking if we have to assume that 'living being' and 'psychic factor' are equivalent. He also asks 'if there are any reasons that would justify the separation of the "living being" from the psyche'. Note that these are formulated *as questions*, and are not positions for which Jung is opting. He is very clear that he thinks a relationship *does* exist between the body and psychic process, which he maintains is a phenomenon dependent on the nervous system (Jung 1972: 606–607). He concludes that the psyche consists of 'reflected images of conscious processes in the brain and of reproduction of these images in an almost infinite series'. That, of course, raises the issue of what consciousness is, a problem that Jung does not want to tackle.

He does, however, suggest that an association between psychic process and the ego produces consciousness. No association means that content remains unconscious. His discussion of the ego leads to his asserting that there is a relationship of dependence between ego and consciousness, the latter being the necessary precondition for the former. He also points out that, paradoxically, consciousness is unthinkable without the ego, which is itself composed of many interplaying processes. Jung explicates the relation between what he calls the sense-consciousnesses and the ego complex, and he uses the term 'ego-consciousness' to suggest that relation.

The complicated sets of relationships postulated here give us an inkling into the complexity of Jung's thinking around mind and body. He holds that mind and body, 'presumably a pair of opposites', are an *expression* (my italics) 'of a single entity whose essential nature is not knowable either from its outward, material manifestation or from inner direct perception'. In my view, Jung's conclusion, that the separation of mind and body 'may finally prove to be merely a device of reason for the purpose of conscious discrimination – an intellectually necessary separation of one and the same fact into two aspects to which we then illegitimately attribute and independent existence' (Jung 1972: 619), is the key to his views regarding mind and body.

Between paragraphs 619 and 626 of the same essay, Jung's discussion of dualism is a development of two points: 'the realistic standpoint of scientific thinking' and the psychological standpoint (or what we might call the phenomenological point of view). Jung claims that he is dubious about the 'exclusive validity' of the scientific standpoint, and proposes the psychological standpoint as an alternative. And it is here, finally, that we come to the tendentious piece of text to which both Brooke and Romanyshyn take exception.

We need to note that Jung's contention that 'what we are immediately aware of in ourselves, are conscious contents that flow from remote obscure sources' is an epistemic claim about our knowledge of the world. The status of that world is, for him, not something he wants to contest, and he is very clear about that. Nor does he want to opt for an idealistic standpoint, which is what both Brooke and Romanyshyn seem to imply he does. Indeed, Brooke's claim that we are left with a world drained of human habitation and Descartes' *'res extensa'*; and Romanyshyn's claim that Jung leaves 'soul without world and world without soul' are conclusions that Jung would deliberately seek to avoid, as we see in what comes next in his text.

While Jung does argue that we live in a world of images, he is keen to develop a position midway between the 'extreme opposites' of full-blown realism and full-blown idealism. That is to say, he does not want to accept a reductionist view that would claim either that there is only physical matter or only psychic 'presence'. He seems to be proposing a phenomenology based on what it is like to have certain kinds of experiences, a phenomenology that lies outside scientific verification.[5] He does not want, though, to ditch scientific verification.

For him, that someone has an experience of a certain kind is not open to question: but he focuses on the *having* of the experience and not on the *content* of that experience. In Jung's view, the claim that someone has experienced God or seen a ghost is not open to empirical investigation from the point of view of demonstrating the existence of the objects of the person's experiences. He makes a similar point in the Terry Lectures, and when he is talking about phenomena as facts (Jung 1938: 3).

As I read him, though, he would not be averse to scientific investigation of the existence of either God or ghosts, although that is not the concern of psychology as he understands it. To reiterate, he makes a distinction between the *having* of an experience (experiencing) and the *content* of that experience (or object of experiencing). The ontological status of the 'contents' of an experience, or what the experience is of (not the concern of psychology), is different from the ontological status of the having of that experience.

Jung's distinction between the factuality of having of an experience in terms of the *consciousness* of content and the *ontological status of that content* discloses his investment in the idea of a world *with* soul, and a soul *with* world. Neither endorsing the realist nor the idealist standpoint, he attempts to capture the importance of the soul (*esse in anima*) as a middle way that embodies spirit, and inspirits body (compare this with Brown's suggestion that, for Descartes, the mind in-forms the body (above)). In my view, his emphasis on *spirit* and its relation to conscious ego and the unconscious is an attempt to ensure a connection between life as manifested in the living body, and spirit as manifested in the psyche. 'Life is a touchstone for the truth of the spirit . . . (s)pirit gives meaning to his life' he maintains (Jung 1972: 647–648). Importantly, Jung here gives a strong indication of his leaning towards a phenomenological account of the psyche. His essay 'Analytical Psychology and 'Weltanschauung' provides us with an elaboration of this middle or third way. But more about this later.

Elements of Plumwood's account of dualism are not evident in what Jung argues about the body and mind relation, although a superficial skimming of his text might lead one to be sympathetic with the view that his work is rife with dualistic assumptions. Further, the invocation of value as an integral part of dualism needs defending, and not mere acceptance. As I see it, there are some good reasons to maintain very strict boundaries between 'opposing' and value-laden categories (like, for example, moral goodness and badness: is paedophilia ever morally good?). Jung's insight that the separation of mind and body might be a 'device of reason for the purpose of conscious discrimination' may provide a means to think further about dualism in general.

For now, we can see that we have good grounds for doubting the inferences that Brooke and Romanyshyn draw from the troublesome quote. Jung does not appear to be making a radical separation between different orders of being, or establishing a hierarchy of paired terms. Rather, he is attempting to do what both Brooke and Romanyshyn tell us he is *not* doing: Jung is adamant that spirit, soul, psyche permeate the life world of which he speaks. This leads to the possibility that their attributing to Jung a version of Descartes' philosophy that invokes a dualism of the kind identified by Plumwood is limited or mistaken; it leads to the possibility that, initially, their reading of Descartes is also limited (as may also be the case for Plumwood). What is in evidence is that there is a conflation of Jung's views with Descartes' dualistic philosophy, with the result that the way in which each thinker is read is problematic.

Earlier, I identified three points that emerge in discussions of Jung and Descartes that I consider to be central to understanding the conceptual links between them. Let me now return to those themes and explore them more fully. Overall, what these themes suggest is a sentimentalising of the past together with a certain misunderstanding of the interplay between different historical contingencies and events. For example, the effect of religious sensibility and practice, and their changing forms and content from the mediaeval period through the Renaissance and Reformation, seem to be overlooked.[6] While I have no particular complaints about sentiment *per se*, the sentimentalising of a past in which historical context is either avoided or erased seems to appeal to us on an emotional plane devoid of rational framing. This has the potential to ally us with superstition and with a fantasy, historical world as we would like it to be rather than like it was. From my perspective, that has potentially dangerous consequences.

Descartes' real distinction, phenomenologically read

I talked above, in very general terms, about distinction making. If we consider the kinds of distinctions we do in fact all make, we can see that conscious judgement regarding their content is usually involved. We make distinctions for many different reasons, and while we might be able to develop a taxonomy of distinctions revolving around their purpose (why we make distinctions), how we make them, what gets included and what excluded, and the principles we use in distinction making, we can see that distinctions themselves range from the broad to the very narrow. And that is the key, really, to making distinctions: we make them to classify, to sort things out, to make the world either more complex and difficult or more simple and easy to navigate using our judgement, deliberatively or spontaneously.

If we had a bowl of produce from our garden sitting on the kitchen bench, we can classify what we have: maybe we have fruit, eggs, vegetables and herbs. We might have apples, plums, pears and quinces; chicken eggs and duck eggs; courgettes, tomatoes, spinach and lettuce; rosemary, oregano, thyme and chives. Initially, we might refer to our produce as early autumn or late summer, and comment that it's getting cooler so the chickens aren't laying as well as they did. We might decide the chickens being on strike is because of the turn in the weather: laying goes off in the cool days of autumn. So we make judgements using our local knowledge, and our past experience, and our reason, and sometimes our intuition. Even that we can say that there is produce and that it's on the kitchen bench is to use language, one of our modes of distinction making.

Identifying our produce broadly, and then classifying and gradually refining our classifications, say, by deciding what it's used for, whether it's cooked or eaten raw, by itself or with other produce, a principal ingredient or flavouring, means that we are making important distinctions about some very practical matters. Making comments about the seasons and their impact on our produce is also to make distinctions between events and their effects. And underpinning all of these activities is our awareness of the worlds we live in and that we experience; that is to say, what I have been talking about is largely phenomenological. We encounter and engage with phenomena of all different kinds, some 'external' to us, some 'internal'. Jung's Fog Argument notwithstanding, we take the world and our minds to be the way they are.

Underlying our distinction making is the activity of our brains, our innate capacities to think and judge and discern, our abilities to reflect and imagine, to solve problems, *to be conscious* (Blackmore 2006). So the practical activity that we see expressed in the above example is dependent on what we are like physiologically, as human beings. Our distinction making is not entirely practical, however, even as it might involve knowledge of the empirical world and the ordinary everyday. For example, we often make distinctions that require thought and consideration, a deliberate and deliberative withdrawal to consider some matter or other. Descartes' *Meditations on First Philosophy* exemplifies this.

I argued earlier that we can think about dualism methodologically: associated with the idea of existential appropriateness, which is principally descriptive, we can think that we use dualism as a methodological device to help achieve an end we have pinpointed for ourselves. This teleological approach does not, however, attend to what the *content* might be about. A prospective antagonist might argue, for example, that although it might be the case that dualism can be conceived methodologically, as I suggest, the status of the two terms is not decided. To what do they refer? Is there anything over and above the methodological considerations I outlined?

When Descartes discusses the mind and body and their differences, he argues that bodies or material substance are extended, and the mind or thinking substance is unextended. He is engaged in both description and in using his judgement in making these claims. In other words, he says how he understands *what things are like, to him*: we might hear his saying 'look around you, and you will see that the world contains material bodies all of which are extended, and minds (of humans) none of which is extended'. But for Descartes, this was not simply an empirical matter, invoking as he does the idea of *real distinction*. He goes further than simply observing, and, rightly or wrongly, he is moved by his judgement and his cognition. His cognitive activity is not suppressed in his meditation. He is knowledge making and developing a metaphysics that he sees as the ground of his knowledge. Indeed, he makes a metaphysical claim based on his belief that there is a guarantor of the distinction, a divine being who is not a deceiver.

As Carriero says, Descartes' argument is an attempt to show that 'there is a truth corresponding to my grasp of the body as an extended thing' that there is a 'distinct cognition of body [that] involves true and immutable natures' (Carriero 2009: 281). In other words, Descartes' focus is not simply to report some empirical fact that we can know by observation, or even to use a dualistic distinction to achieve a methodological step forward: reason kicks in here as the arbiter of establishing what ultimately corresponds to an epistemological certainty.

The distinction to which Carriero is referring appears in *Meditation VI*. What exactly a real distinction is, is important not only to our understanding of Descartes, and also to our understanding of Jung. It is important to our understanding of Jung because the kinds of distinctions he himself makes benefit, I think, from being understood within a Cartesian framework. For example, there is a real distinction between the collective unconscious and the personal unconscious just as there is a real distinction between archetypes and archetypal images. Because there is a real distinction between them, it does not follow, as we shall see, that there is no *connection* between the personal and collective unconscious, or archetypal images and the archetypes. So in this section, I am going to explore Descartes' notion of real distinction and then show how and why it is important for getting to grips with aspects of Jung's analytical psychology. Importantly, I am not going to explore in detail the metaphysical arguments around Descartes' real distinction; numerous Cartesian scholars have done that work (Gaukroger 1995; Rozemond 1998; Brown 2006). However, I am going to accept that there is actually a metaphysical distinction between mind and body, that it is a real distinction and that it is both an intuitive and a structural distinction for Descartes.

Here is what Descartes says:

> First, I know that everything which I clearly and distinctly understand is capable of being created by God so as to correspond exactly with my understanding of it. Hence the fact that I can clearly and distinctly understand one thing apart from another is enough to make me certain that the two things are distinct, since they are capable of being separated, at least by God . . . Thus, simply by knowing that I exist and seeing at the same time that absolutely nothing else belongs to my nature or essence except that I am a thinking thing, I can infer correctly that my essence consists solely in the fact that I am a thinking thing. It is true that I have (or, to anticipate, that I certainly have) a body that is very closely joined to me. But nevertheless, on the one hand I have a clear and distinct idea of

> myself, in so far as I am simply a thinking, non-extended thing; and on the other hand I have a distinct idea of body, in so far as this is simply an extended, non-thinking thing. And accordingly, it is certain that I am really distinct from my body and can exist without it.
>
> (Descartes 1984: 54)

Any antagonist to Descartes' analysis of mind and body could be envisaged leaping up and down with joy at this passage: here we have a very transparent case for his metaphysical dualism, for the distinction between mind and body that makes of the mind the very essence of human being, conceivable without a body. QED! What is more, God has to do a lot of work in this argument – God as guarantor of the veracity of Descartes' ideas assumes the existence of God. Yet Descartes' proofs for God's existence are very problematic, as many commentators have argued, and it would seem that Descartes' argument can work only if God does exist. So there are problems . . .

The modal language of Descartes' argument, that what he clearly and distinctly understands is *capable* of being created by God, that two things are *capable* of being separated by God, does not, in my view, entail that God has so acted. Having argued that God would not deceive him, because deception is contrary to God's nature, Descartes can rest in the knowledge that his clear and distinct understanding of the distinction between mind and body is guaranteed not to be erroneous given God's capabilities. So the arguments show what would be the case if certain things obtained.[7] What is important to us is what Descartes reports about his perception of the world.

Commentators as early as Arnuald worried about the real distinction argument (Descartes 1984: 140ff), and what it did or did not show. There are differing views about precisely what Descartes' clear distinction argument is. Likewise, there are differing views on what the precise relationship is between mind and body, and its union, the human being. John Cottingham, Marleen Rozemond, and Eugenio Zaldivar, to name just three recent Cartesian scholars, debate the nature and status of the union of mind and body: is a new, a third substance, the human being, envisaged by Descartes apart from thinking substance and material substance? Where is sentience to be located in the mind or in the body or is there any other possibility? Some scholars regard the union as the metaphysical claim that material bodies and the mind are two distinct substances which then, somehow, become united; others argue that the clear distinction argument is about the separateness of the mind and body (Cottingham 1985; Rozemond 1998; Zaldivar 2011).

But that is by the bye. My interest here is not so much with who has the 'correct' view, if there is a correct view, or, indeed, if metaphysical dualism is a viable theory and Descartes' notion of a real distinction is capable of verification. To that end, I acknowledge the scholarship done around these issues and which is extensive.

My focus is on the phenomenological underpinnings of the real distinction and its usefulness as a methodological tool: as I see it, the practice of meditation in which Descartes engages is the ground for his distinction and that means that in some fundamental sense the distinction has an experiential and thus phenomenological aspect. Let us concentrate here on where Descartes comes from and then where he gets to – his full realisation that in his meditative mode he is conscious only of his thinking – having bracketed his body from any consideration whatsoever, his attention is restricted, and deliberately so, to what remains; and that is his doubting or his being deceived, from which he intuits that he must exist. In an immediate intuition, Descartes clearly and distinctly exemplifies his own existence.[8] It is not that he *reduces* himself to his thinking, it is, rather, that having subtracted everything else, he cannot simultaneously subtract his thinking and *be aware of his own existence.* What remains after the bracketing of his body and his senses is a discursive awareness or consciousness that is completely *revealed* as his being, the essence of who he is. This is not a reduction but a revelation. *For him, that awareness is encapsulated in his thinking.* Put in another way, Descartes' attention is so focused that there is only his thinking, but it is self-reflective or self-directed, rather than other-directed. He 'purifies' his being at the moment of revelation, if you like, to such an extent that he is able to conclude that there is only his discursive consciousness.

So, in my view, the foregoing is the basis of Descartes' metaphysical commitment to the real distinction between body and mind. Certainly, that mind and body are distinct *as a matter of fact* relies on the existence of God and his goodness, which means that he would not deceive Descartes.[9] From Descartes' clear and distinct, and immediate intuition of himself as a thinking thing, he is able to understand himself, considered as that thinking thing, as really distinct from body. But note that he has a distinct idea of body 'in so far as this is simply an extended, non-thinking thing'. One question we might raise here concerns the status of body and mind considered together. Is Descartes referring to his own body, or to body generally? We might be inclined to say that he *must* be referring to *his own* body. But if it is the case that his mind and his body are really distinct, then how can they act on each other, for that is what he does claim?

What he later argues is that mind is *embodied* mind (although it need not be if God had made it otherwise). The mind acts on the body and the body acts on the mind: but it is not *any* body and *any* mind: *his* body acts on *his* mind and *his* mind acts on *his* body. We can deduce this from his letters to Elizabeth in May and June 1643. In the letter of 21 May, he tells Elizabeth that there are two things we can know about the soul: 'that it thinks, the second is that, being united to the body, it can act and be acted upon along with it'. He then goes on to confess that he has already identified 'the notions that belong to the soul alone by distinguishing them from those that belong to the body alone'. He now has to explain 'how to conceive those which belong to the union of the soul with the body as distinct from those which belong to the body alone or to the soul alone' (Descartes 1991: 218). Then, in the letter of 28 June 1643, he says that there are three primitive notions[10] with which he is concerned, 'each of which is known in its own proper manner and not by comparison with any others: the notions we have of the soul, of body, and of the union between the soul and the body' (Descartes 1991: 226).

In what I think of as quite a remarkable turn, Descartes, in the same letter, says to Elizabeth that 'it is the ordinary course of life and conversation, and abstention from meditation and from the study of the things that exercise the imagination, that teaches us how to conceive the union of soul and body'. This is a remarkable turn, for Descartes is not here appealing to any metaphysical principle, or any meditative technique or method. His is an appeal to the ordinariness of life. He explains to Elizabeth that he has always had a rule that one should not spend too much time meditating and exercising the imagination; and that he does not think that the human mind 'is capable of forming a very distinct conception of both the distinction between the soul and the body and their union; for to do this is necessary to conceive them as a single thing and at the same time to conceive them as two things; this is absurd' (Descartes 1991: 227). Fundamentally then, the union of mind and body is beyond human comprehension; it is a taken-for-granted thing, acted out in everyday life.

It seems to me that this is not a very satisfactory place to end up. It is possible to think of this apparently almost naïve position here, though, as provisional, requiring some further thought and reconsideration. And indeed, Descartes seems to have thought so too, judging from his later work, *The Passions of the Soul*. This work can be seen as a result of his correspondence with Elizabeth, and as an attempted response to her inquiries about 'the manner of [the soul's] actions and passions in the body' (Descartes 1991: 325). In so far as Descartes is concerned, there are properties of mind or soul, and properties of the body. Brown regards the passions as 'the lynchpins of the mind–body unity, and to play this role passions must have a dual status, consisting in bodily processes and thoughts' (Brown 2006: 7).

In *The Passions of the Soul*, Descartes argues that there is one soul and that is 'at once sensitive and rational' (Descartes 1985: 346). Its passions are 'those perceptions, sensations or emotions of the soul which we refer particularly to it, and which are caused, maintained and strengthened by some movement of the spirits' (Descartes 1985: 338–339). Note here that the body has an effect on the passions, because the spirits to which Descartes is referring are the animal spirits responsible for carrying neural impulses around the body and into the pineal gland. Further, he maintains that the soul is joined to the whole body, even though the pineal gland is 'where it exercises its functions more particularly than in all the others' (Descartes 1985: 340). And, we also have Descartes distinguishing between imaginings of the body, that the will is not involved in forming, and imaginings of the soul. Of the former he says, '[s]uch are the illusions of our dreams and also the day-dreams we often have when we are awake and our mind wanders idly without applying itself to anything of its own accord' (Descartes 1985: 336).

Descartes orders and enumerates the passions: wonder is the first of the passions and it occurs in the context of surprise. In his catalogue of passions, Descartes talks about all kinds of passions – what we might think of now as tied to character: 'love and hatred', 'desire', 'attraction and repulsion', 'how joy causes blushing', 'how we weep from sadness', 'why children weep and old people weep readily' and 'why some children grow pale instead of weeping'. At the risk of begging the question, this is hardly the sentiment of someone living in a world drained of human habitation!

There are problems with Descartes' real distinction between mind and body. There are metaphysical problems about the notion of mind as thinking substance and body as extended substance. There are problems with Descartes' proofs of God's existence. Yet, his idea that the passions bring the soul and body together, and that imagination can have a corporeal origin, goes some way to redeeming his thinking in the *Meditations* that has fuelled the intellectual debate. But there are even greater problems with casting Descartes in the dualistic fashion that we have seen earlier in this chapter: such overly simplifying readings do not do justice to his thinking. I would go so far as to say that, although there are problems, and big problems at that, Descartes' conception of human being suggests a deep awareness not only of our corporeality, our fleshy existence, but of that existence in a relational way. *The Passions of the Soul* situate the body/soul unity in a world where there is veneration and scorn, love and hatred, joy and sadness, derision, pity and envy, favour and gratitude. This is most certainly not the world assumed by Romanyshyn or Brooke. And it is also not the world, we can assume, that Jung encounters when we read his texts and the *Red Book*. The worlds there are the worlds at which he wonders.

We have seen, then, that it is the case that Descartes maintains there is a real distinction between mind and body. My reading of this distinction is that it has its origins in his phenomenological experience of his teleologically inspired meditational method. But we have also seen that Descartes understands that the body and mind are a unity which we experience as we live our lives, and which is beyond human comprehension. Finally, we have just seen that the passions are critical to our understanding of the unity that is mind and body – the human being about which Descartes speaks in *Meditation VI*.

At this point, we need to remind ourselves of Jung's consistent claims about the unity of mind and body, and of the notion of the living being that we saw earlier in this chapter. Jung does not justify or argue for his positions. In a way, he takes on the naïve natural attitude[11] we have just seen in Descartes' provisional conclusion that we cannot comprehend the body/soul union. I would also add that Descartes' immediate intuition of his own existence in/through his thinking seems to me to be spot on. The thinking revealed to him is the very thing that makes us human. It is conscious thinking, without which we would have no conception of ourselves at all. So the *cogito* is ontologically primitive for us as human beings who pursue the kind of programme Descartes pursues. As meditational practice, Descartes' radical bracketing of his body and systematic denial of his senses can only be thought of as existentially appropriate – where else could and would he start other than with his own conscious experience?

And, as a matter of fact, that is Jung's starting point as well, in his parallel quest for the truth of the unconscious. As I understand Jung's position in the Fog Argument, it is not Cartesian. Descartes' hyperbolic doubt follows a methodological process, that, couched in terms of spiritual practice, pre-empts, albeit with a quite different *telos*, Jung's confrontation with the unconscious. In both cases, they open themselves to existential possibilities through phenomenological experience, the outcome of which is uncertain. And in order to achieve any advance at all, they each require some real distinctions with which to operate; the ontological veracity of such distinctions is secondary to the phenomenological experience itself. At least that is my view.

The distinction between the mind and its images, in Jung's case, and Descartes' mind as a thinking thing should, by now, be obvious. Descartes' mind as thinking thing – his soul or mind – is the condition of his *awareness* of his being; he begins in his body and he returns to his body, a body more highly conceptualised through his account of the passions. Jung maintains throughout his work that the living body, the living being, is a unity. Yet he so easily defers to the psyche as an inner/outer phenomenon. To reiterate a point made earlier, Plumwood may well be correct in her analysis and assessment of some forms of dualism: the existential appropriateness we find, though, in Descartes' and Jung's more and less well-developed accounts of the mind/body relation, and for Jung, the psyche/body relation, needs careful consideration.

Of course I do not think that the matter ends there. There are many loose ends which I cannot possibly hope to tie up here, principally because they are better dealt with by metaphysicians. We do, though, need to attend to a very tricky question around boundaries – the inner and outer trope – and it is to that I now turn in the next chapter.

Chapter 4

Inner and outer troubles

> The Cartesian dualism of an interior, subjective knowing mind sealed off from an exterior, objective world to be known and exploited repeats itself in the European movements of expansion into the New World.
>
> (Romanyshyn 2000: 29)

> When the opposites unite, all energy ceases: there is no more flow.
>
> (Jung 1954: 467)

The inner/outer trope and its cognates, which seem to invoke spatial delimiters, fall under the umbrella of dualism, the pairing of oppositional terms which, it is argued, creates untenable divisions that end up constituting an alienating world. The trope, conceived of as exemplifying the very dualist structures we have just encountered, thus needs some detailed examination. So, in this chapter, I explore in detail aspects of Roger Brooke's critical appraisal of Jung's use of the trope.

We saw that Val Plumwood identifies hyperseparation or radical exclusion as one of the elements of value dualism and that there need be only one characteristic different from another in an ordered hierarchy of master and inferior (Plumwood 1993: 49) for there to be a dualistic structure. In my view, the notion of hyperseparation underlies the critique of Jung as an inheritor and proponent of Descartes' dualism. Romanyshyn, Brooke and Abram argue that Descartes' view ideates a separateness of self and world, which I now explore and evaluate in light of what we have seen so far. As I proceed, I begin to tread a path to philosophical phenomenology, and then to the psychological dimensions of phenomenology by looking at Brooke's approach to Jung-as-phenomenologist. I wonder how much there is, in the end, separating philosophical and psychological phenomenology: the two are closely intertwined. Descartes' argument that his thinking is his essence, as I have suggested, gestures towards a philosophical phenomenology that I do not believe is all that foreign to analytical psychology, focusing as it does on *prosoche,* the immediacy of the present moment and one's attention to it.

Carl Jung is a metaphysical dualist. His metaphysics is influenced by Descartes' philosophy, with specific, identifiable, mind/body and subject/object distinctions operating throughout his work. Or so a succession of claims might go. Even with the analysis in Chapter 3, issues about two-term distinctions that can be conceived dualistically remain for Jung, and for Descartes. How body and mind are capable of interacting remains an issue, even though Descartes' analysis of the passions might be seen as a linchpin between body and soul. This is, as I have said, difficult material, and a resolution is not immediately forthcoming. At this stage, the best option seems to be to live with the ambiguity. Maybe Descartes is right – we humans cannot comprehend the union of mind and body. Likewise, we may not be able to comprehend the relation between psyche and body, and how a collective unconscious can influence personal psyche, conscious and unconscious.

When one reads Jung, as we have seen, one often comes across comments, ideas, concepts and views that are reminiscent of Descartes' philosophy, even if such similarity is manufactured from oversimplified readings of Descartes. Both men are dealing with apparently perennial problems about the nature of reality, and of knowledge, even though their overt concerns are quite different. Jung's focus on the separation of psyche and world is an interesting point of departure for an examination of thematic similarities, so let us begin there.

Jung seems to be agnostic about the existence of an external world; and what is more, he gives ontological precedence to the collective, over the individual, unconscious. He maintains, for example, that 'we are so wrapped about by psychic images that we cannot penetrate at all the essences of things external to ourselves. All our knowledge consists of the stuff of the psyche which because it alone is immediate, is superlatively real'. Jung also analyses 'our practical conception of reality', arguing that we perceive nothing but images, and that 'our world is not a material, but a psychic world' (Jung 1972: 680).

Straight away, we seem to be in a divided world – the psyche, which can be seen as an inner or interior domain of mental entities on the one hand, and on the other, a world of material objects, 'things' outside or exterior to the psyche. Jung's claim that our world is not material but psychic seems to imply that he is some kind of idealist: there are only ideas, and nothing else, and the human mind is the maker of the world. And from the small scrap of Jungian discourse, just cited, we might be prepared to say that there is strong evidence for the claim that he was, indeed, a metaphysical dualist, just like Descartes before him and in whose shadow he sits – Jung is ontologically committed to the reality of the psyche, and the reality of the material world could be seen as problematic. Likewise, we might also be led to say that he is an epistemological dualist: we know only our minds and cannot know an outer world. Put like this, there is a clear relationship between metaphysical dualism and epistemological dualism: we know about different domains of being, a psychic domain and a material world domain, which are ontologically distinct from each other.

Yet we need to be careful with the implications we might draw from these Jungian snippets. In the first place, 'psyche' is simply not an inner domain of mental entities. Rather, for Jung the psyche consists in two psychic systems which form a 'conscious-unconscious whole' (Jung 1972: 397) and which have both personal and collective dimensions. The personal psychic system (conscious and unconscious) is that which we might think of as 'internal' to ourselves; the collective psychic system is both conscious and unconscious, yet the latter is uniquely characterised in terms of archetypes and archetypal expressions or images (Jung 1968: 90) that pre-exist individual embodiment and so might be considered 'external' to any individual psyche. On Jung's view, as we know, there is an interplay between the two 'systems'. Jung's alleged dualism, is then, ameliorated by his sophisticated notion of the psyche, the domain of inner, and outer, the domain of conscious and unconscious life. What effect does this have on his conception of knowledge, and how are we to understand that conception?

In my view, there is a very obvious sense in which Jung's claim, that the stuff of the psyche alone is superlatively real, is true: we are cognitive and sensory beings, both *connected to* and *separated from* our worlds in which we find ourselves. Our brains and our minds are the media through *and in which* this happens. On the one hand, one might say that our knowledge can be *nothing but* socially constructed, that is to say, produced through the interaction of sociocultural factors, our psyches, and our embodiment. On the other, one might also say that we know things apart from our experiences, that some knowledge is not socially constructed *per se* but a product of the way we, innately, are. Either way, Jung is pointing to the complexity of the material and psychic worlds. We find such sentiment echoed in Edmund Husserl's work: 'the complete world is not merely physical; it is also psychophysical and it is a practical world, a world of manifold cultural formations, which for their part, are relative to psychophysical subjectivity' (Husserl 1982: 124 fn78). Jung is not unique, therefore, in struggling with these very issues, as we see here in Husserl, and in Kant before them.

So, although we 'cannot penetrate at all the essences of the things external to ourselves', Jung's claim could be read as amounting to the rather bland and uncontroversial assertion that our psyches are fundamental to our knowledge making. Our *knowledge,* and indeed, our opinions and beliefs *are* psychic in so far as our minds are products of consciousness, collective and personal. Jung is keenly aware that consciousness exists within the world, influenced by that world and our experiences, and thus the effects of the worlds we inhabit. The mind/consciousness/unconscious/psyche complex is both social-collective and personal-innate.

The important point here is that Jung acknowledges that we do not *make* our worlds, that we appear in a ready-made, ready-to-hand changeable world, in which material objects, their relations with each other and with us, help to make us who we are. Things external to ourselves are ontologically prior to our being. Jung operates with a metaphysical dualism that distinguishes between thing and that of which it is a perception. That means that what is in my head when I see a tree is not the tree itself, but an image or representation of the tree.

Philosophers, including Descartes, have debated this relationship between an object and its mental representation. For example, there is a discussion in *Meditation III* and also Descartes' opening remarks to *The World or Treatise on Light* where he discusses the connection between words and the objects they signify, and where he points out that words and objects bear no resemblance to each other (Descartes 1984: 27ff; 1985: 81–82). The distinction between 'thing out there' and 'what's happening in here' construes inner and outer domains of being, then, that appear to be related. But how? Is this a valid distinction, anyway? And what effect does his notion of psyche have as a whole system of conscious and unconscious whole? It is way beyond the scope of this book to answer the first question. However, the validity of the distinction is precisely what is questioned by Brooke and Romanyshyn. What does Jung say and how can the issue be dealt with?

Within Jung's world view, the distinction between interior and exterior is fundamental to his epistemological, dualistic, standpoint. There have been several critiques of Jung's dualism that attempt to come to terms with his open acceptance of inner/interior and outer/exterior tropes. In *Jung and Phenomenology*, for example, Roger Brooke addresses a circularity problem he finds in Jung's writing and which revolves around these tropes. Brooke describes the origin of the problem in terms of a 'subtle but fateful epistemological turn' (Brooke 1991: 106). Brooke quotes Jung's view that 'we are so wrapped about by psychic images that we cannot penetrate at all the essences of things external to ourselves. All our knowledge consists of the stuff of the psyche which, because it alone is immediate, is superlatively real' (Jung 1972: 680). Brooke comments that, in these remarks, Jung is claiming that we 'have no direct access to the "real world" but only to psychic images which may or may not be an accurate representation' (Brooke 1991: 106).

The Fog Argument remains a problem for Jung unless we can see our way forward to a reading that lifts the fog. Brooke also mentions several other instances where Jung seem to be making claims about the status of the world and the psyche, amongst which we find these claims: that 'far from this being a material world, this is a psychic world', and that 'the psychic alone has immediately reality' (Jung 1972: 747); Brooke reads these quotations in light of Jung's commitment to the thesis that 'the phenomena of the world, including the human psyche, show themselves through the psychological perspectives of the observers'. Ultimately, Brooke argues, this is a 'self-enclosed position', that leads to a circular definition of the psyche and to an unpalatable psychologism (Brooke 1991: 106). That said, Brooke attempts to re-vision Jung's position and refigure it within a phenomenological framework.

Brooke pursues the theme of self-enclosure and of an '"outer world" drained of meaning and human habitation', arguing that the latter is Descartes' *res extensa*. Jung, on this reading, he asserts, 'becomes, like Freud, a "Descartes of the depths", to use Romanyshyn's phrase' (Brooke 1991: 109). Robert Romanyshyn is similarly critical of Jung's apparent separation of psyche and world. Romanyshyn's claim that projection 'rests upon our unacknowledged stupidity' that is an expression of Cartesian dualism and its 'subjective knowing mind sealed off from an exterior, objective world' is not a particularly scholarly reading of Descartes. Nor is his related claim that Jung's psychology in its commitment to projection theory 'is haunted by a dualism of inside and out, leaving soul without world and world without soul' takes into account the subtleties of Jung's metaphysical commitments (Romanyshyn 2000: 29, 31). It is not obvious that the inside/outside trope is intrinsically dualistic in the metaphysically loaded sense suggested by Plumwood. Yet, as these theorists take up the issue, we are reminded of Plumwood's argument (Plumwood 1993: 110ff) that Descartes' hyperseparating philosophy articulates a non-agential mechanism resulting in a nature 'represented in mechanistic terms as inferior, passive and mindless, whose only value and meaning is derived from the imposition of human ends' (Plumwood 1993: 110ff; 2002: 49).

I am not convinced that the inside/outside trope implies that the soul is left without world or the world without soul, the meaning of which, in any case, Romanyshyn does not explain. We might take him to be saying that, in view of the hyper-rational stance adopted by generations over the past three or four hundred years, any intrinsic value that nature might have has been trumped by instrumentalist concerns that make of nature a slave to human reason in that it can be manipulated and defeated in an imaginary war we have declared. Perhaps we can take it that Romanyshyn is proposing a view similar to Plumwood's notion of hyperseparation. Plumwood's defence of the intentionality of nature is very strong and, in a profoundly argued manner, maintains that the value intrinsic to nature requires acknowledgement in word *and* action. While we cannot conflate 'nature' and 'world', we can, as a heuristic device, appeal to her reading to help us to come to terms with what might be going on in Romanyshyn's analysis.

As I see it, Romanyshyn's claims about projection and the inner/outer trope is a rather thin reading of metaphor, and of Descartes. He invokes a Descartes who is the subject of rather superficial scholarship, and then extrapolates what he finds there, Jung. In so doing, Romanyshyn appears to overlook the complexities of each thinker. The idea that Descartes' philosophy is an expression of a 'spectator-self, imprisoned in a body made into a specimen' (Romanyshyn 2000: 31) perpetuates the myth of a Cartesian dualism that, as I argued, is not very sophisticated. In terms of the inner/outer trope, we need further an exploration of its alleged place amongst other forms of dualism; so let us see how we can address what seem to be some major issues with the

Descartes–Jung connection, and their attitudes to what goes on 'in' us, and what goes on 'outside' us.

We might agree that Jung's comments contain some metaphysical assertions about the nature of the mind, and of the world, that 'they' are different kinds or orders of being. What the nature of those metaphysical assertions is, and how they might or might not relate to each other, though, is moot. We can see, for example, that the knowable 'stuff of the psyche' seems to be distinguished from the unknowable stuff of the world. Hence Jung might be seen to be raising a question about what we *can* know and what we cannot know; or, he could be raising a question about 'direct' knowing. He could be saying that our knowledge of the world is secondary to our knowledge of the contents of the psyche which might make him play right into the hands of Plumwood's analysis of dualism. On his mental-is-primary view, we would have immediate, untrammelled, *direct* access to the psyche, and which is 'superlatively real'. Our access to anything apart from the psyche would be indirect or mediate and its reality status would be uncertain.

Would this mean that what is *in* the psyche, in being 'superlatively real' and that to which we have direct access, is the singular, and only, reality? If so, what would be the status of tables and chairs and elephants and rainbows, and other people? Since they are not *in* the psyche, we do not have direct access in the required sense. Yet, if it is the case that we are born into the psyche, then there is no issue at all: tables and chairs and elephants and rainbows and other people are all there, within our psychic horizon, given as part of the furniture of the psyche. Still, we might wonder about their status as existents in their own right, if they do have such status, as beings with ontological independence and autonomy irrespective of the psyche in which we are supposedly always already located. Where does this take us?

In a move designed to refocus his issues with Descartes' philosophy that he sees reflected in Jung's work, Brooke invokes 'phenomenology's two fundamental reciprocal criticisms' of Descartes: that inner life is solipsistic and self-enclosed to the degree that 'it is impossible to speak coherently of any real relationship with other beings' and that the world is emptied of any intrinsic meaning 'other than that prescribed by natural science' (Brooke 1991: 109). Brooke's claims here echo Plumwood's analysis of hyperseparation. In my view, however, Brooke's summary dismissal misrepresents the relationship between Descartes and phenomenology and also appeals to an orthodox and very uncharitable reading of Descartes. While it may help to reframe Jung's approach to these issues, his argument depends on some quite suspect assumptions about both Descartes and phenomenology.

That said, the positions that Brooke and Romanyshyn attribute to Jung are, in my view, not sustainable as critiques of either Jung or of the philosophy – Descartes' in fact – that both implicate in their reading of Jung. If, for example, Brooke's critical assessment of Jung rests on a clear and critical assessment of the *cogito*, it would be important for Brooke to sketch out his critique of the *cogito*. If Brooke's critique implies that Jung is an antirealist, indeed, even an idealist, then an appraisal of Jung's epistemological commitments is called for as well as an account of what realism consists in. And since Brooke is dealing with Jung's relationship with phenomenology, he needs also to acknowledge the relationship between Descartes and the phenomenology of Husserl and Merleau-Ponty, which I think he does not do satisfactorily. It remains the case that the *cogito* is central to Husserl's and to Merleau-Ponty's phenomenologies, either assumed or refigured.

Thus, given the import of the *cogito* to Descartes' philosophy and to later phenomenologies, and Descartes' recovery of the body in *Meditation VI*, together with the his work in *Passions of the Soul*, I argue that Brooke's analysis is difficult to sustain, even though he himself wants to see Jung in phenomenological terms. I hold that the impossible positions attributed to Jung, and argued as derivative of Descartes, can be reframed within a Husserlian phenomenological framework, its problems notwithstanding. So let us now turn to Brooke's claims around the relationship between 'inner' life and solipsism, before moving to a discussion of the status of the concept of 'intrinsic meaning' and the world.

Self-enclosure

As a start, let me say that we can look even further afield across Jung's *oeuvre* and find more examples of what Brooke and Romanyshyn are pointing out. Even if we grant both Jung's understanding of knowledge *and* his metaphysical commitments, we can already see that Brooke and Romanyshyn are highly critical of what they understand is an explicit ontological dualism in Jung and also seem to exhibit Plumwood's notion of hyperseparation. However, in my view, we cannot simply assume that, because we use the interior/exterior trope, a radical, irreparable tear between psyche and world has been made, that hyperseparation is the upshot. Certainly Descartes assumes the interior/exterior trope as well; but that it does the work of division in quite the way that Brooke and Romanyshyn maintain is contestable. Yet Jung's insistence on the reality of the psyche and its contents as distinct from the reality of the world and its objects *outside* the psyche is no fiction, and seem to open the possibility of radical, unbridgeable separation. How are we to understand this dualistic framing of Jung's thinking?

Brooke himself admits that Jung's dualism does not fit into traditional accounts. He says that when Jung 'speaks of "autonomy of the psyche" he is referring to a dimension of investigation and functioning that is inextricably linked to the existential ambiguity of the living body' (Brooke 1991: 113). Brooke lauds Jung's acknowledgement of the embodied subject here; as we have seen in Descartes' *Passions of the Soul*, though, Jung could be construed as following in Descartes' footsteps. The unity of mind and body constitutes the wholeness of human being. However, claims Brooke, the problem with interiority versus 'outside world' remains (Brooke 1991: 118).

In my view, the interior/exterior trope is an important psychophilosophical, ethical, and phenomenological distinction. The idea that we are autonomous beings who are responsible for our actions and who are in relationship with other autonomous beings similarly thought of, that we are oriented towards those beings, and they to us, is constituted in part by the inner/outer trope. Thus a dissolution of the inner/outer trope would have far-reaching ethical and existential implications simply because we are all in the world, part of the world, yet able to bracket the world and turn in upon ourselves. Bearing this in mind, and reflecting on how to approach Jung's dualism, let me construct a possible position that Jung could represent here.

Jung countenances different meanings of 'real' and its cognates. For example, in his essay, 'The Real and the Surreal', he distinguishes between Western and Eastern ways of thinking that, he argues, have different ontological commitments. These are the points he makes:

1. 'Reality . . . contains everything I can know, for everything that acts upon me is real and actual. If it does not act upon me, then I notice nothing and can, therefore know nothing about it' (Jung 1972: 742). Jung here, does not tell us what reality is, nor does he distinguish what is real and what is actual. He posits a relationship between knowledge and what is real; and a relationship between oneself, and what acts on oneself. At this stage, Jung is not talking about the *status* of what acts upon oneself.
2. He quotes the very phrase we find in Descartes' *Meditations*, the phrase that had been an article of faith for Descartes pre-doubt. This is what Jung says, and mind you, he, too, is sceptical about its whole-hearted acceptance:

   > This restriction of the so-called material or concrete reality of objects perceived by the senses is a product of a particular way of thinking – the thinking that underlies 'sound common sense' and our ordinary use of language. It operates on the celebrated principle, '*Nihil quod intellectu quod non antea fuerit in sensu*', regardless of the fact that there are very many things in the mind that did not derive from the data of the senses. According to this view, everything is 'real' which comes, or seems to come, directly or indirectly from the world revealed by the senses
   >
   > (Jung 1972: 742)

   In this view, a world of material and concrete objects (presumably trees, cats, people, horses, buildings, flowers, computers) is posited and these objects affect our senses: these are objects that act upon us, it would seem, in the way he has just identified. For him, this is material reality.
3. Contrary to the material reality view, he posits a 'dark penumbra which one would have to call unreal or surreal'. Jung regards the unreal or surreal

as a feature of Eastern reality, a feature which is menacing to those who accept our 'arbitrarily delimited reality' (Jung 1972: 743).

4. In relation to Westerners, by which I assume Jung means those of us with a European as opposed to an Asian, or African, or Indigenous North or South American heritage, Jung describes the psychic as disturbing, the menacing, and in so doing, he distinguishes between psychic reality and material reality. He says that we think of the psychic as derivative of the material, 'an effect at third hand, produced originally by physical causes'. Thus Jung claims that we attribute only an 'indirect reality' to the psyche that also knows itself as mind (Jung 1972: 744). In his view, this is mistaken: for him, the psychic has a reality with which we are directly in contact.

   Thus Jung seems to operate with a two-tiered epistemology and a two-tiered ontology: we can know psychic reality directly, and material reality indirectly.

5. Jung proposes a theory of mind and body frameable in terms of 'psychoid' phenomena (Jung 1972: 368). Jung's use of the adjective 'psychoid' is deliberate as, if I understand him correctly, he wants to distinguish psychoid phenomena from the purely psychic and ensure a connection between psychic and quasi-psychic phenomena. He, like Descartes, admits that there is a relationship between the nervous system, the sense organs and the psyche, which effectively produces images in consciousness. Yet he argues that, in the transmission between sense organs, nerve endings and consciousness, an unconscious process is interpolated between physical process and the resultant psychic image (Jung 1972: 745).

Jung builds up a knowledge base from experience, while at the same time he clearly conceives of innate activities of the psyche, such as the action of the archetypes which structure much of our experience. So he takes an eclectic view of epistemological process and effect. By this I mean that his comments around the relation between images in the psyche and the material world are to do with the capacity and role of the human psyche in its apprehending that material world. Human knowledge is a result of the activity of the psyche; human knowledge is, *essentially*, a psychological matter, if you like. What else can it be? This means that psychological activity must be brought to the forefront if we are to gain insight into the cognitive activity that founds knowledge. Cognitive activity is the activity of human being, psyche and body; innate processes and structures are responsible for such activity. And psyche, recall, is an already given, always.

This is where point 1 above becomes important. In distinguishing between different meanings of 'real' and its cognates, Jung establishes a pattern of epistemological and ontological mediacy and immediacy. I say 'pattern' because of the outward/inward movement that is the interplay between mediacy and immediacy.

One of the features of psyche is that it can intuit its own existence, as the *cogito* attests. As I argued earlier, the *cogito* can be seen as an instance of exemplification, as a self-evident intuition. I take this also to be an instance of cognitive immediacy, that is to say, I take it to be an example of the psyche's reflexive self-aware knowledge unmediated by anything apart from its own nature. The conscious realisation of its own being is due to the peculiar nature of the immediate intuition that accompanies the *cogito.* And 'its own nature', that of which the psyche is immediately aware, is ontologically immediate in so far as even the doubting mind can never be absent from its own doubting.

On this view, the *cogito* has an epistemological priority over any other cognitive activity, even though the *cogito,* most often, postdates other, chronologically earlier, cognitive activities. It seems to me that Jung is working with a conception of directness or cognitive immediacy that can be considered as originary perception. This does not mean that we, as humans, must secure the *cogito* before anything else. What it does mean is that, in a process of doubt such as that engaged in by Descartes, the bottom line for all cognition, and all doubt, is, precisely, the *cogito* and the *cogito* as a phenomenological experience or event in one's biography. Implicit in Descartes' and Jung's comments is the idea that we are immediately aware of the 'contents' of our psyches, an awareness that is comparable with the self-evidence of the *cogito.*

What we know directly, immediately, then, is limited to our psyches. That is to say, we have direct access to, or an immediate intuition of, what is going on in our psyches, limited, that is, by our consciousnesses. In this reading, Jung seems to be assuming a relationship between directness or immediacy and knowledge. We know only that of which we are directly aware. The rest is belief. Hence Jung raises the question of direct knowing and alleges that one can know only the contents of one's psyche; from this he deduces that we cannot 'penetrate' what is outside us.

What we *think* we know about the material world is mediated through the psyche as an effect of sensual input. That means, in effect, that material-world knowledge is also mediated by the human body through which the senses are operative.

For Jung, the psyche is not simply a matter of a set of functions internal to a body. The psyche pre-exists individual existences as unconscious and, in that sense, we are all *in* the psyche. Note that this is a claim about the collective rather than the personal. For Jung, the personal conscious and unconscious are both internal phenomena. In various places he speaks of the objective psyche – the psyche we are all in. He also deploys Driesch's term 'psychoid' in an adjectival sense only, in terms of quasi-psychic relating to organic reflex (that is to say, related to the functions of physiological organs) and to distinguish psychoid processes from 'merely vitalistic phenomena on the one hand and from specifically psychic processes on the other' (Jung 1972: 368). For Jung, the term 'psychoid phenomena' evokes a relation between consciousness and the sense functions as well as the body (see above).

The human body, on this view, is a kind of interface between material reality and psychic reality, both conscious and unconscious. In other words, the psyche through the human body mediates its own presence in the world, as it brings its special character into relation with that world. The psyche, through the body, 'touches' the world as the world 'touches' the body in mutual embrace, as it were. The body is a permeable boundary that interacts with the psyche, the body's own being and the being of the material world. Such a view allows of the possibility of a phenomenological account of psyche and world. Because of this, the earlier understanding of reality can be reframed in terms more faithful to a phenomenological standpoint, as Jung would put it. Note that how we are to understand the concept 'material world' is not evident.

But, given all of this, is Jung a metaphysical realist? Is he an idealist? Dan Zahavi argues that metaphysical realism:

> assumes that everyday experience combines subjective and objective features and that we can reach an objective picture of what the world is really like by stripping away the subjective. It consequently argues that there is a clear distinction to be drawn between the properties things have 'in themselves' and the properties which are 'projected by us'. Whereas the world of appearance, the world as it is for us in daily life, combines subjective and objective features, science captures the objective world, the world as it is in itself.
>
> (Zahavi 2010: 295)

As we have seen, Jung alludes to this very distinction. Whether or not a scientific capturing of the world is possible, however, is highly contentious. Yet, if we think back to the Fog Argument, it suggests that, in terms of epistemology, Jung has idealist tendencies.

I doubt that Jung is wholeheartedly either. So, for now, let us assume that this constitutes a good-enough account of Jung's theory of knowledge and of his ontological commitments: a two-tiered epistemology and ontology, consisting in direct and indirect knowing of psychic and material reality that is mediated by the living body and existing in a pre-given psyche. We leave in abeyance the question of his realist or idealist tendencies. Perhaps we can sometimes read him as one, then as the other. Either way, Jung does seem to have a commitment to the inner/outer trope.

Thus our focus on Jung's onto-epistemology, for the time being then, draws us into an engagement with the question of the interior/exterior trope. We note that on such an account the immediately knowable is constitutive of innerness or interiority and the mediately knowable constitutive of outwardness or exteriority. The latter is the case because of the existence of beings (objects, people, animals, clouds) not 'contained' in or by the personal psyche.

Brooke, as we have seen, holds that the fundamental issue is to do with what he calls the 'spatialising' of the metaphors we use to describe our places in the world that, for him, begin with Descartes.

> Somehow, and I think this is crucial, a way needs to be found to understand our vital engagement within the life-world symbolically without spatialising that understanding and hauling psyche out of the world . . . one way to forget this primordial reality is to spatialise the metaphor by locating its meaning in one's head . . . the Cartesian interiorisation of psychological life loses an essential quality of metaphor, namely its capacity to intensify reality.
>
> (Brooke 1991: 98–99)

Much the same is the case with Romanyshyn's critique of projection theory.

Bearing in mind the distinction between kinds of reality and kinds of knowing, we might ask what Brooke means here: the question of metaphor is important, both to him and to Romanyshyn, who also alludes to issues with spatial metaphors. We might also wonder how psyche can be hauled out of the world when the psyche enables the world, is the condition of worldness. Descartes' repeated affirmation of the causal relations between body and mind and then his placing the body in a relational world of the passions suggests otherwise. And if we accept that the psyche is composed of two psychic systems, a conscious and an unconscious, that is expressed at a personal and collective level, it is very difficult to resist talk of interiority.

Now I do not dispute that *some* metaphors do indeed have the capacity to intensify reality through their poetic or aesthetic turn of phrase. However, as some theorists have argued, that is not the only function of metaphors. Janet Martin Soskice's working definition of metaphor, for example, says that a 'metaphor is that figure of speech whereby we speak about one thing in terms which are seen to be suggestive of another' (Soskice 1985: 15). David Hills contends that metaphors function to bring together 'two different and disparate subject matters' that 'are mingled to rich and unpredictable effect' (Hills 2011). Max Black identifies different forms and functions of metaphors: substitution, comparison and interaction metaphors. He argues that interaction metaphors are of most interest to philosophers and that '[t]heir mode of operation requires the reader to use a system of implications (a system of "common-places " – or a special system established for the purpose in hand) as a means for selecting, emphasizing, and organizing relations in a different field' (Black 1954: 293). Eva Kittay identifies first- and second-order meanings or orders of discourse and argues that metaphors break first-order semantic rules (Kittay 1984: 158). These different views on metaphors argue around the possibility of metaphors not only having the capacity to intensify reality, but, indeed, to be the very building blocks of the reality that comes to us through language. Metaphors, then, could be regarded as being indispensable to how we see and understand the world, and to the ontological commitments we all might make.

So, assuming that metaphors have at least some of the roles to which I just alluded, we might wonder in what way a metaphor's capacity to intensify reality is lost through an interiorisation of psychological life. That is to say, the use of spatial metaphors to talk about psyche and world may well point to some significant features of human perception and cognition, *and experience*. If, as is the case, it seems, with Jung, there are (at least) two readings of 'reality' expressed in the language of two spatial locations, we are not simply talking about the intensification of reality: we are talking about the *construction and depiction* of reality which, as a matter of fact, can be seen as having two different dimensions: interior or psychological, and exterior or material world. (And are conscious and unconscious disguised spatial metaphors?) Even though talk of different kinds of reality might be metaphorical on this account, the metaphors function as reality depicting. On this view, there are not problems with spatialising our metaphors; our metaphors are already spatialised because they depict 'the way things are'. Brooke's claim, then, that the 'Cartesian interiorisation of psychological life' loses its capacity to intensify reality, needs to be rethought within a more specific framing of metaphor.

With this reading of onto-epistemology and the construction and depiction of reality through metaphor, we might be able to see a way through the unbridgeable divide alleged by Brooke and Romanyshyn. Firstly, metaphors function to structure the psyche, and the mind and consciousness in particular, together with the material world, to produce the phenomenon of inner and outer as the way we and the world are. This is how we 'naturally' see the world. Secondly, my rather tentative reading of Jung's onto-epistemology casts doubt on both Brooke's and Romanyshyn's aligning 'orthodox' reading of Descartes' philosophy with Jung's philosophical assumptions in analytical psychology.

After this discussion we may recognise that Jung's claim needs re-evaluation:

> it is my mind, with its store of images, that gives the world colour, and sounds . . . "experience" is, in its most simple form, an exceedingly complicated structure of mental images. Thus there is in a certain sense that nothing is directly experienced except the mind itself.
>
> (1954: [8] 327)

The above reading of Jung's onto-epistemology cannot stand as it is, for, as we shall see, it ignores to a large extent the phenomenological backdrop to his analytical psychology. Romanyshyn, quoting the preceding text from Jung, observes that '(t)his passage is not from Descartes' (Romanyshyn 2000: 31). Why would we think it is from Descartes? If anything, there are very strong Kantian overtones in the passage, as there seem to be in his onto-epistemology. A close reading of Descartes' philosophy does not find him holding the views we find here in Jung. Indeed, one wonders how Descartes would actually respond to the issues Romanyshyn raises. We have already seen that his views about ideas (in the mind), and their relation to objects, are fraught.[1]

Jung's claim that '[w]hat we know of the world, and what we are immediately aware of in ourselves, are conscious contents that flow from remote, obscure sources' (Jung 1954: [8] 623) problematises the acceptance of an objective world that we can know directly. It does not make claims about that world, what it's like: indeed, it implies that there are difficulties with such a position. Did Descartes hold this view? Well, maybe, because he did believe that he had been deceived by his senses. Yet do not forget that, in his view, that the world is there as he perceives it is guaranteed by the goodness of God, who is not a deceiver.

Descartes' *cogito* does not serve the purpose of relativising everything but the mind, although that may be an effect of his hyperbolic doubt. As an immediate intuition, the *cogito* does not even imply the view being expressed by Jung here. Sure, on some readings of both Descartes and Jung, we could slip into a kind of default orthodoxy that would let Brooke's and Romanyshyn's assertions appear to contain some truth. But this is to ignore the very important point that Descartes' onto-epistemology is quite different from Jung's, even though they are both committed to the notion of the embodied mind or psyche.

It is not clear to me that projection theory has the effects that Romanyshyn claims, nor that it results in 'stuffing the person with subjective soulfulness and leaving the world a slagheap from which all projections, personifications and psyche have been extracted', as Brooke says James Hillman claims (quoted in Brooke 1991: 94).

The romantic vision that Romanyshyn (and Hillman) interpolate into their interpretations of Jung, and which they suggest is part of the ambiguity of Jung's cognitive and ontological commitments, demonises post-Enlightenment thinking. A mechanical, rational world is contrasted with an embryonic, caring, spirit-filled, pre-Enlightenment world where all creatures, including humans, are 'connected' with an apparently benign, spiritualised nature. Brooke argues that Jung also had a tendency to promote a spiritualised view of the world, one compatible with the pre-Enlightenment vision. The theme of connectedness is prominent in such a view. Even if Jung did have the tendency Brooke points to, the degree of compatibility is questionable.

Brooke, however, remains critical of what he sees as Jung's tendency to see the psyche as an interior domain. Brooke remarks that Jung's articulation of projection meant that he was caught in a bind between a despiritualised world and a world that was populated by animate projections (Brooke 1991: 175). One might wonder what this says for Brooke's compatibility claim. From a phenomenological perspective, even Brooke's reading of the body as the *lived* body, in line with Merleau-Ponty, portrays Jung as wedded to an orthodox reading of Descartes that promotes the ontological precedence of interiority. Consider, for instance, this claim:

> It has been shown that Jung failed to follow through a consistently psychological analysis of the lived body. In other words, although Jung seems to have understood, even better than Freud, the body as a *psychological* body, he did not conceive of that psychological body as the bodying forth of human existence. Thus his insight into the nature of psyche as the

> experiential realm of the lived body still tends to be an interiority placed over and against the world 'outside' . . . For Jung, however, the psyche seems to be conceived as an inner world, radically separate from an incarnated life-world. Moreover, although Jung tends to separate outer and inner worlds along Cartesian lines he also tends . . . to view the phenomena and relations of the outer world in terms of the interplay of psychic images.
>
> (Brooke 1991: 118)

Brooke is still asserting that Jung conceives of a radical distinction between inner and outer, and Descartes is seen as the dualist pro-generator, the culprit at whose feet this apparently unacceptable division lies. The point for Brooke, though, is that he regards Jung's reading of the psyche as a whole, consistently and principally, in terms of the 'inner' or interior domain through which the external world is viewed, thus tending 'to retain the Cartesian separation of psyche and world' (Brooke 1991: 135). Yet, I maintain, from a phenomenological perspective, it is difficult to deny the aptness of this trope. I suggested above that if we tease out the threads of Jung's onto-epistemological commitments, then we can see that he operates with a two-tiered epistemology and ontology. Brooke, undoubtedly, would reply that, even with this dual structure, the inner and outer trope reinforces rather than addresses a division that is unbreachable. Indeed, his discussion of the subjective and objective psyche, as we shall see in the next chapter, is an attempt to ameliorate the issue. In my view, as we shall see, Brooke does not succeed but further enmeshes Jung in the problem; but that is largely an issue for Brooke and not for Jung because of the way in which Brooke reads phenomenology.

So the question of innerness in Jung's work persists as a problem for his critics, notwithstanding their, at times, sympathetic reading of Jung's work. However, this bind can be filtered through a phenomenological re-reading of Jung's understanding of the relationship between psyche and the world, a reading that accepts a version of interiority, without the adornment of pre-Enlightenment yearnings so apparent in Romanyshyn's work in particular. Brooke attempts such a phenomenological re-reading to erase the troublesome trope. However, I hold that the notion of interiority can be preserved, and, indeed, is a condition of, a phenomenological understanding of human being. What is more, this trope underpins the relationship between the psyche and the world, and it is through addressing the curious notion of a world emptied of meaning that we can understand how that is the case.

An 'outer world' drained of meaning and human habitation?

Recall that Brooke invokes Descartes' *res extensa* when he comments that, after Descartes, we are left with an outer world drained of meaning. He implies that

Jung, because of his focus of the primacy of the psyche as that which we can know directly, is likewise disposed to the world. According to Brooke, psychic images dominate reality for Jung, and the effect of that is semantic: 'the meanings of an event are separated from the event itself' (Brooke 1991: 118–119). In either case, I am not sure what Brooke means by 'meaning' so I want to pause and explore the question of meaning in this context, for a short while. From what Brooke is saying in the latter, he seems to be presuming that meaning is relational in some way. In the former, he seems to be thinking that meaning is somehow a property of the world. Jeff Speaks, following David Lewis (1970), argues that we can distinguish between two types of 'meaning':

> One sort of theory of meaning – a *semantic theory* – is a specification of the meanings of the words and sentences of some symbol system. Semantic theories thus answer the question, 'What is the meaning of this or that expression?' A distinct sort of theory – a *foundational theory of meaning* – tries to explain what about some person or group gives the symbols of their language the meanings that they have. To be sure, the shape of a correct semantic theory may place constraints on the correct foundational theory of meaning, or vice versa; but that does not change the fact that semantic theories and foundational theories are simply different sorts of theories, designed to answer different questions.
>
> (Speaks 2011)

Given this, we can argue that Brooke seems to be assuming a foundational theory of meaning which is explanatory of the relation between symbols and their makers. The difficulty is, then, to provide an account of the relation between an event and its meaning. Are meanings of events given *in* or *with* an event, or do they pre- or post-date them? That meaning is *already* given implies a giver, and a giver with attitudes, beliefs, ideas and intentions. This suggests some form of consciousness on the part of a meaning giver and maker. The person or group that is the meaning maker might have several different ways of expressing and deciding meaning and, undoubtedly, that will take place within a broader sociolinguistic and cultural context. Hence meaning will be influenced by many factors, and expressed in different ways. Of course, there is an unavoidable personal and/or group psychological dimension in that expression because meaning is intimately connected with various mental/cognitive/affective attitudes, beliefs, ideas and intentions.

An alternative reading can be given to Jung's discussion of synchronicity which Brooke cites as evidence of the separation of event and meaning. Indeed, contrary to his interpretation, Jung's discussion can be interpreted as an affirmation of the position that Brooke seems to hold: that there is some continuity between event and meaning (and even if there is continuity, it does not follow that event and meaning are not logically, or theoretically, separate, and separable). Rather than arguing for a separation, however, Jung is discussing the *correlation* between events and meaning and their cosmological dimension. In his discussion, Jung maintains that it is man[2] who now has exclusive providence over meaning; but Jung seems to be thinking that the cosmic meaning dimension, 'benighted', represents a loss to human being. Regardless, the idea that meaning is given, either cosmologically (by God, for example) or by 'man', instantiates a foundational theory of meaning. There is separation, but a separation in which a link between event and meaning is made by the meaning maker.

I suggest, then, that we need to acknowledge that we are meaning makers, that event and meaning are separate or distinct, and that our sources of meaning making can be various. I do not mean to suggest, though, that we all make our meanings up as we go along. As I argued above, there are social meanings into which we are born. So there are different *sources* of meaning, either social or collective, and personal. On this reading, the psyche can very easily be seen to be a source of meaning making. Our lives are *meaningful* according to our contexts and our own personal experiences mediated through the psyche. Whether or not it is Jung's exclusive source is moot.

In a sense, it is trivially true that continuity and correlation are logical relations between events and their meanings. An event takes place. It is interpreted and given a meaning. Or an event with an already ascribed meaning takes place. Each occurrence of that event's taking place might be accompanied by further interpretation. Thus meaning – and there may be more than one – emerges from the event's having occurred, its context and a group's or individual's understanding and interpretation of that event. But the relation is not a *necessary* logical relation. Multiple meanings are possible, so we are dealing here with a *contingent* relation – the very possibility of multiple meanings implies that the meaning(s) given could be otherwise. Almost perversely, then, a corollary of this view is that any correlation or continuity between event and meaning is, itself, an *effect* of meaning making. In giving a meaning to an event we link that event to our understanding of the world and, perhaps, of ourselves.

Consider the event of my having a dream; say that I am being chased by a monster. I wake up terrified. That I am terrified does not give my dream event a meaning in and of itself. But I might wonder what my terror means, why I am having this dream now. That I think about the dream and its effect on me, and then come up with some explanations and perhaps some interpretations out of which I build meanings, postdates the dream event. I connect the dream with the rest of my life, as it were.

Now consider the celebrations that occur every year on 26 January in Australia. The events surrounding this day are commemorative: they celebrate the arrival of the First Fleet into Botany Bay, so, the beginning of the Europeanisation of Australia. Meanings, in this case, are given in advance of the celebratory events, and based on some initial event or state of affairs. The meanings belong to the First Fleeters, succeeding generations, and their descendants. They are the meanings of the most powerful, those in charge, those authorised by the British government. Such meanings are re-visioned and refashioned with the passing of time. Yet for many Indigenous People of Australia, the (allegedly non-existent human?) inhabitants of *terra nullius*, this is a day marked by sadness and loss. The meaning given by them to 26 January links the celebratory events, and the event itself, to their oppression and demise, loss of language and culture, loss of land and autonomy, loss of identity. On this view, there is no intrinsic meaning specific to any event: that meaning is given does not entail, or imply, that meaning is always already there, to be uncovered. Of themselves, events have no meaning. So meaning is always external to and imposed upon events by a meaning maker.

If this is the case, how are we to understand the idea of a world drained of meaning? Meaning, on the above view, cannot be a property of a world, something that can be drained out of it. For implied in the claim that the world is drained of meaning is the idea that, somehow, the world itself is intrinsically meaning*ful*, which, I take to suggest is that the world is full of meaning in and of itself, say by its mere existence. That is to say, the assumption that the world has meaning of which it could be drained as a consequence of mind and body separation, and as a consequence of extension becoming the identifying property of material bodies (such as the world), seems facile. If the human construction of meaning thesis holds, the world does not have meaning before the existence of human being, and, presumably, then only after the development of certain human psychological properties, the acquisition of language and symbolic systems.

Let us approach this issue in another way. We saw that Jung distinguishes between living body, considered as a natural object, and the living being, the human. In this context we might reflect on a similar distinction made by Husserl, who argues in his preliminary discussion of the natural attitude. For Husserl, the natural theoretical attitude consists in 'the collective horizon of possible investigations that '*Nature as mere nature, contains no values, no works of art* etc., though these are indeed objects of possible knowledge and science' (Husserl 1989: 4; italics in the original). We will see further development of 'natural attitude' in the next two chapters. However, Husserl is clearly conceiving of nature as devoid of *value* (and not meaning) in itself. His idea is that 'world' is a scientific reality, and can be seen in terms of physical forces, quarks and electrons, energy flows, the world of 'objective science' (Boghossian 2006; Searle 2008; Daston and Galison 2010). Descartes' mechanistic theory would be a related model. Yet Husserl, as we shall see, saw problems with his notion of life world and objective science (Husserl 1970: 121ff).

Perhaps what Brooke is trying to get at is the question of value; in other words, that the world has meaning in terms of its value. For example, one could argue that, regardless of anything we think about the natural world, it is valuable in and of itself because the world supports life forms, relationships, webs and networks that are part of a life far greater than anything anthropocentrically oriented. There is no human attributer of value. Typically, deep ecologists would hold such a view. In that case, meaning emerges out of value – indeed, the more valuable something might be, the more meaningful. I shall return to this point shortly. Even so, Husserl's distinguishing between, broadly speaking, an object as given, and an object as valuable, opens the door to considering how we actually do come to create both meaning and value in our worlds. And it also helps us to see that there is a conceptual, and real, distinction between a merely existing world and a world that is valuable and meaningful.

What is this world of which we can all speak so readily? The meaning of 'world' can be interpreted in any number of ways – there are turns and differences in meaning that suggest the multifaceted concept it is. We may speak of the *natural* world – furry animals, trees, flowers, lakes, seas, mountains, birds, rainbows, cyclones, thunder storms, forests, deserts, stars, their networks and relationships. We might think of this as Earth world, the world that is the blue sphere held in the solar system and the cosmos by the natural laws of which it is a part. This world is independent of human being: it pre- and post-exists human occupation of planet Earth, and in this sense, it coincides with Husserl's conception of nature devoid of value. From this, however, it does not follow that the world is valueless. What follows is that any value attributed to the natural world emerges from human experience and understanding. A question to be raised here, though, is what is the place of human being in such a conception? Are we separate from or part of the natural world? In what ways can we and do we describe our relationship?

Earth world, it might be said, is the *'real'* or ontologically fundamental world, a world of systems and their relations, and is the world studied, characteristically, by ecologists, scientists, environmentalists. Claims about this world and its existence are metaphysical claims. They deal with the kind of reality that is constituted by Earth world. On this understanding, Earth world persists through time and space. A view consonant with this, which has clear ethical implications, is that Earth world might be seen as purely instrumental – the world is there for human use, to be mined and grazed and logged and built upon.

An alternative view might argue that Earth world, in all of its complexity and biodiversity, has intrinsic value irrespective of what anyone believes. The very complexity and beauty seen in biodiversity is an expression of the value of such a system in an overall conception of the cosmos. On this view, and depending on our ethico-epistemological assumptions, such a world might be said to be intrinsically valuable or meaningful, regardless of human perceptions or beliefs.[3]

Another view proffered might see humanly constructed worlds of business, of science, psychology, and so on, that supervene on some understanding of the world as given. On this account, which is fundamentally phenomenological and existential, what it is like for individuals and groups to be members of different kinds of self-constituting communities counts as 'world'. Here, 'real world' is reinterpreted, and now includes the dominant experiences of those involved in these particular existential settings (Ricklefs and Miller 2000; Molles 2010). Related to this, we can deny the existence of any *one* world and argue that there are multiple worlds which are expressed through different cultures and lived in different ways by individual members of those cultures (Young 1990a). This phenomenological and psychosocial model is seen in postmodern political and existential theories around deconstruction, difference and social constructionism (Berger and Luckmann 1967; Derrida 1981; Irigaray 1985; Said 2003).

On such accounts, worlds are enacted within built and natural environments, and seen as varyingly independent from, and interdependent with, other worlds. There may be overlaps between worlds because of trade, arts, science, politics, travel and war, and Earth world. All of these worlds contribute to a multifaceted notion of world: the world is the sum of all of these particular worlds; or something in excess of that sum; or, alternatively, is a concept abstracted from, say, family resemblances amongst those worlds. One of the issues with this account of 'world' is dependence on the tendentious notion of social construction.

Jung's claims about the world seem to me to be consonant with what I am calling the phenomenological and psychosocial model. His assertion that without the psyche there would be no world, and no *human* world at all, appeals to a deliberately ambiguous reading of 'world' in which meanings would arise according to different understandings and different metaphysical framings of 'world'. By that I mean that, for Jung, the centrality of the psyche as a constituter of the nature of reality (as we have seen above in my reconstruction of his onto-epistemology) is fundamental to his own understanding of the being of the world and of human being. But Jung's understanding can also encompass the idea that there are particular worlds with their own properties constitutive of a world of work, or of illness, or of the psyche. Furthermore, if Earth world is the fundamental reality, it is inescapably the case that Earth world must be always a presence, even if a silent one. This seems to be the world to which Jung alludes in his indirect onto-epistemology.

But there is another issue here. The idea that the world has *intrinsic meaning* is problematic given the account above, where meaning making requires a minimally psychosocial activity. Yet if that is the case, the world cannot have intrinsic meaning at all, except in so far as humans are part of that world. And that is precisely what the work of phenomenology does – it endorses human being's presence *in* the world effecting and affected by that world. In the accounts above, humans, as meaning makers, make and give meaning to events precisely because of their attitudes, beliefs, values and because of their taken-for-granted being in the world, regardless of the degree to which it is acknowledged. Assuming that what I have argued with respect to the meaning(s) of events can easily be extrapolated to the meaning of other states of affairs and occurrences, then it can be applied in the case of the world. The meaning of 'world' in any of the above senses is, therefore, dependent upon human being, and the human psyche. And, as I indicated before, it is possible to construe a relationship between meaning and value. Recall that, on that account, the value of Earth world is independent of anything we might think, feel or believe.

Abram suggests that 'the world in which we find ourselves before we set out to calculate and measure it is not an inert or mechanical object but a living field, an open and dynamic landscape subject to its own moods and metamorphoses'. The world of scientific objectivity, to use Husserl's phrase, alluded to here by Abram, is, indeed a problem if it devastates the Earth. But is it because of Descartes and Galileo that this has occurred? Abram's account acknowledges an intertwining of oneself and the world and argues that:

> the scientist never completely succeeds in making himself into a pure spectator of the world, for he cannot cease to live in the world as a human among other humans, or as a creature among other creatures, and his scientific concepts and theories necessarily borrow aspects of their character and texture from his untheorized, spontaneously lived experience.
>
> (Abram 1996: 33–34)

The scientist Abram envisages may well be a caricature, since many of the problems engaged in by scientists over the past four hundred years have been an engagement with the world and its problems. Public and personal health and sanitary issues, the discovery of the importance of basic things like cleanliness and antiseptics, transport, new and better building technologies can all be seen as a response to human habitation and the environment. However neglect and ignorance of the environment cannot be gainsaid.

With Descartes' mechanistic view of the body, it is difficult *not* to implicate him in such a view. However, it does not follow that a mechanistic account such as we find in Descartes' analysis of material body leads inevitably to a valueless and thus meaningless world, except for its scientific and instrumental value. One wonders if either Descartes or Jung subscribed to the mechanical, lifeless view of Earth world, or the world in general, or to the bloodless version of the scientist that Abram envisages. One also wonders if Descartes or Jung saw themselves as pure spectators of a world sealed off in the way Abram, and also Brooke and Romanyshyn, describe. To place this always in the context of Descartes' philosophy is, from my point of view, very problematic.

Jung's remark, that the 'psyche and body are not separate entities but one and the same life', reiterates Descartes' view of human being. Jung also writes that 'self, as an inclusive term, that embraces our whole living organism, not only contains the deposit and totality of all past life, but is also a point of departure, the fertile soil from which all future life will spring' (Jung 1972: 619). We might note that, according to Jung, we cannot, in the end, explain the whole of human being by appealing to the physical sciences. A human being is always in excess of her or his physical properties both personally and collectively. A human being is neither *principally* mental nor physical: it is an *organism* of a specific kind that is a human being. So why, one might ask, does he speak in such apparently dualistic terms?

In order to explain that, it is important that we consider Jung's relationship to phenomenology, which we shall do shortly. But the question of the interior/exterior trope is not entirely settled. My tentative construction of Jung's onto-epistemology fails if it does not take into account the phenomenological aspects of analytical psychology. It also fails if it does not take seriously the idea of the human being as a whole organism. I should like to offer another reading, which I shall do in the next chapter. While I have been defending the interior/exterior trope and its cognates, the issue remains unresolved because it is certainly the case that this trope is used or implied by both Descartes and Jung. However, it is very difficult to understand the criticisms of the trope when the findings of the previous chapter are taken into consideration. Put bluntly, the trope is entirely existentially appropriate and, in my view, the trope could not be abandoned without simultaneously abandoning Descartes' phenomenological insights. If we regard the trope as intrinsic to the methodological intentions of spiritual practice, such as I have outlined, then its metaphorical inflections are not ontological, but phenomenological.

If one puts oneself through the same processes as Descartes put himself through, with the same assumptions and teleological aspirations, one needs to be able to perceive oneself as having an 'inner life'. So the inner and outer trope becomes a condition of the possibility of Descartes' hyperbolic doubt, and also a condition of the possibility of his phenomenological encounter with himself as thinking thing. And, I would argue, a similar situation obtains with Jung: the conscious and the unconscious are manifested as internal phenomena first and foremost. The images he creates in the *Red Book*, for instance, are an expression of an *internal* phenomenological awareness that arises in his encounter with the collective unconscious as it represents itself to him.

What both Descartes and Jung do is to give precedence to one aspect of the trope in order to uncover some truth or other with which each is concerned. And if we think of the inner and outer trope as part of the metaphorical context that conditions our awareness of the world and our place in it, we can see that it should be understood as fundamental to the natural attitude. Lastly, the erasure of the trope would have dire consequences for individuation because it would result in an abandonment to the collective. Assuming that individuation is possible and desirable, it involves a withdrawal of projections and the ownership of one's whole self, including one's shadow. It is difficult to conceive of ownership, which, in this context, involves a sense of responsibility to oneself and to one's community, without some operative notion of a personal psyche to which one has exclusive access. This entails a boundary around oneself, and a conception of interiority that is both productive and beneficial to oneself and one's world. In other words, there are several layers of importance that the trope has both phenomenologically and metaphorically. And what is important then, about phenomenology?

Chapter 5

Jung and the phenomenological standpoint

At the beginning of 'The Phenomenology of the Spirit in Fairytales', Jung says the following:

> One of the unbreakable rules in scientific research is to take an object as known only so far as the inquirer is in a position to make scientifically valid statements about it. 'Valid' in this sense simply means what can be verified by facts. The object of inquiry is the natural phenomenon. Now in psychology, one of the most important phenomena is the *statement*, and in particular its form and content, the latter aspects perhaps being the more significant with regard to the nature of the psyche. The task that ordinarily presents itself is the description and arrangement of events, then comes the closer examination into the laws of their living being. To inquire into the *substance* of what has been observed is possible in natural science only where there is an Archimedean point outside. For the psyche no such point exists – only the psyche can observe the psyche . . . Consequently, knowledge of the psychic substance is impossible for us, at least with the means presently available. This does not rule out the possibility that the atomic physics of the future may supply us with the said Archimedean point . . . I do not think it superfluous to acquaint my reader with the necessary limitations that psychology voluntarily imposes on itself, for he [*sic*] will then be in a position to appreciate the phenomenological standpoint of modern psychology, which is not always understood.
>
> (Jung 1968: 384)

Fourteen years previously Jung had written 'Basic Postulates of Analytical Psychology', which contained the epistemologically disturbing remarks we saw in the previous chapter. In the above, we see Jung make a very clear distinction between, on the one hand, scientifically 'valid' statements, made from an Archimedean point of view, a bird's-eye, or God's-eye point of view, *external* to the relevant phenomena; and on the other, the limits of the psychological standpoint, a standpoint that does not, and indeed cannot, participate in an Archimedean point of view. Why not? Well, Jung assumes the legitimacy of first-person statement making about one's own psyche – he seems to be claiming that, in one's own case, one cannot get the same kind of viewpoint on one's own psyche as one could on, for example, the trees and sky and birds outside the window. There is a relation that I have to myself and to my own psyche that is different from anything else, that I do not identify as my psyche.

Of course, he might argue, *you* could say something about my psyche, but, it might be held, it is doubtful that such a statement would have the same validity as a statement you might make about the colour of my shoes, or the way in which my hair is cut. Jung is suggesting that something would be valid according to verification by the facts. What could and would count as the facts? You cannot look at my psyche, or touch, or smell, or weigh or otherwise measure it. Jung puts his finger on some of the very difficult issues about psyche – mind and consciousness – in general. Where is 'it'? Do I have a special access to my mind that I don't to yours, and vice versa? What counts as verifiability in the case of my mind and yours? While these are interesting and important questions, I cannot answer them, especially here. I want, instead, to focus on the following.

Jung refers to the phenomenological point of view – what is it and what does it mean in the context of this book? In his discussion of the role of experience and science in psychology, Jung claims that there has been a:

> general shifting of the scientific standpoint point in favour of phenomenology. Nevertheless, it cannot be maintained that the phenomenological point of view has not made much headway. Theory still plays far too great a role, instead of being included in phenomenology as it should be.
>
> (Jung 1968: 111–112)

The text that follows is not particularly illuminating on this matter. Jung talks about the lack of knowledge of a general phenomenology in relation to a psychology of neurosis, of Pierre Janet's descriptive methodology, and the biographical descriptions of Théodore Flournoy and the attempted synthesis by William James in *Varieties of Religious Experience*.[1] Even so, we cannot glean much from what he says, except that context, perhaps biography, and description appear to him to be elements of a phenomenological standpoint.[2]

Even in other places, Jung does not give any clear indication of what he understands by 'phenomenology' and by 'phenomenological standpoint' except to say, for example, that the phenomenological standpoint is 'concerned with occurrences, events, experiences, in a word, with facts' (Jung 1938: 3). In my view, this is not particularly illuminating. History, science, anthropology are also concerned with occurrences, facts and experiences, as we saw above. They do not operate from a phenomenological standpoint (although they can). So we need to find out exactly what it is that Jung means.

Jung's use of the term 'standpoint' is noteworthy, echoing as it does, consciously or unconsciously, Franz Brentano's use of the term in *Psychology from an Empirical Standpoint* (Brentano 1995). The idea of standpoint not only suggests possible multipositioning of statement making, but different relations that one might have to different objects or phenomena. In the case of natural objects that are publicly observable, for example, trees and sky and birds, there is a sense in which such objects are not-me where 'not-me' stands for the observing consciousness. In other words, the not-me creates a distinction between what is an aspect of myself and what is not. While I might perceive trees and sky and birds, and my perceptions are *mine*, that of which they are perceptions (the objects or phenomena) are other than me: they have an autonomy and independence, I might argue, beyond the existence of my psyche and my consciousness. We have already touched on this issue.

In the case of one's psyche, as distinct from natural objects, two things are going on:

1. Only I, it might be argued, can observe my own psyche so the observing consciousness in my own case is always and only myself.
2. If point 1 is the case, you cannot have access to my psyche because it is not a publicly observable object like trees and sky and birds.

Whether or not my psyche is an 'object' is moot; let us agree, though, that the psyche is a phenomenon, a conscious and unconscious centre that is peculiar to me or to you as the case may be. It is not publicly observable in the required sense – a something 'out there' capable of coming into the public perceptual field or of being an object of scientific enquiry. Sure, you can see my actions in the world, form views about my intentions and desires from my behaviour, but you cannot see what sits under such activity. That is part of the point Jung is making. He does not, however, argue the rightness or wrongness of any of his claims. What he terms the scientific standpoint he, quite plainly, accepts in terms of observation of natural phenomena; and observation of the psyche is of a different kind, involving only a subject in question. Questions of validity in each case entail different standpoints that are perhaps incommensurable.

The status of consciousness, the soul, the mind and associated concepts, has been the topic of debate for a very long time. Some of these debates featured in the establishing of psychology as a discipline in the nineteenth century. Franz Brentano, for example, focused his psychology on mental phenomena, arguing 'for whether or not there souls, the fact is that there are mental phenomena' (Brentano 1995: 18). Brentano argues that 'no mental phenomenon exists which is not . . . consciousness of an object'. Consciousness is 'synonymous with "mental phenomenon," or "mental act."' He characterises mental phenomena in terms of the 'intentional inexistence of an object'. His idea of intentional inexistence originally incorporates an Aristotelian conception of perception in which an object (of perception) is thought to exist in the soul. His discussion of the nature of mental phenomena and acts precedes a lengthy philosophical interrogation of inner consciousness (Brentano 1995: 120).

Given his analysis of conscious mental phenomena, he raises this issue: 'All mental phenomena are states of consciousness; but are all mental phenomena conscious, or might there be unconscious mental acts?' which Brentano encapsulates in the expression 'unconscious consciousness' (Brentano 1995: 102). Brentano weighs the arguments for the idea of an unconscious consciousness, acknowledging the 'lack of unanimity' amongst psychologists.

Ultimately, he rejects the idea after a lengthy and comprehensive consideration of 'four different ways' of arguing the point:

1. The facts of experience might point to unconscious mental phenomena as their cause.
2. Facts of experience 'bring about an unconscious mental phenomenon as its effect'.
3. There is a relationship between the intensity of conscious mental phenomena and the consciousness associated with those phenomena.
4. If, for every mental phenomenon, there is a mental object of that phenomenon, this would result in an 'infinite complexity of mental states' that is 'intrinsically impossible and contrary to experience'.

(Brentano 1995: 101–137)

This short commentary on Brentano's concept of intentional inexistence opens us to some of the historical background and context to Jung's own hypothesis of the unconscious, either personal or collective. I do not mean to suggest any relationship between the two thinkers though. Brentano had little, if any, influence on Jung as far as we know, even though it is known that he did have an effect on Freud.[3] Note that Jung's reasons for maintaining the existence of the unconscious are largely based on induction, to which Brentano objects in his analysis. More's the pity: who is to know how Jung's own philosophical underpinnings and then his own practice would have been affected by conscious engagement with Brentano, whose idea of intentional inexistence of the mental subsequently influenced the development of phenomenology so strongly? In Brentano's work, we see the seeds of the phenomenology to come.

But just what is the phenomenological standpoint of modern psychology that Jung invokes? He says that it is a:

> standpoint that does not exclude the existence of faith, conviction and experienced certainties of whatever description, nor does it contest their validity. Great as is their importance for the individual and for collective life, psychology completely lacks the means to prove their validity in the scientific sense.
>
> (Jung 1968: 384)

Yet these are not really the concerns of phenomenologists in the tradition of Brentano and Husserl, and then Merleau-Ponty and Heidegger *et al.* Their deeply philosophical expositions focus so much more on the method and structure of phenomenal experience together with detailed argument and analysis. Jung's is largely descriptive and profoundly undertheorised – the case histories, examples and commentaries he uses are contextualised almost backwards, into the past, rather than in the literature cotemporaneous with his own intellectual milieu. Even his rather brief exposition in *Psychology and Religion* does not give us much insight – he reiterates his concern for psychological experiences that are subjective as distinct from their objective acceptance 'by a *consensus gentium*'.

Jung's focus on phenomena implies that he considers himself to be a phenomenologist – he says that he represents the method of the phenomenological standpoint (Jung 1938: 3). We saw above that he identifies 'the statement and its form and content' as phenomena, and that he thinks that content is 'perhaps more significant' (than statement *per se* and its form). Presumably, Jung is here referring to the content of his patients' tellings, what and how they say what they say, in therapy. Already then, we are, in all likelihood, dealing with different conceptions of 'phenomena': the telling or statement itself, its contents and its expression.

In Jung's analytical psychology it is possible to discern other conceptions of 'phenomena'. For example, a patient may 'tell' something about his or her psyche without, or in combination with, words, as in Jung's 'A Study in the Process of Individuation' involving a Miss X who painted a series of watercolour landscapes (Jung 1968: 525–626). The dream, for Jung, is also considered a phenomenon in both form and content. This, together with the symbols, paintings and other artifacts and art forms, that Jung explored and analysed throughout his life, suggests a vast panorama of possible meanings for 'phenomena'. It could perhaps be summarised in the expression 'presentation to consciousness'. On this reading, a phenomenon is anything that is presented or appears to, or in, consciousness.[4]

The idea of a presentation or appearance to consciousness resonates closely with Brentano's conception of 'presentation, judgement and emotional attitude as the basic three classes of mental reference' (Brentano 1995: 78–80, 278–281). A phenomenon that is presented, or appears, to or in consciousness clearly connotes Brentano's idea of intentional inexistence (meaning 'existence in x' rather than non-existence):

> Every mental phenomenon is characterized by what the Scholastics of the Middle Ages called the intentional (or mental) in-existence of an object and what we might call, though not wholly unambiguously, reference to a content, direction toward an object (which is not to be understood here as meaning a thing), or immanent objectivity. Every mental phenomenon includes something as an object within itself, although they do not all do

> so in the same way. In presentation something is presented, in judgement something is affirmed or denied, in love loved, in hate hated, in desire, desired, and so on.
>
> (Brentano 1995: 88)

Brentano traces the notion back to Aristotle, Philo, Augustine, Anselm and Aquinas. He argues that only mental phenomena exhibit intentional inexistence which becomes the defining mark of the mental because 'no physical phenomenon exhibits anything like it' (Brentano 1995: 88–89).[5] Brentano does acknowledge the controversial nature of intentional inexistence, noting that Hamilton had denied this characteristic to all of mental phenomena like feelings: 'pleasure and pain in all their most diverse shades and varieties' (Brentano 1995: 89). Brentano, however, responds by arguing that not all objects to which feelings refer are external objects, and claims that the notion 'subjectively subjective' (as distinct from the subject–object relation) is self-contradictory. Thus a mental phenomenon may have as its object something that does or does not exist and something that is internal or external to a subject.

Brentano later modified what he came to see as, according to Oskar Kraus, an 'imperfect' Aristotelian conception of intentional inexistence, that is, 'as a mode of being the thing has in consciousness'.[6] His preferred articulation of intentional inexistence emphasises that the characteristic of every mental activity 'is the reference to something as an object' (Brentano 1995: 271). This has become known as the intentionality of mental acts, events, objects or, more generally, of consciousness. We might say that, fundamentally, Brentano has pointed out that mental events, acts or phenomena are always in an of- or to-relation: that means that they are always directed towards an object.

Given this understanding of the intentionality of consciousness, we can see that Jung's work, since it concerned consciousness and the psyche generally, was in fact right in the domain of Brentano's mental phenomena. Yet his comments about the phenomenological standpoint of modern psychology do not deal with the material we find in Brentano's work; and Brentano, with his directedness thesis, lays the foundation for the phenomenological standpoint and its subsequent developments and re-visioning in Husserl, Heidegger, Sartre, Merleau-Ponty and others. Edmund Husserl was the key figure in this development, as is well known, and it is to his idea of phenomenology that we initially turn in our exploration of Jung's reading of phenomenology.

The Husserlian factor, and beyond

What is the link between Brentano and Husserl? In the *Logical Investigations,* Husserl briefly discusses Brentano's classification of mental phenomena before turning his attention to his primary interest:

> that there are essential specific differences of intentional relation or intention (the generic descriptive character of 'acts') . . . We take intentional

> relation, understood in purely descriptive fashion as an inward peculiarity of certain experience, to be the essential feature of 'psychical phenomena' or 'acts', seeing in Brentano's definition of them as 'phenomena intentionally containing objects in themselves' a circumscription of essence, whose 'reality' (in the traditional sense) is of course ensured by examples.
>
> (Husserl 2001 (1901): 213–214)

Intentionality became part of the fabric of phenomenology and, in spite of its difficulties and the controversy it has attracted, it remains central to our understanding of, broadly speaking, mental and affective states. There is always an object – existent or not – of our thoughts, ideas, loves, hates, passions *et alia*.

At the beginning of Lecture IV of *The Idea of Phenomenology*, Husserl claims that:

> [c]ognitive mental processes (and this belongs to their essence) have an *intentio,* they refer to something, they are related in this or that way to an object. This activity of relating itself to an object belongs to them even if the object itself does not. And what is objective can appear, can have a certain kind of givenness in appearance, even though it is at the same time neither genuinely *(reell)* within the cognitive phenomenon, not does it exist in another way as a *cogitatio*.
>
> (Husserl 1964: 43)

Quite plainly, Husserl is adopting the Brentano thesis about intentional objects and, for him, any intentional object is metaphysically neutral – whether or not an object of intention exists is irrelevant. Husserl claims that not all conscious experience, for example, the data of sensation, is intentional (Husserl 1982: 75). Thus Husserl incorporates the intentionality thesis into his phenomenology as an aspect of his understanding of genuine immanence (which arises, as we shall see, from the direct intuition that is Descartes' *cogito*) (Husserl 1999: Second Meditation *passim*).

Let me go back, though, to Jung's claim that the object of inquiry of scientific research is natural phenomena. Broadly speaking, Husserl would accept Jung's claim. In *Ideas Pertaining to a Pure Phenomenology,* Book II, for example, Husserl discusses the natural scientific attitude. There, he identifies nature as the '*object of natural science* . . . the total spatio-temporal "universe", the total domain of possible experience . . *the field of transcendent – specifically, spatio-temporal – realities . . . the* intentional correlate of experience as carried out' by someone who thinks in 'the natural-scientific way' (italics in the original). He refers to 'nature, as mere nature' a nature that 'contains no values, no works of art' (Husserl 1989: 3). It is possible, and legitimate I think, to interpret Husserl's description of 'nature' as what Jung had in mind as the object of scientific research.

Jung's view of the relationship between psychology and science is curious: he holds, for example, that the phenomenological point of view 'is the same as that of natural science' (Jung 1938: 3). That does not quite gel with his view that there is no Archimedean point of view in psychology, as there is in science.

Jung's view is not Husserl's view. Husserl distinguishes between natural thinking and philosophical thinking, a distinction not deployed by Jung. Jung was keen to separate analytical psychology from philosophy. Yet he also seemed to think of himself as dealing in the domain of empirical science, and so it seems that he would want to embrace empirical psychology as a science perhaps describable in just the terms identified by Husserl.

Husserl's focus is not on the psyche, it is on the possibility of cognition. Cognition, he maintains, cannot be dealt with in the 'natural thinking' scientific model. He regards cognition as 'a fact of nature' that can be an object of scientific enquiry 'in a certain manner'. It can be described and investigated (Husserl 1964: 13–21; 1989). Jung's observation that atomic physics may one day provide an Archimedean point from which to view the psyche might parallel Husserl's remarks here. From his perspective, there is a tension between the demands of a natural science concerned with nature, and presumably empirical on the one hand; and, on the other, an empiricism concerned with a non-objectifiable self-conscious psyche. Jung does not seem to recognise this tension, although he does admit that psychology would be limited if conceived of *only* as a science (Jung 1971: 86). Yet Husserl's comments do not contemplate the possibility of such a point: how could subjectivity be thought of ever in terms of an Archimedean point? one might ask. His focus is on the relation between cognition and cognised.

Here is how he sees the problem:

> Cognition in all of its manifestations is a psychic act; it is the cognition of a cognizing subject. The objects cognized stand over and against cognition. But how can we be certain of the correspondence between cognition and the object cognized? How can knowledge transcend itself and reach its object reliably? . . . In perception the perceived thing is believed to be directly given. Before my perceiving eyes stands the thing. I see it, and I grasp it. Yet the perceiving is simply a mental act of mine, of the perceiving subject.
>
> (Husserl 1964: 16)

Husserl is also highly critical of attempts to make of philosophy a natural science after the models of science developed in the seventeenth century. His attempt to establish a method for dealing philosophically with the issues of cognition sees him claiming that '*philosophy lies in a wholly new dimension*. It needs an *entirely new point of* departure and an entirely new method of distinguishing it in principle from any "natural" science' (italics in the original). He argues that 'pure' philosophy must disregard the achievements and methods of the natural sciences to begin in critical reflection, a reflection that suspends our belief in any science and its methods. He sees this as a method set 'over against the "natural" method' (Husserl 1964: 19–21). Consequently, Husserl distinguishes between experiential sciences involving matters of fact, and eidetic sciences or the sciences of essences (Husserl 1982: 7ff). If Jung is anxious to see his theoretical work as scientifically legitimate, we do not see that here with Husserl. Jung's focus on matters of fact is not of the same order as those of Husserl. In the domain of cognition, Husserl is much more concerned to deal with matters lying outside scientific facts – that is part of what makes his work phenomenological.

Husserl points out that any object is both contingently placed and contingently constituted: 'in respect of its essence', it could be otherwise. That said, he argues that this contingent factualness, in which something, say a material body, is what it is in respect of its own essence, and also has the character of both eidetic necessity and a relation to eidetic universality. What does this mean? Husserl argues that there is something empirically ungraspable beyond the empirical phenomenon, that an object has 'its *own specific character,* its stock of *essential predicables* which must belong to it (as "an existent such as it is in itself") if other secondary, relative determinations can belong to it' (Husserl 1982: 7–8; italics in the original). The aim, then, of this new eidetic science is to apprehend the pure essence of an intentional object, the *a priori* (not given in experience) and in order to do that, one must put into question, and suspend one's natural attitude to, the world. What Husserl is talking about here is the *phenomenological epochē* and he is talking about intelligible essences, rather than about something observable.[7]

Now when we read Jung, we come across nothing like the process I have just described. Yet it seems to me that Jung's work plays around and through the relationship and tensions between the *a priori* (for example, the collective unconscious, the archetypes) and the empirical. Husserl's is very demanding material with which to deal, yet it gives us some idea of an intellectual milieu in which we can better understand Jung's philosophical commitments and issues. And what that does is to show the potential richness of Jungian psychology. Jung's focus, though, is in establishing his psychology as a legitimate form of therapy, rather than on establishing the grounds on which that might be built. And that is a way in which we might understand Husserl: as providing the theoretical underpinnings for cognition, and thus for the possibility of a grounded psychology. I am not claiming that, from a theoretical perspective, Jung should be doing the same thing as Husserl was doing and thus actually 'doing philosophy'.

In my view, Jung notes problems, either substantive or methodological, and works through them in a systematically descriptive fashion. His discussions often take the form of critical commentary. But they do not explore his own assumptions and ideas beyond finding textual evidence perhaps, for instance, in philosophy or in the literature of alchemy or of Eastern philosophy.[8] What is important here is that it is quite evident that Husserl understood phenomenology as a philosophical method that went back to the fundamentals of cognition. Jung did not or, at least, it does not appear that he did. So although the problems both Jung and Husserl are dealing with echo each other, it is a faint echo, and their language and orientation differ. Jung's phenomenological standpoint might or might not refer to the phenomenological tradition stemming from the work of Husserl. Methodologically and substantively they have different concerns so we are left wondering what it is to which Jung is referring.

When we turn to the idea of the *phenomenological epochē* we are led into Husserl's world of radical re-evaluation of what we, from an onto-epistemological perspective, take for granted. In his elucidation of phenomenology as a critique of cognition, Husserl puts into question the natural world, all sciences, and the natural attitude that accompanies them (Husserl 1964: 22; 1989: 189ff). The natural attitude is basically the attitude with which we engage in the world on an everyday basis, an attitude that accepts the world as we perceive it, as if there were objects – natural and otherwise – in their own right. On this basis, the world is as we think and believe it to be. According to Husserl we take these natural objects – natural because they are the objects of this attitude – to be transcendent, to exist in themselves (Husserl 1964: 37). He says that 'transcendence' is ambiguous, and he distinguishes between those objects as a genuine concrete part of the *cogitatio*[9] on the one hand; and those objects that are genuinely given 'beyond what can be *directly "seen"* and *apprehended*' (Husserl 1964: 28). We could construe the latter as problematising the (ontologically independent) existence of objects external to the psyche in much the same way as Jung's claim that we are unable to 'penetrate at all the essences of things external to ourselves' that we saw in Chapter 4. From a philosophical *and* a phenomenological perspective, then, Jung could be seen as a (common-sense) natural attitude dissident – as Kant had before him. Hence the concrete reality of the world questions articulated by both Kant and Jung can be seen to interrogate the natural attitude.

Husserl ponders the problem of how the critique of cognition can begin when everything has been suspended, with the result that nothing at all can be assumed, including any cognitions. The reduction, the suspension of the natural attitude, entails 'the annihilation of the world of physical things', leaving the being of consciousness 'untouched' (Husserl 1982: 110). He argues that a direct intuition that is immediately given, and that would count as a 'self-giving' cognition, can be admitted. In his view, such a cognition would be 'immediately evident and of such a kind that, as absolutely clear and indubitable, it excludes every doubt of its possibility and contains none of the puzzles that led to all the skeptical confusions'. Husserl calls on what he sees as the self-evident nature of the *cogitatio*.[10] He assumes Descartes' immediately given intuition as a model for phenomenological method and argues that Descartes' method of doubt, even if it was used 'for other purposes', is a starting point for phenomenology (Husserl 1964: 2ff, 23ff; 1999).

On this reading, we might see Descartes' method of hyperbolic doubt as a founding moment for phenomenology, and certainly for Husserlian phenomenology. And we also see that Husserl is developing the idea of a transcendental consciousness, that is, the point of view from, and at which, the reduction is carried out. This transcendental consciousness is what emerges from, and is simultaneously established by, the *cogito.* And it is what is activated in the meditative mode. Basically then, Husserl is arguing that we have to suspend everything we perceive, apprehend, believe about the world – get rid of the clutter as it were – and see what's left. Consciousness persists as the mode of consciousness capable of immediate intuition – a self-presence that can function within a pure domain of consciousness. What is required in order to achieve this? The 'pure subject of the act' of the cogito emerges as an effect of the *epochē.* Husserl calls this the pure Ego (Husserl 1982).

Having said that, we need to be aware that the link with Descartes is important for phenomenology in general. Husserl refers to Descartes as 'France's greatest thinker [who] gave transcendental phenomenology new impulses through his *Meditations*' (Husserl 1999: 1). There are limits to Descartes' prototypical philosophical reflection, however, and Husserl also argues in *Cartesian Meditations* that he deviates from Descartes and 'plunge[s] into the task of laying open the field of transcendental experience'. For him, the evidence of the *cogito*:

> remained barren because Descartes neglected not only to clarify the pure sense of the method of transcendental *epochē*, but also to direct his attention to the fact that the ego can explicate himself *ad infinitum* and systematically, by means of transcendental experience, and therefore lies ready as a possible field of work.
>
> (Husserl 1999: 31)

In my view, that takes us right into the arena of the spiritual practice, to *prosoche.* I take this up again in the next chapter.

It also points out a methodological difference between Husserl and Descartes. While Husserl mentions 'annihilation', Descartes' hyperbolic doubt is a cautious scepticism that leaves open the possibility of the continuing existence of the world.

Not only is Descartes identified as an intellectual inspiration and progenitor for twentieth-century phenomenology, a link with Brentano is also indicated. He mentions Descartes in relation to the problem of the existence of objects in consciousness and also, although not always approvingly, in relation to other matters (Brentano 1995: 140, 305, 361). In reference to this, Dermot Moran argues that Brentano frequently:

> refers to Descartes' distinction between objective and formal reality in explanation of the status of the intentional object. In fact Brentano is replaying a debate which took place between Descartes and his Thomist critic, Fr. Caterus, a debate between the Scotistic and Thomistic interpretations of *realitas objectiva*. Indeed, the terminological similarities between Brentano and Descartes strikingly demonstrates Brentano's debt to what I call the Scholastico-Cartesian tradition indebted to Brentano for the idea of intentionality even when he did not agree with Brentano in his totality.
>
> (Moran 1966: 8)

On this account the relationship between Descartes, Brentano and Husserl is spelt out in terms of the intentionality thesis on the one hand, and method on the other. In my view, the methodological orientation of Descartes' and Husserl's work that implies the existence of a transcendental ego can help us to understand Jung's work in the context of phenomenology. In other words, transcendental considerations, of which the subject is the centre, reflect an important face of Jung through which we can understand the various arcane references he makes to apparently obscure matters.

That said, we need to bear in mind that this is a very brief exposition of Husserl's work that serves merely to situate other discussions of Jung's relationship with phenomenology. Much of what I have been discussing above is controversial. Aspects of Husserl's phenomenology have been mined and rejected and modified by his followers and detractors (as have aspects of Jung's work). Notorious amongst them is, of course, Heidegger. The dust has not settled on Husserl, however, and he has not been relegated to the dungeon to be left and forgotten. There has been a recent revival of Husserlian scholarship led by Dermot Moran, Dan Zahavi, Natalie Depraz, and Sara Heinämaa, amongst others. An extensive survey of Husserlian literature, read in relation to an equally extensive survey of Jungian literature, is beyond the scope of this particular project here, so my reading is necessarily limited. If we are to appreciate fully attempts either to read Jung phenomenologically or to construe him as a phenomenologist, it is wise to take seriously the Husserlian context of, for example, Merleau-Ponty's descriptive phenomenology, which has a highly ambiguous relationship with Husserl's phenomenology. Similarly, the deployment of Heideggerian hermeneutic phenomenology needs to be read against a Husserlian backdrop.

Jung's reference to the phenomenological standpoint with which we began this short survey might include some of the perspectives that we have seen emerge in the discussion so far. One might assume in good faith that the issues around the idea that only the psyche can observe itself and the apparently resulting circularity are precisely such perspectives. But perhaps an equally big issue is the question of the body and its 'place' in the world. Certainly, Husserl devotes a lot of attention to intersubjectivity, the body and the world, and by

Book II of *Ideas,* there is specific concern with the body as *living* body, or 'animated flesh' ('*Leib*') as distinct from body as 'inanimate physical matter' (Husserl 1989: xiv). The themes of time and consciousness which we see emerge in Heidegger's work are pre-empted by Husserl, just as the notion of flesh or lived body comes out of Merleau-Ponty.

For Heidegger, the question is the question of Being, not the question of cognition. His book, *Being and Time,* is an exploration of that question through his analysis of *Dasein*, the manner of being in the world for the entity, 'man himself' (Heidegger 1962: H12). Undoubtedly, patently, Heidegger is influenced by Husserl: *Dasein* is interpreted in terms of temporality and his discussion of 'phenomena' and phenomenological method bears the marks of Husserl ('to the things themselves' says Heidegger (Heidegger 1962: H28)). Even Heidegger's discussion of *poiesis*, as I shall shortly suggest, takes off from Husserl's deployment of phantasy.

Merleau-Ponty adopts and adapts some of the themes of Husserl's work and fashions them after a style all his own. We should not read Merleau-Ponty's phenomenology as a completely radical departure from Husserl, because in those very themes, he engages in some of the problematics identified and explored by Husserl.[11] That is not to say that Merleau-Ponty reiterates Husserl's thought, without innovation, without creating a different horizon within which consciousness and the body and the world are schematically intertwined. Methodologically, his approach is different, eschewing, as he does, any extensive analysis of the *epochē.*

From our perspective what is interesting and important is that Merleau-Ponty rejects a conception of the body which sees it as one object among many; and he rejects a psychology that separates mind and body, that results in the interiority of subject and exteriority of world. As I noted above, the concept of the lived body is highly derivative of Husserl's own view.

Merleau-Ponty argues that the 'return to the phenomenal' enables and recognises the ambiguous domain that is the phenomenal field in which we are constituted, and constituted as living bodies with a point of view upon the world (Merleau-Ponty 1962: 26ff, 66–70). In *Phenomenology of Perception*, Merleau-Ponty comments on the *epochē*, and claims that the:

> most important lesson which the reduction teaches us is the impossibility of a complete reduction. This is why Husserl is constantly re-examining the possibility of the reduction . . . The unfinished nature of phenomenology and the inchoative atmosphere which has surrounded it are not to be taken as a sign of failure, they were inevitable because phenomenology's task was to reveal the mystery of the world and reason.
>
> (Merleau-Ponty 1962: xiv–xxi)

In thinking phenomenology's task in this way, in remarking on its unfinished nature, Merleau-Ponty is not closing off the possibilities for phenomenology. His own project, however, brings a different emphasis that, after critique, is a descriptive analysis of the lived body in the world, its interrelations and intersubjectivity. Thus Merleau-Ponty's orientation to the question of perception highlights themes like intersubjectivity, the body and the world. His account develops and emphasises the intersubjective relations that enfold and situate us in the world.

The basic point I want to make here, however, is that I think it is unwise to dismiss Husserl's phenomenology and opt for either a Heideggerian or a Merleau-Pontyan reading of phenomenology without a full acknowledgement of the range of his influence. When it comes to considering Jung's view of what the phenomenological standpoint consists in, we may never know exactly how he conceived that standpoint. Clearly it is not Husserlian and his influences are obscure. In a sense, that does not matter. In another sense, it does, because even if Jung is not himself a phenomenologist (except maybe in a very weak sense), it is possible to read him phenomenologically, as Roger Brooke and Robert Romanyshyn do. So I now turn to their construction of a relation between Jung and phenomenology.

The Jung–phenomenology connection?

The dualistic positionings, of subject and object, knower and known, inner and outer, arise as a consequence of the natural attitude, the pre-reflective state in which we take the world to be as we perceive it to be, as we encounter it. How we construe that dualism is highly controversial: Husserl's phenomenology problematises the dualist structure, but only upon the deployment of the *epochē*. That does not mean, however, that we abandon the natural attitude altogether, only that it is suspended for the purposes of the philosophical endeavour. With Descartes, the analysis that emerges in the context of his secluded meditating is a grounding, a foundation for understanding and certainty. With Husserl there is a way of conceiving cognition and consciousness that sees intersubjectivity, and the world, as constitutive of consciousness. We see in his analysis a rethinking of what comes to us in the natural attitude.

The relationship between Descartes and Husserl is intimately nuanced even if their aims are different and the results that emerge from the ways their distinctive methods evolve lead to alternative theoretical perspectives. Something of Descartes' dualism has clearly persisted, even with recent challenges, such as we saw in earlier chapters.

It is not surprising that Roger Brooke has a commitment to a phenomenology that overcomes Descartes' dualism. In Descartes' work, Brooke sees the ultimate expression of a dualism that has informed much of Western thinking since the Enlightenment. He refers to the 'dichotomy of subject and world, knower and known', and says that an effect of Descartes' dualism is that human consciousness is located in the mind, itself separated from the natural material world (Brooke 1991: 30–31). For Brooke, the problem of location is a serious onto-epistemological issue. One way in which he addresses this issue is to read Jung's work in terms of *poiesis*. How does that work?

We saw in the preceding chapter that the interior/exterior trope was a problem that, in Brooke's view, persists for Jung. What we have not noted, and what is important to acknowledge, is that Jung makes an important distinction between the subjective psyche and the objective psyche. Brooke points this out. He states that the:

> 'subjective psyche' refers essentially to the ego complex and the 'objective psyche' to no more than what Jung had called psyche all along . . . the psyche is not to be confused with or limited to the boundaries of the individual person, whose personal psychology is organized around the 'ego'. . . *the psyche is not in each of us, we are in the psyche.*
>
> (Brooke 1991: 62; italics in the original)

In and of itself, the distinction does not erase the apparently troublesome trope (but, perversely enough, reverses it because the 'in-relation' remains, and thus the in/out trope is still active). The distinction, though, when seen from either a Cartesian or a Jungian perspective, seems to rely on some (minimal?) concept of spatiality that implies the deployment of the inner and outer trope.

Part of the difficulty may well be Jung's own failure to be consistent with the distinction. Perhaps Jung does not indicate to which aspect of psyche he is referring every time he uses the distinction – it seems reasonable, though, that context is revealing on that point (as I think it is). And part of the problem might be that Brooke does not make as much use of the distinction as he might, especially in view of his reading of phenomenology. Unfortunately, however, he seems promptly to forget what he has pointed out.

But is there an inconsistency with Jung's use of the distinction? Brooke argues that Jung reaffirms the notion of the internalised psyche in his discussion of projection in which he 'flatly contradicts personal experience of psychic development' (Brooke 1991: 125). Why, though, do the externalised collective objective psyche hypothesis and the internalised personal or subjective psyche hypothesis contradict each other? Surely if the collective objective psyche pre-exists the individual, and the individual becomes conscious as an aspect of its development and indeed as a consequence of its participation in the collective object psyche, then contradiction does not operate here. Rather it would be a case of commensurability, co-operation and inter-relation. A well-thought-out relational thesis could easily comprehend this distinction, just as Husserl tries in the case of intersubjectivity (Husserl 1982, 1989). Ironically, it is also one of the problems embedded in both Heidegger's and Merleau-Ponty's phenomenologies.

As we have seen, the critics of Jung argue that he, in implying the existence of an inner psyche, constructs an unbridgeable gap between a subject and its world. But, according to some of these critics, Brooke and Romanyshyn included, phenomenology saves the day by providing a 'sustained legitimation of the ontological priority of the life-world – that is, the world constituted through and disclosive of human existence' (Brooke 1991: 126). Bertha Mook remarks that the:

> unique contribution of existential phenomenology to analytical psychology lies primarily in overcoming the Cartesian separation of subject and world by providing an ontology and an anthropology of the human world as a network of human relations.
>
> (Mook 2000: 236)

And David Abram's analysis of Descartes mirrors the opinions of Jung's critics. He also has phenomenology recognising the intertwining of subject and world, on the assumption that this was absent from Descartes' work (Abram 1996: 31–32).

There are a number of issues with the embracing of phenomenology, understood here as Husserlian or a derivative of Husserl's phenomenology, as a remedy for the subject/object, inner/outer trope and their dualistic relatives. Phenomenology is a broad church with differing ontological commitments; and the inner/outer trope does not automatically disappear from phenomenology 'simply because it's phenomenology'. Of course Brooke and others recognise the different phenomenologies of Husserl, Merleau-Ponty and Heidegger; this recognition, though, is limited because of their lack of familiarity with Husserl's texts, and an acceptance of his influence on later phenomenologies that actually did emerge as a response to Husserl's ideas. His reading of Heidegger and Merleau-Ponty is similarly parsimonious.

Brooke claims that phenomenology is 'primarily and thoroughly descriptive' and he, using Merleau-Ponty, identifies 'phenomenal reduction, the search for essences (eidetic reduction) and intentionality' as its other aspects (Brooke 1991: 59). Note that, in light of what I just said, Brooke's reading of Husserl is rather limited, and he relies heavily on either Merleau-Ponty or other commentators for his discussion of Husserl's and Husserlian-inspired phenomenology. Brooke refers very briefly (pp. 62 and 67) to Boyce Gibson's translation of *Ideas* (Husserl 1931). His rather superficial direct acquaintance with Husserl's writing is surprising since Brooke recognises Husserl's foundational importance to phenomenology and he is clearly prepared to dismiss Husserl as someone who can contribute to an appreciation of Jung. *The Idea of Phenomenology* has been available in English translation since 1964 (Husserl 1964), as we have seen, and he develops the principal ideas so much more fully in later works like *Ideas Pertaining to a Pure Phenomenology,* Books I and II (*Ideen* I and II) (Husserl 1970, 1982). Presumably Brooke would have access to these texts, and one is surprised that he does not make more use of them, or of the texts of Heidegger and Merleau-Ponty.

In my view, Brooke's minimalist reading produces a rather less than robust extrapolation and critique of Husserl on which he can base his further discussion of Heidegger and Merleau-Ponty. For example, Brooke's contention that description and interpretation are not opposed concludes with the remark that 'interpretation is required to remain intrinsically descriptive' (Brooke 1991: 60). This completely overlooks the role of the theoretical attitude and judgement so carefully spelt out by Husserl. It is not only description that is involved in Husserl's concepts and interpretations. The highly theoretical aspects of his work are illuminating and worth working with, over and beyond an acceptance of a watered-down thesis about description that returns 'repeatedly to the phenomenon itself so that it may show itself in ever deeper, richer, and more subtle ways', as Brooke puts it.

Indeed, Husserl, in discussing 'the authentic concept of the psychic' argues that the task (of phenomenology) is to:

> examine, *in eidetic intuition, the essence of the experienced in general and as such,* precisely as it is made explicit in any experience, whether carried out actually or imaginatively (by means of a fictional transfer of oneself into a possible experience) in order then to grasp intuitively, in the unfolding of the intentions essentially involved in such an experience, the sense of the experience as such – the sense of the class of regional objectivities – and to express this sense in rigorous analysis and description.
>
> (Husserl 1989: 97; italics in the original)

Clearly, Husserl is committed to more than description of a phenomenon. Even if one rejects his notion of essences, to grasp what the psychic is about – what he terms the authentic concept of the psyche – will involve more than simply describing. An 'object's showing itself in deeper, richer, subtler ways' will involve observation, analysis of observation, attention and an active mind. That is to say, the depth, richness and subtlety of an object, existing as it does in an inter-relational world, is dependent as much on the observer's conscious receptivity and openness as it is on showing itself. And what is meant by 'showing itself' also needs to be wrestled with. A rock's showing itself, it seems to me, will be heavily dependent on the consciousness of the observer. Rocks are not conscious, so no intersubjective relation exists between an observer and a rock. This is in contradistinction to an intersubjective showing where two consciousnesses, two *intersubjective consciousnesses,* show themselves. Such would be the case in analysis of dreams and in the use of active imagination. Analysis – and rigorous at that – is an integral part of Husserl's method.

Brooke rejects the early phenomenology of Husserl and seeks to read Jung 'in the light of existential phenomenology' (Brooke 1991: 19). Brooke is very clear that his sympathies lie with Heidegger and with Merleau-Ponty. So what do Heidegger and Merleau-Ponty have to say that Brooke finds useful in reading Jung? Let us begin with relationships with Descartes. We will not be surprised to learn that Heidegger was scathing on the question of Being as he read Descartes.

Heidegger argued that the question of Being is the question 'that today has been forgotten'. He claimed that Descartes neglected the temporal aspects of the *cogito* and that he had not interrogated the kind of Being that belonged to the *cogito*. Indeed, in his 'Introduction' to *Being and Time*, Heidegger states that his interpretation of the meaning of Being will show that Descartes thought he had exempted himself from exploring that question (Heidegger 1962: H1–H25). His extensive criticism of Descartes (Heidegger 1962: H89–H101) is an analysis of the alleged self-exemption. Unfortunately, it is beyond the scope of this book to explore Heidegger's analysis but, as I see it, Heidegger does not take account of Descartes' historical context and, furthermore, reads his own phenomenological ontology back into Descartes' metaphysics, despite his protests to the contrary (Heidegger 1962: H98–H99).

And Merleau-Ponty, what does Brooke find in him? Well, bizarrely, it might seem from Brooke's point of view, Merleau-Ponty clearly sees in Descartes' mind–body union thesis something highly laudable:

> The Cartesian idea of the human body as *non-closed*, open inasmuch as governed by thought – is perhaps the most profound idea of the union of the soul and the body. It is the soul intervening in a body that is *not of the in itself* (if it were, it would be closed like an animal body), that can be a body and living – human only by reaching completion in a "view of itself" which is thought.
>
> (Merleau-Ponty 1968: 234; italics in the original)

Merleau-Ponty's reading of the union of soul and body, *apparently* congruent with Jung's own approach to the notion of human being, distinguishes soul from body yet sees soul as acting upon body, a body already not simply an object. That is to say, thought, and human consciousness of thought, is crucial to human being. But it is not only that: Merleau-Ponty seems to be alluding to the idea that human being is completed as human being *because* the soul enables self-consciousness. For it is surely that a '"view of itself" which is thought' points to the self-reflexivity that is self-consciousness. Merleau-Ponty also argues that thought involves a 'step into the invisible', the 'reverse side' of visible Being (Merleau-Ponty 1968: 235).

The 'view of itself' perspective is central to the idea of transcendental subjectivity to which I alluded above. In my view, this is a legacy from Descartes that is repeated and adapted into the phenomenological tradition through Husserl. Sara Heinämaa, for example, remarks that Simone de Beauvoir, whom she regards as a philosopher in the phenomenological tradition in her own right, 'affirms the Cartesian notion that gives priority to what is evident in experience'. Heinämaa also maintains that Merleau-Ponty actually develops Husserl's account of embodiment in *Phenomenology of Perception* (Heinämaa

2003a: 5–27). She reiterates her point about Merleau-Ponty when she points out that Merleau-Ponty held that 'the usual understanding of Descartes as dualist is biased or anachronistic'. After a careful analysis of the soul–body union and sensations and sense perceptions, she remarks that Merleau-Ponty has a paradoxical reading of Descartes' metaphysics (Heinämaa 2003b: 24, 36).

We see here, as we also did earlier, some alternative ways of thinking about Descartes in the phenomenological tradition, that addresses positively what has been held to be Descartes' dualistic construction of mind and body. Thus Descartes' work, albeit not in a totally uncritical manner, comes into the limelight through these early phenomenologists. And we need to take note of this: we need to step with care, then, when we make assumptions about phenomenology's possibilities for mending the alleged scissions of Descartes' metaphysics.

I have been arguing that a review of more orthodox readings of Descartes is important in order to come to a different understanding of Jung's work. While I am sympathetic to Brooke's and Romanyshyn's projects in relation to phenomenology and Jung, I think that the intellectual aspects of Jung's work recede into the background in favour of developing a Jung who can be understood with only superficial acknowledgement of his intellectual commitments and their philosophical complexity.

For instance, if we were to ask the question, 'What is it analyses, evaluates, contextualises and interprets psychic material?' one appropriate response would be to look to some idea of subjectivity that allows for the possibility of transcendence. The notion that the subject can reflect herself by turning on herself, a kind of folding back, would be captured by 'transcendence' suitably articulated. This is an extraordinarily difficult concept with which to come to terms, and it would mean that we would have to take very seriously Jung's debt to Descartes and to Kant. What is more, it is not a very 'fashionable' idea embedded, as much current intellectual culture in social constructionist, immanentist and subjectivist is, in rhetorical discursive practice. In my view, Merleau-Ponty's soul intervening in the body who has a '"view of itself" which is thought' is indeed that transcendental subject.

I argued above that Brooke uses Merleau-Ponty as his entry point into Husserl's phenomenology. In principle I do not oppose an intervention of either Merleau-Ponty or Heidegger into a reading of Jung. But I think a very compelling case can be made out that will allow such an intervention. And I think that Husserl needs, with this aim in mind, to be the entry portal into his own work. Let us take a look at what Brooke says about Husserl's conceptions of intentionality, phenomenal reduction and the search for essences (eidetic reduction). I outline the three aspects as Brooke reads them. I keep my own comments to a minimum.

Intentionality

Brooke conceives of intentionality as 'always and necessarily directed towards an object *that is other than consciousness itself*' (my italics). In this case, Brooke fundamentally misreads Husserl who, as we already have seen, suggests that objects of attention, or intentionality, can be 'inside' or 'outside', existent or non-existent, that is, can be a 'mental process of consciousness' as well as being 'physical things' (Husserl 1970: 70–71).

Brooke rejects the idea of intentionality as a 'relation between' and he claims that 'intentionality undermines the foundation of western thought, which conceives of subject and object as separate, self-contained entities only contingently and unnecessarily related to each other'. But then he argues that the:

> placing of a someone here and a thing 'here' and 'there' is a derivative of consciousness-as-intentionality, and is not its precondition . . . consciousness is that irreducible, non-optional occurrence within which the world comes into being.
>
> (Brooke 1991: 75–76)

If it is the case that spatiality, actual or imaginary (the here–there reference) is derivative of consciousness-as-intentionality rather than its precondition, then we are in a bit of a quandary. It makes the subject/object distinction unchallengeable because consciousness as intrinsically intentional will always already have to have some object within its intentional orbit in order to be active, in other words, in order to be consciousness. If that is not the case, then we would seem to assume that there is consciousness that is originally not a consciousness-of, which is self-contradictory.

This means that that subject and object necessarily imply each other, and that consciousness is the ground of that distinction. Without the distinction, consciousness is void. This means that consciousness is a metaphysical, and a phenomenological, condition of objects and the world. It does not make consciousness a *causal* condition, however: consciousness does not *cause objects to exist.* Rather, in the case of Husserl, consciousness enables the world as its other. As Dan Zahavi points out:

> Husserl's decisive point is that reality far from being some brute fact that is detached from every context of experience and from every conceptual framework is rather a system of validity and meaning which needs subjectivity, that is, experiential and conceptual perspectives if it is to manifest and articulate itself. It is in that sense that reality depends upon subjectivity, which is why Husserl claims that it is just as nonsensical to speak of an absolute mind-independent reality as it is to speak of a circular square.
>
> (Zahavi 2010: 290)

Presumably, where there is subjectivity there is objectivity, and thus a 'relation between' subsists. So it is not a matter of eliminating either the relation or the subject/object duality. Rather, it is how one *describes* subject and object in their relation that counts. Is that relational causal, phenomenological, experiential, metaphysical, synchronistic? Hence Brooke could actually harness such an interpretation of reality, retain a robust sense of subject and object, and read it in concert with a notion of intentionality that does not, and need not, undermine the subject and object distinction. It would be a view with which Jung might have some sympathy. So one wonders why intentionality precludes the subject and object distinction: it is completely feasible, as we have just seen, that one could come up with a theory of consciousness and its objects which involves giving those objects some ontological integrity.

Brooke's claim that intentionality 'calls into question our modern western identities, our sense of ourselves as pre-existential subjectivities, self-contained imperious in relation to a matter-of-fact world' demands some explanation (Brooke 1991: 76). How? Why? The slip into Jung that follows this remarkable claim, remarkable because it seems entirely unfounded and is given no explanation, has Brooke talking about Jung's theory of types and their 'effect of loosening the ontological ties to the world' (Brooke 1991: 78). There, Brooke continues to read Jung's introversion and extraversion typology, again in the dualistic, unproblematised fashion upon which he insists. He argues that the connection between Jung's *Psychological Types* and Jung's later works is fantasy. Then Brooke discusses intentionality *as* fantasy (my italics) and later declares that 'intentionality *is* fantasy' (Brooke's italics). This conflation cannot be sustained, even with Brooke's use of *poiesis.*

Ironically, Husserl has a lot to say about *phantasy,* its role in eidetic cognition and the perception of essences, and its role as free phantasy, in exploring reflective perception (that Brooke does mention later in his discussion of essences). Husserl argues that *'free phantasies* acquire *a position of primacy over perceptions* and do so *even in the phenomenology of perception itself, excluding to be sure, the phenomenology of the Data of sensation'* (Husserl 1982: 158–159; italics in the original). The main point I want to make at this juncture is that the logical leap from intentionality as fantasy to the identity statement he comes up with disempowers the notion of intentionality because it potentially restricts the subject to occupying a fictional world. There is more to Husserl's notion of intentionality than that, even given his emphasis on the primacy of free phantasy in the eidetic reduction and clarification.

Now it is not the case that Jung discusses the notion of intentionality as we have examined it here. Certainly, he mentions the idea in *Symbols of Transformation* during his discussion of libido. He relates an idea of intentionality to energy value, and dynamism and Schopenhauer's 'Will' (Jung 1967: 197). It is pretty inconclusive that Jung has in mind any notion of directedness of either mind or consciousness or psyche or the unconscious as we saw it developed by Husserl. Yet Brooke is keen to make a connection between Jung and the phenomenological notion of intentionality through fantasy. But principally, he develops a theory of intentionality around Jung's idea of types and their orientation. Interestingly, Marilyn Nagy appears to read Jung's idea of intentionality as purpose. Nagy associates intentionality of the libido with 'Will and its manifestation in Schopenhauer' and remarks that intentionality 'is the theme of Part III' of her book (Nagy 1991: 130). And then her theme does work itself out in terms of purpose, goal or *telos*. Altogether, Husserl's sense of intentionality is not what either Jung or his commentators appeal to.

As I see it, Brentano and Husserl paved the way for a substantive reading of intentionality which must subtend any discussion of mind, consciousness and psyche after them. However it is extrapolated, we need to be aware that fictional objects, objects of fantasy, sense data objects and sensations on some accounts all come within the intentional fold; but they do not define that fold. Thus I think that Brooke has done himself quite a substantial intellectual disservice in not attending to Husserl as he could. And that disservice spills over into Jungian scholarship which could benefit from its analysis.

Phenomenological reduction

The language in which Brooke describes the phenomenological reduction suggests a complete abandonment, rather than a bracketing, of theoretical and practical assumptions. Brooke eschews a full discussion of the 'subtle distinctions' found in Husserl's account of the reduction. It is disappointing that he does. He argues that the *epochē* (which he calls the bracketing of being) represents a return to original experience. Further, he argues that 'the reduction ensures, at least in principle, that phenomenology is essentially descriptive'. Yet his relationship with the *epochē* is ambiguous. On the one hand, he seems, based on Merleau-Ponty's comment about the impossibility of the reduction (quoted above), to dismiss the *epochē*. What Brooke does not comment on, though, is Merleau-Ponty's remarks that follow immediately about the 'unfinished nature of phenomenology' and his observation that the impossibility is not a sign of failure 'because phenomenology's task was to reveal the mystery of the world and reason'. In other words, the impossibility has to be seen in the context of the mystery that is never completely solved (if at all). Brooke does acknowledge that the turn-away from the natural world is extremely difficult.

On the other hand, he seems to think of the *epochē* as a return to the 'wonderful meaningfulness of phenomena' within which he reads Jung's work and to which scientific colleagues cannot be persuaded to return (Brooke 1991: 62–63). We saw earlier that Husserl regards mere nature as a value- and culture-free domain. Very clearly, then, Brooke has quite a different perspective on the phenomena that are implicated in the *epochē.* Indeed, Husserl is very specific that phenomenology is concerned with essences ('a *descriptive* eidetic doctrine of transcendentally pure mental processes as viewed in the phenomenological attitude' (Husserl 1982: 167)). What Brooke seems to be doing here is refusing Husserl's concern with the eidetic reduction, and opting instead for a reduction that focuses on phenomena *per se*, above all, *natural* phenomena. It is worth noting that in the 'Supplements' to *Ideen II,* Husserl distinguishes between phenomenological description and scientific description (Husserl 1989: 326). What he is suggesting in the return to the meaningfulness of phenomena is *not* a return to scientific objects held and reframed within a domain of value. This echoes closely the discussion in the previous chapter around the notion of meaning and value in the natural world.

The eidetic reduction

Brooke's hesitancy with the eidetic reduction concept is quite understandable given its theoretically controversial nature that has clearly resonated within Jungian scholarship. According to Brooke, 'it is achieved through free imaginative variation' (Brooke 1991: 67). Free imaginative variation is one possible avenue of intentional exploration within consciousness, related as it is to *phantasy*, as we saw above. Interestingly, Edward Casey remarks that Jung's notion of active imagination 'is a process parallel to Husserl's technique of free variation'. He then argues that there is a resemblance between Jung's archetypes as pure forms and Husserl's *eidē*; the process of getting to either the archetype of the essence involves multiple approaches (Casey 2000: 216). Were the processes parallel, we have even further reason to revisit a potential Husserl/Jung relation.

Brooke comments that there are issues around the relationship between existential phenomenology and Husserl's phenomenology, referring, one would think, to the Husserl/Heidegger tension over authorship of ideas (Pietersma 1979; Zahavi 2003; Moran 2005). He suggests that there are four interlinked departures from 'pure' or 'eidetic' phenomenology, thus from Husserl: there are no immutable essence, essences are seen as less 'pure' or eidetic, every act is an interpretation, and phenomenology becomes hermeneutic phenomenology because of the emphasis on the significance of language (Brooke 1991: 68–69). In my view, this exemplifies Husserl's assessment of Heidegger's philosophy: that 'he disapproved of Heidegger's starting point', and that Heidegger had produced 'an anthropology written from the natural attitude' (Moran 2005: 37). Whether or not Heidegger had abandoned essences is moot (Crowell 2005: 60). Brooke's analysis, however, takes him to a point where he can begin to explore more fully a specific relationship between Jung and existential phenomenology. He does that through drawing on Heidegger, to whom we now turn.

Jung and poiesis

Brooke reads Jung so as to identify his work as *poiesis* (Brooke's 'poesis'). I am sure that Brooke would not want his interpretation to be the *only* and final word on how we are to understand or read Jung. However, unless a full discussion of *poiesis* takes place that would uncover its difficulties and intellectual complexity, especially the relationship between thought and *poiesis* which we find in Heidegger's work (Heidegger 1982, 2001) the full import, and limitations of, reading Jung through *poiesis* cannot be appreciated.

According to Jung, argues Brooke, analytical psychology becomes 'intrinsically metaphorical, *or* poetic' (my italics) because Jung appeals to archaic experience *contra* physical explanations of the psyche and psychic events. Brooke seems to be saying here that metaphor and the poetic are one and the same thing. In proposing this, however, Brooke deploys an inclusive disjunct that is misleading. Metaphor and the poetic might traditionally be associated, but, as we saw in Chapter 3, metaphor is not the sole domain of poets and artists. It simply does not follow that we must portray Jung as a poet, or his work as poetic, because he uses metaphor. But it is on this basis – that Jung is a poet – that Brooke finds for Jung a soul mate in Heidegger. Brooke argues that Jung introduced a poetic perspective to analytical psychology – a work of *poesis*[12] – that 'remains caught a self-enclosed, almost solipsistic ontology' (Brooke 1991: 25–27). Brooke maintains that his own use of phenomenology will radically re-read this solipsistic tendency.

It may well be the case that we *can* understand Jung's work as *poesis* – or the work of making involving the maker and the raw materials of what is made – that produces an 'intrinsic, irreducible, and mutually transformative relationship between him and his subject matter', as Brooke puts it, stressing that Jung's *poesis* is 'not merely a product of empty fantasy' (Brooke 1991: 27). But whether or not acknowledging poetic strands in Jung's work because he uses metaphor really comes to grips with issues like inner and outer or the status of the collective unconscious or the archetypes is highly questionable.

Brooke's characterisation of Jung's work as readable within a Heideggerian sensibility fits, he argues, because Heidegger saw a poet as 'given in that fallen and profane time between the retreat of the gods and the emergence of Being'. Brooke remarks that the 'poet is thus a pivot in cultural history through which his fellow mortals are turned towards the advent of the divine presencing of Being . . . In these terms Jung is a poet through and through'. He then claims that if we portray Jung's work as *poesis* then we are able, following Ludwig Binswanger, to 'go to the heart of "the fatal defect of all psychology" . . . the dichotomy of subject and object, knower and known [that had] achieved its clearest philosophical expression with Descartes' (Brooke 1991: 27–29).

In sum, Brooke seems to be assuming that *poesis* can address the complex philosophical issues associated with dualism. In reading Jung phenomenologically, the problems he encounters in Jung's *poesis* (for example, retention of subject/object distinction and inner/outer trope) and consequent solipsism can be reframed. In other words, *poesis* and phenomenology together provide the ground for eliminating the bothersome subject and object distinction which Brooke reads into Jung's claims about, for example, all of our knowledge consisting of the stuff of the psyche, the spectre of subject and object. It seems as if *poesis* becomes a kind of panacea capable of mending some deep ontological fissures even when there is a question about the language of poetry and poetry itself. Given Heidegger's association of thinking with *poiesis*, that may well be the case. I am not arguing that poetry cannot do as Brooke seems to be suggesting; I am simply saying that we must err on the side of caution.

So I have reservations about Brooke's assumption. Brooke (1991: 27) remarks that to:

> think poetically as Heidegger did, however, is not to begin writing poetry . . . It is to establish the poetic sensibility as valid in the ontological claim it makes upon us, a claim which tends not to survive the knife of Western rationalism. Thus if we want Jung's psychology to be thought poetically

we cannot return to Cartesian materialism or reified entities. I take it that Brooke means by 'poetic sensibility' a kind of sensitivity to aesthetics, to beauty, perhaps a capacity to wonder, a story telling or narrative sensitivity, and a feeling for the subtleties and power of language. That is certainly in Jung's work – and certainly in Descartes' as well!

Given this, the poetic sensibility undoubtedly does make, and perhaps has always been capable of making, valid ontological claims upon us. It does not follow from that, though, that the knife of Western rationalism does not survive, because poetry is capable of many things: it is evocative, descriptive, epic, historical, narrative, and so on. One has only to think of the epic poetry of Homer, or Hesiod, or *Beowulf*, or *Faust* by Goethe in this regard where, for example, moral points are intertwined with serious ontological claims about the nature of destiny and human endeavour.

There is, I maintain, a big difference between our thinking Jung's psychology poetically, by which I assume Brooke means that we either think of Jung's work *as poetry* or of his work *being expressed poetically*, and Jung, *himself, thinking poetically*. In principle, we should be able to identify those passages of Jung's work where he does think poetically but, clearly, this does not *necessarily* mean that Jung is a poet. Brooke does not identify such passages. Having made the distinction between thinking poetically and being a poet, though, Brooke makes the transition to calling Jung a poet, as we saw above, as if the transition were smooth and unproblematic. It is not.

How *we* think about Jung's psychology – as poetry, or as using poetic language, or as philosophy, or as empirical research, or anything else – depends on a whole lot of factors that have as much to do with our imagination, understanding, reasoning, perspective and orientation as it has to do with Jung's words written there, on the page in front of us. 'If we want Jung's psychology to be thought poetically' seems to imply that Jung's psychology can be thought of in a number of ways, amongst which is 'poetically' (because of his use of metaphor). Our reasons for wanting to think his psychology poetically would have to include amongst them, one would assume, some inadequacy in other ways of thinking Jung, some incompleteness that the appeal to *poesis* can redress. So we might then ask ourselves the question: what is it that thinking Jung poetically can add to our understanding of his psychology? Does this bring another dimension to his work? And can it do the work that Brooke is claiming for it?

Lastly, we might note that in his introduction to *Poetry, Language, Thought*, translator Albert Hofstadter remarks that Heidegger held that the 'speech of genuine thinking is by nature *poetic*'. He then asks the question, 'Is there in the end any fundamental difference between the thinking poet and the poetic thinker?' Not, he responds if the thinking of the poet is first-rank, and if the thinker of first rank thinks in such a way that his 'thinking has all the purity and thickness and solidity of poetry, and whose saying *is* poetry' (Heidegger 2001: x–xi).

We can see from this, then, that Hofstadter is prepared to conflate thinking poetically and poetry. If we regard Jung as a thinker of first rank (whatever that might mean), then it would seem that he is a poet. Hofstadter's view repeats Heidegger's own sentiments as Heidegger expresses them in his (Nietzschean-inspired?) verse 'The Thinker as Poet'. We might think of Heidegger's verse in terms of exemplification, consisting as it does of a set of almost aphoristic-type verses (Heidegger 2001: 3–14). Even in his early work, *Being and Time*, Heidegger argues that in '"poetical discourse", the communication of the existential possibilities of one's state-of-mind can become an aim in itself, and this amounts to a disclosing of existence' (Heidegger 1962: H162). This suggests specific Heidegger's commitment to his own forging of poetic prose, as an existentially focused end in itself, something that is not undertaken self-consciously by Jung.

For myself, I think that this excursion into the poetic refocuses the impact of Jung's work in part because it is an option that ignores difficult questions around *poiesis.* It also overlooks the profound philosophical issues of subject and object that elide some hard philosophical questions in Jung. Ultimately, poetry deals with the world in a very different way from the language of philosophy and also the language of psychology, both of which can be poetic without being undemanding. That said, if there is the link between *poiesis* and thinking that Heidegger proposes, then the question of reframing Jung in a way that honours his intellect should be addressed.[13] As it stands, the change of emphasis envisaged by Brooke seems to me to be an anachronistic turn-away from the central business of Jung's analytical psychology.

I end with these questions and their answers as I see them: Do we really know what Jung thought phenomenology consisted in? No. Was Jung a phenomenologist? No. Did he use the language of phenomenology typical of the phenomenologists we have encountered? No. Can we read Jung as a phenomenologist? No. Can we read Jung phenomenologically? I am quite uncertain about how to answer this question, for I would want to know what it would mean to read someone phenomenologically. In order to read someone phenomenologically one would need to understand both what the language of phenomenology is and how that language is used. Let us ask the question: What is that language? How would we go about answering it? Would we refer to and explain the concepts that (acknowledged) phenomenologists employ in their articulation of phenomenology? If so, then we seem to have a range of available vocabularies from which to choose. I suggest, though, that we do need to be aware of chronology and intellectual debt in order to make that selection; and then I think we need to treat the text under scrutiny within the framework in which it was articulated.

Several questions remain. They may prove to be impossible to answer adequately. If Jung was so wedded to the inner/outer trope in the pejoratively constructed Cartesian way we have seen in the literature, why did he also think of the psyche/body as a whole living organism? And if the human being is in the psyche rather than the psyche being in the human being, how are we to understand that? And what does spiritual practice have to do with all of that, at any rate? These are the questions with which I go to the next chapter.

Chapter 6

Flesh, reflection and transcendence

> Individuation has two principal aspects: in the first place it is an internal and subjective process of integration, and in the second it is an equally indispensable process of objective relationship.
>
> (Jung 1954: 448)

> In the last analysis, if my body can be a 'form' and if there can be, in front of it, important figures against indifferent backgrounds, this occurs in virtue of its being polarized by its tasks, of its existence towards them, of its collecting together of itself in pursuit of its aims; the body schema is finally a way of stating that my body is in-the-world. As far as spatiality is concerned . . . one's own body is the third term, always tacitly understood, in the figure-background structure, and every figure stands out against the double horizon of external and bodily space. One must therefore reject as an abstraction any analysis of bodily space which takes account only of figures and points, since these can neither be conceived nor be without horizon.
>
> (Merleau-Ponty 1962: 115–116)

One can imagine the importance of solitude to the performance of the *cogito* and the *epochē.* As a situational context, it is existentially appropriate to the task of meditation. This solitude must be characterised within the context of two aspects, one's body and the intersubjectivity in which one is always already embedded and intertwined. We see that the notion of 'intersubjectivity' occurs within the Husserlian *corpus.* It is extensively dealt with in *Crisis*, where Husserl so often in his later work contextualises the ego and the living body within the horizon of the other and the resulting 'we'.

> Thus in whatever way we may be conscious of the world as universal horizon, as coherent universe of existing objects, we, each 'I-the-man' and all of us together, belong to the world as living with one another in the world; and the world is our world, valid for our consciousness as existing precisely through this 'living together'.
>
> (Husserl 1970: 108)

Husserl analyses the 'we', claiming that there is a problem with the 'constitution of intersubjectivity', the idea that there are many Is 'among whom I am one', an idea that sees ' "all of us" – from my point of view, indeed "in" me'. He says we need to stop and go into self-reflective mode, raising the question, 'who are *we*, as subjects performing the meaning – and validity – accomplishment of universal constitution – as those who in community, constitute the world as a system of poles, as the intentional structure of community life?'

The answer to this question involves Husserl in a discussion of the ego, the I, of the *epochē,* the I that is attained, and thus, of transcendental intersubjectivity. Towards the end of his discussion he claims that each human subject 'bears within himself a transcendental "I"' (Husserl 1970: 182, 186). The transcendental I is revealed in carrying out the *epochē*, which is realised through a methodological move. Intersubjectivity thus exists on two levels: on the level of the natural attitude, where each human being is constituted as human being, as an I in relation to all others Is, who similarly are Is and the we co-constituted through this I-ness; and on the level of the transcendental, where each human being realises her transcendental I-ness provided she has performed the *epochē*. This is quite distinct from the natural attitude, as we shall see. Method is absolutely basic in all of these considerations. In the final chapter, I argue that there is yet another step we need to consider in the attainment of transcendental subjectivity.

In this discussion, Husserl is clearly attempting an answer to the circularity problem in the *epochē*: if I bracket everything, if I suspend all knowledge claims, and radically doubt the existence of everything, how can I function at all to perform the reduction? As I read it, the ego of the *cogito* is transcended by the immediate intuition of one's own existence, resulting in the illuminative realisation of one's persistence (through time) in one's own conscious self-presence. We see here, then, a sophisticated *explanans* that recognises an intrinsic spatiality as a conceptual dimension of consciousness, and the psyche. Put more crudely, we can 'move' around our own minds, take up different positions within our own psyches, reflect on ourselves. We adopt different attitudes in relation to ourselves depending on our existential needs at the time. We do this having suspended our belief in, but *not* having denied, the existence of our bodies and the bodies of others like ourselves, all of whom can perform the reduction. I return to this theme at the end of the chapter. The communal nature of one's existence as a body and its inter-relations with all other bodies is the ground from which one proceeds. This is how I shall understand the notion of intersubjectivity as it is used here.

Through and in the living body and its relations with all other bodies – their intertwining, as Merleau-Ponty puts it – we discover ourselves; but we can move beyond the immediate now-ness of this 'ourselves' by self-reflection and self-objectification. We can become more or less objects to ourselves as we are drawn inwards in self-exploration. The conscious activity in which we engage is of a different register from the conscious cognitive and imaginative activity in which we ordinarily engage. However, the former is not possible without the latter. One highly schematised way of thinking about this is in terms of the bi-conditional 'I if other': I and the other exist in an ontologically co-dependent relationship. Certainly, for Jung, this applies in the case of the personal and collective psyche conscious and unconscious. The body, as a living organism affected by its environment, and the psyche, too, are brought into this conceptualisation of the relationality of human being. But as backdrop, never foregrounded in its fleshy human being?

Note that the *epochē* and the reduction are part of a possible movement, a fluidity and mutability that is human existence. However, the secondariness of epochal reduction to my pre-reflective experience of my own being remains always hovering in the fact of my corporeal being: the echoes of that being can be silenced only temporarily. A return to my own flesh is inevitable, a *desideratum*. The solace of the *epochē* is a confirmation of the being of my own flesh.

Imagination plays a central role in all of this at a level where I have moved beyond the merely mundane and immanent, and where I begin the self-reflective exploration that marks a psychic deepening. Can we suppose or think that wonder might accompany this deepening? Descartes' declaration that wonder is the first of the passions modulates this whole enterprise of exploration of psyche/living body. We find in ourselves as well as in the world, through our bodies, our existence. This happens before we know whether or not this is beneficial to us – it just is. Husserl, we have seen, echoes this sentiment in his discussion of the natural attitude. Our sense of wonder and astonishment in our self-apprehension and the apprehension of the world that always already contains and emancipates us permeates the very being we are, pre and post reflectively.

The importance of corporeality, of the living body, acts as mere backdrop to the drama of psychic existence in Jung's work. But does it? Can we envisage Jung to be speaking in wonder at the self-exploration made possible by the architectonic he mobilises through the collective that incorporates and gives voice to the personal psyche? If the body and its relations is backdrop, if Jung's epistemic scepticism confronts us, is this a *necessary* backdrop, and a *necessary* scepticism expressed, as we saw earlier, in the Fog Argument? Is there a choice to go with the psyche, the body remaining a given, a pre-reflective assumption of the flesh that hosts the psyche?

We must constantly remind ourselves that any suspension of the natural attitude, the way we are in the world where we take the world as what is given to us in our perception as natural, is momentary. It is not our ongoing state of being. Rather, its *telos* lies in either certainty, a quest for absolute ground, or even in simple retreat from a world that can engulf us. 'Leaving the body behind' is a methodological device for elemental deepening, a device that is through and through imbued with existential appropriateness. Clearly, being in the body, *being the body* with its intersubjective relationality, is the original condition of its being left. What is left behind, not as remainder, but as *that which is left,* the 'vacated site of being'?

Corporeal intersubjectivity – the flesh

Husserl points out that one's physical body (*Körper*) is essentially different from one's living body (*Leib*), 'the only body that is actually given [to me as such] in perception'. Husserl says that we deal with objects differentially, thematically: we pay attention to objects 'according to our interests'. In perception, our consciousness of the world 'is always in motion' and our consciousness of our affective states remains with us as we function as subjects. Yet he retains the subject/object trope, talking of consciousness of the world and its objects, talking of the we-subjectivity and its togetherness (Husserl 1970: 107–109).

Merleau-Ponty begins with unified experience that he analyses as the fundamental given on which our consciousness of unifying activity is based when we take up the analytic attitude. Perception takes 'advantage of work already done' by the synthesising activity of consciousness. He argues that body and senses 'are precisely that familiarity with the world born of habit'. In other words, we become aware that the world is already given to us, as a synthesised whole and that we are part of that world. 'In perception we do not think the object and we do not think ourselves thinking it, we are given over to the object and we merge into this body which is better informed than we are about the world' (Merleau-Ponty 1962: 238). Merleau-Ponty later deploys the term 'flesh' which, he says, 'is more like the elements, like water, air, earth and fire' (Merleau-Ponty 1968: 139). This suggests the basic nature of flesh, its elemental constitutiveness. He argues that we must not think flesh 'starting from substances, from body and spirit – for then it would be the union of contradictories – but we must think it, as we said, as an element in the concrete emblem of a general manner of being' (Merleau-Ponty 1968: 147). This turn from union of mind and body to a conception of corporeality as flesh marks not the rejection of the inner and outer trope, but a reconceptualising of human being as lived body in the world simultaneously one with, yet distinct from, that world. This general manner of being is not lost in Jung's approach to corporeality and the psyche.

As we have seen, Jung refers to the body as a living organism, as a union and as a correspondence: he argues that the 'whole psychic organism corresponds exactly to the body'. He also argues that the living body is environmentally adapted. Likewise, he claims, the psyche corresponds with 'regular physical occurrences' (Jung 1972: 322, 326). He remarks that 'the physiological and the mental are indissolubly connected . . . not that the tie between mind and instinct is necessarily a harmonious one' (Jung 1954: 185). He asserts that:

> just as the material of the body that is ready for life has need of the psyche in order to be capable of life, so the psyche presupposes the living body in order that its images may live . . . It would probably be more correct to speak of an unknowable living being concerning the nature of which nothing can be said except that it vaguely expresses the quintessence of 'life'.
>
> (Jung 1972: 619)

From this it appears that he has a complex understanding of human body, its relation to psyche, its relation to collective, to community. It seems to me that Jung's work expresses a corporeal sensibility that underpins an implicit openness to embodied human being reminiscent of Merleau-Ponty. This does not make him into a phenomenologist, however. It simply indicates that his thinking about embodiment is not frameable by an orthodox dualistically inspired problematic reading of Descartes.

Thus there are at least two things worth noting in the above: Jung's reference to the mental/mind rather than to the psyche; and an overall disposition to conceptualise body/mind/psyche/environment as parts or aspects of what he seems to understand as a whole. The significance of the former lies in its apparent distinctiveness from the psyche as a phenomenon in which the whole human being is embedded. On this reading, the mind is particular, individual, related only to one body. In other words, we are not dealing here, in this instance, with a collective concept. Yet Jung's context is so often the context of the collective and its underpinning claims on individuals. We need sometimes to speak only of the individual, bracketing the collective; conversely, we need, sometimes, to speak only of collective, bracketing the individual. Any suspension or bracketing marks a movement with a possibility of return, but a return transformed, a seeing with new eyes; perhaps.

I have made several references to possible resonances between Jung's concept of active imagination and Husserl's notion of free phantasy apart from Brooke's analysis. In my view, a transformational return to the everyday can be found in each of their work. Husserl's discussion of transcendental intersubjectivity involves some kind of personal revelation. It is not simply theory that he is talking about. We saw this above in his discussion of 'we'. Jung's distinction between reductive and synthetic technique in the 'elaboration of fantasy images' sees the latter as developing:

> the material into a process for differentiating the personality . . . The synthetic method elaborates the symbolic fantasies resulting from the introversion of the libido through sacrifice. This produces a new attitude to the world, whose very difference offers a new potential.
>
> (Jung 1971: 427)

'New attitude' and 'new potential' are indicative of transformation, presumably emancipatory, and, with a withdrawal of projections, a new sense of relationship with the world. As I see it, Jung is here talking about intersubjectivity.

Indeed, in Jung's 'The Psychology of the Transference', he outlines what I take to be a model of intersubjective relationality, the transference/countertransference relationship. Jung, following Freud, discusses the doctor's and patient's mental health and their responses and reactions to each other. Jung interprets the first ten illustrations from the alchemically inspired *Rosarium Philosophorum*, *as if* they parallel the aim of psychotherapy, presumably which is to bring about a resolution of a patient's issues. He claims that:

> alchemy describes, not merely in general detail, but often in the most astonishing detail, the same psychological phenomenology which can be observed in the analysis of unconscious processes . . . The doctor must go to the limits of his subjective possibilities, otherwise the patient will be unable to follow suit . . . It must be a genuine process of purification.
>
> (Jung 1954: 399, 358)

That said, it is not clear to me that Jung engages with intercorporeal intersubjectivity. For him the first, and foremost, consideration is always the psyche. That in a therapeutic situation there are two living *bodies* encountering each other bears little on the analysis itself as a fundamental consideration.

For example, the illustrations of the *Rosarium Philosophorum* are explicit representations of male and female sexual embodiment (king and queen). Jung reads them symbolically throughout: these sexed bodies are interpreted relationally as psychological engagements at an archetypal level. This has the effect of noting, and then suspending, consideration of the body on the one hand, while at a symbolic level, maleness and femaleness are resolved as masculine and feminine psychic archetypes – *anima* and *animus*. Certainly he comments on the naked images: 'man and woman confront one another in unabashed naturalness'; the 'frank eroticism' of the images in coitus as they 'conjoin'; their death and becoming one body with two heads that he reads as a 'new body, a *hermaphroditus* . . . one half of the body is masculine, the other half feminine' (Jung 1954: 451, 460). Bodies do not mean what they are, but what they symbolise: that is why I say that Jung notes the bodies, and then suspends them.

We can see this in Jung's discussion of the *Rosarium* figures. He argues that it 'would be quite natural to suppose that the king and queen represent a transference relationship in which the king stands for the masculine partner and the queen for the feminine'. Not so, says Jung, continuing his analysis. This is about projection of unconscious contents: although, he argues, man is conscious of himself as man and woman conscious of herself as woman, we see depicted in the illustrations 'a projected fragment of personality'. Hence the woman/queen represents the man's *anima* and the man/king represents the man's *animus*, so a cross-over is to be read into the illustrations (Jung 1954: 421).

I do not want to embark on a long discussion of Jung's claim here, and I am not entirely sure why he makes this assumption: for Jung the emblematic flowers play a role in signalling the cross-over. The sequence of the illustrations shows that the male and female figures 'swap sides' during the process as they lie in the coffin (at 'The Ascent of the Soul' ('*impregnatio*')). Remarkably, Jung does not point out this out, and if this change of sides has something to do with the alchemical process of transformation, then Jung does not explain how. I find Jung's discussion of the cross-over not terribly illuminating, and his appeal to Rider Haggard does not help, nor does his diagrammatic explanation and his recounting of folktales (Jung 1954: 421–437). While folktales might explain *anima/animus* projection, they do not explain the cross-symbolism of the king/queen figures.

One way in which we might understand Jung's focus on symbolic meaning is that it mirrors a more general neglect of the body, as body, as specific ontological dimension to human being, in his work. This is symptomatic of the unease that the body still brings to understandings of what it means to be human even more generally. Yet Jung actually remarks on the Freudian psychotherapist's practice of sitting behind the patient during analysis. Jung's explanation for this practice is that it helps to keep the doctor 'as far as possible' away from countertransference (Jung 1954: 171 fn 16). Jung, it seems, is critical of Freud's technique, but he does not mention what effect the visual co-presence of patient and doctor might have. He might hold, for example, that two *bodies* facing each other, visually present to each other, have the potential to magnify the corporeal nature of the psyche. Facial expressions, hand gestures, comportment all inflect on the profound and difficult moments of encounter. This would be consistent with Jung's belief that a patient's emotional state is the starting point for the production of free fantasy. The range of possibilities he outlines indicates the importance of the body – from modelling of plastic materials to dance, to drawing. Note, however, that these need not indicate intersubjective relation, yet the encounter between psychotherapist and patient will be mediated by whatever the patient produces, together with the persona of the doctor.

We might, however, see Freud's practice in a different frame if we return to the idea of suspension of corporeality that we saw as a pre-condition for Descartes' *cogito.* If the body were to be a source of distraction, it makes sense to reduce its impact on a potentially psychically loaded situation. Thus sitting behind a patient and limiting one's physical interaction would help to bracket one of the many variables that could have an impact on the psychotherapeutic session as well as on other aspects of the patient/doctor relationship. This amounts not so much to a neglect of the body, but to an acknowledgement of its importance, with a simultaneous refocusing of interest. It is not a matter of neglect, but of emphasis.

That said, neither Descartes nor Husserl neglects the body. Rather, the body is the site from which they each launch an *epochē.* We have just seen that that the body, even as symbol, is important to Jung. In a sense, then, corporeality is a transparent presence in his work; it is an acknowledgement and a passing-over that we see in comments that indicate that he takes seriously physical presence in the world: projection, for example, is first revealed in relation to 'concrete persons' (Jung 1954: 357).

With these brief remarks in mind, I want now to explore in more detail the notions of the body and of intersubjectivity. My exploration is framed by the idea of spiritual practice as we have already encountered it. In sum, I take the ground of this discussion to be the living body, the individual flesh in which we, each one of us, are personally instantiated, as an I, in relation with each other, across a range of possibilities – cultural, psychological, physical, aesthetic, imaginative. I do not plan to rewrite the Jungian *opus as if* he were a phenomenologist. Nor do I conceive of the phenomenologists about whom I have been speaking as providers of solutions to the issues that come up in Jung's work.

Rather, in dealing with the body, with flesh, as I do, I hope to indicate that the resolution, in *Meditation VI*, of Descartes' decorporealising his experience brings with it an awareness of body that is a kind of template for a future *epochē* that is present, unconsciously, in Jung's work.

Meditating the flesh

We have seen that Descartes treasured the time he had finally made for himself to examine what he could hold as indubitable belief. Husserl speaks of the philosophical solitude required by someone performing the *epochē*:

> *I* am the one who performs the *epochē* and even if there are others, and even they practice the *epochē* in direct community with me, [they and] all other human beings with their entire act-life are included, for me, within my *epochē*, in the world phenomenon which, in my *epochē* is exclusively mine. The *epochē* creates a unique sort of philosophical solitude which is the fundamental requirement for a truly radical philosophy. In this solitude I am not a single individual who has somehow willfully cut himself off from the society of mankind.
>
> (Husserl 1970: 184; italics in the original)

An idea of solitude, either as an activity of contemplative isolation or as a physical cutting-off from sociality, or both (to proceed reflectively in methodological doubt) is not captured in Merleau-Ponty's critique of reflection as a philosophical activity. Myself, alone with myself, is not alien to my own existential sensibilities, nor is it to others who seek such solitude. Merleau-Ponty, it seems, finds in the logic of the *epochē* reasons to reject its existential dimensions.

Merleau-Ponty rejects the dualism of Descartes, and does not retain the transcendental phenomenological structure of Husserl' work. He discards Husserl's methodological reliance on free variation to get to essence, yet we cannot doubt his debt to both Descartes and Husserl (Flynn 2011). His later work includes an essay, 'Reflection and Interrogation', in which he considers the notion of philosophical reflection. We read in his essay a critique of Husserl that highlights the impossibility of the *epochē* on the grounds of 'simultaneously requiring and excluding an inverse movement of constitution'. He points out that the world is not constituted 'after-the-fact', the fact being the reduction and the identification of essences, but that the world is the very possibility of the fact. Both before and after reflection, he maintains, the spectacle of the world had meaning, a meaning which is expressed in 'the intertwining of my life with the other lives, of my body with the visible things, by the intersection of my perceptual field with that of the others, by the blending of my duration with the other durations' (Merleau-Ponty 1968: 45–49). Meaning is temporally mediated from and though the human being and its intersubjectivity.

Merleau-Ponty takes perceptual faith as his starting point. What is this faith? It is the faith that 'we see the things themselves, the world is what we see': it is about the 'deep-seated mute "opinions" implicated in our lives'. Our efforts to articulate the terms of this faith, what it is, the we, the seeing, the thing, bring us into a 'labyrinth of difficulties and contradictions' (Merleau-Ponty 1968: 3). Merleau-Ponty argues that an interrogation of this faith takes place through reflection. In order to get to the truth of the faith, to the truth of the world, the philosopher must reflect, and when that happens, a third dimension, 'beyond the world itself, and beyond what is only "in us" beyond being itself and being for us' (Merleau-Ponty 1968: 28–29); that third dimension is thought. Merleau-Ponty argues that reflective analysis must start from a '*de facto* situation' that is even prior to thought. Because of the risk of infinite regress, he argues, 'we must not say that reflection precedes the experience'.

Merleau-Ponty's examination of the nature of reflection, its orientation and effect, problematises the meditative practice which I have claimed is explicit in Descartes' and Husserl's work. Clearly, both Descartes and Husserl are the philosophers Merleau-Ponty has in mind as he sets up his critique. Rather than seeing Descartes' and then Husserl's philosophical meditation as *totally* legitimate philosophical method and practice, as I have been proposing it might be, Merleau-Ponty's essay suggests that the idea of reflection, because of what it assumes in the radial suspension of the natural attitude, is controversial. We can see here that Merleau-Ponty stresses the importance of the pre-reflective acceptance and experience of the world and its objects. It is there that reflection has its home. Merleau-Ponty rejects reflection as 'methodic doubt and as a reduction of the openness upon the world to "spiritual acts"' such as we have seen in Descartes and Husserl. Merleau-Ponty insists instead on 'hyper-reflection' which, in relation to brute things and brute perceptions 'would not cut the organic bonds between perception and the thing perceived with a hypothesis of inexistence' (Merleau-Ponty 1968: 38–43). He regards Husserl's transcendental reduction (which is simultaneously eidetic reduction) as a departure 'from the flux of life' that involves a disengagement from the totality of the world. In other words, the position espoused by Husserl even when is begins in intersubjectivity and community, because it involves the positing of a transcendental I, absented from its origins, is untenable. In my view, this is not what Husserl envisages at all.

It seems clear that there are competing views on the question of the role of the world and the body in reflection. For Husserl, the body grounds the possibility of transcendental subjectivity, even though the presence of the body is capable of suspension in the *epochē*. Transcendental subjectivity, expressed in the I that can intuit essences, is based on exclusion or parenthesising of the body; he seems to follow in Descartes' footsteps in holding this. For Merleau-Ponty, this is an impossible situation: we remain always bonded to the world through our pre-reflective experience. We do not think the world into existence – rather it is its existence that makes possible any reflection, any theory. For him, the idea of transcendental subjectivity is dissipated because, methodologically, he takes a different point of departure from Husserl. We are still unclear about any precise metaphysical commitment that Jung might have here, but we can be clear that the body is important as the grounding of emancipated psychic being.

There is a sense in which it is fruitless to decide a 'who is right and who is wrong' kind of question at this stage. Dan Zahavi traces the relationship between Husserl and Merleau-Ponty, and argues for the anticipatory nature of Merleau-Ponty's account of intersubjectivity, seen especially in the case of double sensation (Zahavi 2002: 17). There are ongoing debates about relationships between intellectual Husserl, Heidegger, Merleau-Ponty, de Beauvoir, Sartre – debates too extensive and complex either to list or deal with here (Carman 1999; Casey 2000; Toadvine and Embree 2002; Heinämaa 2003a; Beyer 2011). As we saw in the last chapter, Brooke sees Husserl's work as less than helpful in understanding Jung and is more sympathetic to Merleau-Ponty and Heidegger. And even though I am sceptical about Heidegger, and of Brooke's reading of him so as to construct Jung's work as a work of *poiesis*, my principal concerns are with the logic of the argument, and the effect of such a reading. We all read according to our understandings and contexts, and assess arguments according to what our intellectual commitments are. There is an underlying principle that needs acknowledgement in this specific discussion – the notion of existential appropriateness. Consider the following.

No doubt we would all agree that that the body, its relationship with others, intersubjectivity expressed in and through inter-relationality, and the thinking *I*, are fundamental to our conceptions of ourselves, and who *we* are and who *I* am. We go out to the world and the world comes to us as flesh: as self-conscious, active agents who behave and believe and think and create. We are immersed in our worlds. Yet we can leave those worlds, we can vacate our sites of being, our bodies – and one way of doing that is through philosophical reflection in the parenthesising activity undertaken by consciousness.

Recall that, using the work of Pierre Hadot, I argued that Descartes' *Meditations* is in the tradition of spiritual exercises. I also argued that Jung's work can be seen as a part of that tradition and we see that exemplified not only in his clinical work with his clients, but in *The Red Book.* The nature of the spiritual exercises means that they are unremittingly philosophical – they deal with onto-epistemological, existential and ethical issues. A focus on one's nature and one's *raison d'être* is, precisely, philosophical, for these are wisdom questions and issues. The dimension of living as humans that brings us to wisdom and emancipation from desire, as is suggested by ancient spiritual practice, needs cultivation. Principally, this involves cultivation of attention, or *prosoche.*

I remarked above that for Husserl the *epochē* is not merely an intellectual exercise. The process through which Husserl's thinking takes him is patently philosophical, and it involves a practice of attention. As such the *epochē* can be considered a mode of philosophical reflection. You may have noted also that Merleau-Ponty, in his discussion of reflection, is talking about *philosophical* reflection and it is apparent that Merleau-Ponty had in mind Husserl, and Descartes, as he wrote 'Reflection and Interrogation'. In my view, one of the critical issues for each philosopher is method.

The method that is embraced by Descartes and Husserl is reflective: it takes its cue from a turn towards their own consciousnesses, away from the world, yet at the same time retaining some elements of the world – their thought and their thinking processes engage the sociality intrinsic to language and its use. As Gaukroger remarks, Descartes 'reconstructs' the corporeal world (and from clear and distinct ideas, so from mathematical principles) (Gaukroger 1995: 344). Ultimately, we cannot know with decisive certainty if the world we think and the world that exists match each other. Reflection is a turn towards one's own consciousness, even when a source may be external (for example, your reflecting on what I now write); but it essentially deals with a psychic or a conscious or a mental mode of oneself, distinguishable from one's embodiment.

That thought is distinguishable from one's own body, does not entail, however, that the body is extinguished altogether:

> You are reading this text. Perhaps you are sitting, or standing or walking as you read. You can read because you are a body with eyes, a brain, intelligence, a mind, and you have learned to read this language. You know how to follow a text, how to weigh up what you read, how to consider the ideas in the text, how to appreciate, understand or reject what you read. You are a body, and a body amongst other bodies, a body that speaks, looks, breathes and moves. Maybe you are by yourself right now, at home or alone in a library, or in a crowded tram or bus or train, or on an aeroplane, or

sitting in a park. If you are with other bodies, they might be sitting, talking and listening, or looking, attending, reading, eating, laughing, playing, exercising. Their gaze might be directed or undirected, perhaps focused on other bodies around them, female or male bodies, bodies that might be uttering the words to which they attend. They might or might not notice you. If you were to look up at this moment, assuming you are not alone, your gaze might encounter bodily femaleness and/or maleness, colour, ages and the draperies of class. Some of these are bodies caught in intersubjective exchanges of gaze and countergaze.

As a reader, there is something about you that separates you from the world while simultaneously placing you in the world. You are concentrating, absorbed by the text that is a fact in the world, yet your absorption is not there, only, it is here, in this act or reading. In a sense you are alone with your reading, cut off by the very act of reading which has placed you in the world with the text; in another sense the text brings you into the world, for the text is not you, having as it does, a separateness distinguishable from you. Either way, witness the aloneness of yourself; and witness the otherness of yourself in this reading event, this moment of bodily dialectic between reader and text, where language is multiply woven and interwoven into patterns of understanding that arise and dissipate, and arise again to produce meanings that exceed my authorial intention. Witness this against a background of intention, of purpose, of scholarly communion, yours and mine and ours together.

I have written these words, you read, you take in what is being said in my written words. But now I ask you, 'Who or what writes those words and speaks to you? Who or what reads? Do I write and speak as a body? Or am I a body writing and speaking? Do you read as a body, listen to this text as a body, or are you a reading, listening body? How are we to discern this corporeal difference, perhaps so logically subtle? Does this logical differentiation matter?' Let us, though, consider this body, my body that is, a who that wrote these words: is this body a voice, a means, for this execution of text, or is she, the flesh, the speaking text itself, body and written voice indistinguishable? Are you, an attentive reader, a body reader in this performance, or the reading performance itself, body and reader indistinguishable? Are speaking through text as a writer and listening to text through reading constitutive of the one event, a performance necessarily embodied if it is to occur at all? Do we constitute each other's horizons, as not only figures and points inconceivable without each other, but spatiotemporally related through text and engaging psyches?

Are the body writing–speaking and the writing voice a one-ness inadmissible by Husserl, who, meditating with Descartes, to found a first philosophy, assents to the correctness of the Cartesian method of doubt and suspends the natural attitude? Let us think of Husserl's twin claims: 'the Ego with its Ego-life is not a piece of the world' and 'the certainty of sense experience does not withstand criticism' (Husserl 1999: 3). Do they precipitate a potential crisis in the common-sense understanding of human identity as bodily identity? The Ego is not a piece of the world? The certainty of sense experience does not withstand criticism? If the Ego is not a piece of the world, of what is it a piece? Is it a 'piece' at all? And what is it to say that sense experience does not withstand criticism? Is it not sense apparatus that existentially enables even the tiniest doubt to be posed? Does doubting the veracity of the senses gesture only towards a conceptual possibility and does such a possibility, as conceptual, give us grounds for founding an indubitable science? Does thought with its transcending propensity bind the world to a conscious, thinking mind, delimiting sensuous experience as a ground to and for indubitable knowledge?

Now, simply stop for a while and think about how you are at this moment, reading this text. Where are you in relation to your body? Do you feel a twinge, an itch, a pain, a cramp in your foot, a coldness in your fingertips, or the quiet sweat on your forehead? Or has your body 'disappeared' as the reading task takes up all of your attention so that your body becomes background to a more compelling mental experience? Are you aware of your eyes moving across the text, the furrowing of your brow, your breathing, your posture, your heartbeat? Are you experiencing the sensuousness of your body at all? Has your body become an obedient, neglected, silent slave to the mastery of cognitive process?

Redirect your attention: consider yourself in relation to Descartes and Husserl: was it possible for them to inhabit a world capable of exceeding the senses, a world where epistemology is potentially grounded in the activity of mind? Senses bracketed, put out of action, just as yours might now be as you progress through this reading task. Do you, and we all, as a matter of fact, share in systematic bracketing to make our ways through our worlds? Is bracketing the key to philosophical reflection, the key to attending to some tasks that are fundamental to the thinker's, the artist's, the writer's, the reader's worlds?

Suppose, next, that I ask you to focus totally on your mind. What is happening there (and is your mind a 'there')? Think about this: does not Jung require of his patients that they focus on their minds, on their psyches, as they examine their imaginings, their fantasies, their dreams in their dream worlds? Can you do such a thing, that is to say, focus on your very own mind? How do you do that? Is that what Descartes did when he decided that he could doubt everything except that he was thinking, because to doubt is to think? When he reflected on this point, did he have a fundamental awareness of his own being, his thinking being, a doubting being, not a thinking event that was happening to him, but a full-blown, self-constituting moment of being? Did his subjectivity make its relentless presence felt, so that he could not conclude that there is thinking, full stop? What are we to do with a claim that there might only be thinking and no thinker? As you read this, are you thinking (for one thinks, doesn't one, as one reads?) that, yes, intuitively you believe there must always be a thinker or potential thinker, of thoughts? And is this a mind or a body, or both, even? 'Are thoughts always thought by someone, some body?' – that is the question.

So here we are, at a point that might be suggesting that you do not exist. That is to say, you may have forgotten all about your body as you focus on your mind. You may be exploring your mind and considering what is going on, and, prompted by my questioning text, you may be now considering if there is a you, or just a series of thoughts that, that what . . . give the appearance of there being a you? This might be quite dangerous territory for you to be entering. Hasn't psychology tried to establish that there is an ego, an essential you-ness revolving around all your psychic processes, conscious and unconscious, mental, emotional, psychological?

But the thing is, that what I have asked you to do is impossible while you are a reader of this text. And it doesn't matter if you are a subject reading or a reading subject. It simply doesn't matter. The point is you have to go off and do this exercise all by yourself. Not with my giving you instructions, guiding you through a meditation. No: this has to be your experience, your time with yourself. Just as it was with Descartes, just as it was with Husserl; and presumably just as it was with Jung . . .

. . . Return now to your body, to your own flesh, flesh that is reading and responding to these words. Feel your alignment; perhaps you have slumped slightly; twiddle your toes, and think about the expression on your face: maybe smiling, frowning, pursing thelips. This return may sever a transcendence in which you have been participating, a moving out around your conscious mind that marks the peculiar ability we have as human flesh, conscious flesh. In this phenomenal situation we engage as we might in any session that sees speaking and reading and listening as its centre.

In the above, you variously directed your attention according to what the words said to you. Your body awareness may have been minimal when you began reading, or you may have had an ache in your foot that disappeared when you took your attention to the text as you read. More generally, with the focusing of our attention on something other than ourselves, we suspend our self-awareness, including our awareness of ourselves *as body*. But that does not always happen. In other words, we decorporealise our experience from time to time, and it is entirely existentially appropriate that we do so. Sometimes, as was the case with Descartes, we see the beginnings of philosophical reflection: in the above, philosophical reflection began with the movement from the writing's calling your attention to what you are doing, through the development of ideas around reading, the raising of questions, then further questions, especially around your body, your flesh, where and with whom you are in the world, and finally, the instruction to go off and practise the thinking for yourself, as an invitation to think differently about yourself and your world. In other words, philosophical reflection begins with attention and is directed towards an awareness of a particular kind, an awareness related to transformation of thinking.

Paradoxically, by virtue of our embodiment, then, we are able to disengage from that embodiment, decorporealise our experience, through our ability to direct our attention in specific ways. At other times, that is not the case, as we shall see shortly. That directedness of attention is what we find in Descartes' *Meditations,* in Brentano's description of intentionality, and its subsequent development and modification by the phenomenologists we have been discussing. It is, too, a feature of Jung's practice in his psychoanalytic work, and in his writing; and also what he is talking about in his description of the reductive and the synthetic method, together with the notion of the transcendent function he articulates.

The deliberate movement away from the body and perhaps getting involved in one's own thinking to the extent that one follows a train of thought that becomes entirely centred on that thought, might, you may argue, involve a suspension of awareness of one's corporeality. But this is only temporary. It is not like Descartes' doubt or Husserl's realisation of a transcendental ego. Indeed, the deliberate bracketing of the body that we see in their work suggests that there is a qualitative difference between the two cases. You might argue that where there is genuine doubt, as in the case of Descartes, then there is the strong possibility of a final severance, a sinking into solipsism and an impossibility of 'return to the body'. A capture by interiority, never to be released, would follow. And this is precisely the danger that Brooke and Romanyshyn worry about and fear for in Jung's work.

My response to this objection is twofold: on the one hand, recall Gaukroger's analysis of the kind of doubt practised by Descartes – hyperbolic doubt, that is. Such doubt involves *justification* of some belief or other that you might have about, for example, the existence of an external world. It does not involve doubt of an absolute nature – that *in actual fact* there really is not a world, and thus that your body really does not exist. The nature of that world might remain in question – what it is like and if our perceptions match the 'what it is like'. On the other hand, Descartes' robust return to the body in *Meditation VI*, in his epistolary discussions with Elizabeth and in his focus on the passions, and then Husserl's insistence on intersubjectivity, anchor one in/to the body and in/to the world. Theirs is a methodological doubt, part of a procedure or process that is enacted in order to get to a place not available in the natural attitude. This reply suggests that, even if the metaphysics that results from the practice is dubious, the body remediates the result because, in a sense, it is the origin of the process of doubt in the first place: you can't even get off the ground, as it were, without the body. Let us look at this from another perspective. In order to do that, let us return to the theme of 'Eastern thinking' we have already met.

Body consciousness

I argued above that there is not much point in deciding 'who is right and who is wrong' when it comes to considering the arguments of various phenomenologists. How very postmodern of me, you might respond: why bother, in the first place? Doesn't it matter that some theories are more or less closer to the way the world is? It is here that the idea of existential appropriateness can prove to be fruitful, and also a more detailed examination of the natural attitude. In order to develop these ideas, I want to explore consciousness of oneself in a quite specific way, that does not involve a turning directly towards one's consciousness. It involves direct engagement with one's body, and taking seriously the inner/outer trope as a case of genuine phenomenological experience and thus as an existentially appropriate principle of human being.

Jung analyses, respectively, 'Western' and 'Eastern' minds in terms of his extraverted/introverted typology. He acknowledges that the mind can exist without an ego in Eastern philosophy. Is Jung, I ask you, complicit in what has been characterised as a Western Cartesian-inspired reduction of ego to a thinking subject in even thinking the East/West split? Is his further claim that he 'cannot imagine a conscious mental state that does not relate to a subject, that is, to an ego' evidence of this complicity?

Jung's analysis of 'Eastern' (by which he presumably means Indian and Chinese) and 'Western' (European) conceptions of mind opens our eyes to what is at stake. He mounts an argument to show that these two conceptions of mind are quite different. He claims that the 'Western' notion of mind has more to do with consciousness than does the 'Eastern' notion and that in the West the 'consciousness is inconceivable without an ego'. He holds the philosophical view that an ego is a necessary condition of there being consciousness at all for 'if there is no ego there is nobody to be conscious of anything'. In this vein, he also claims that he has no problem conceiving of mental states that transcend consciousness. Jung argues that the case if quite different in 'Eastern thinking' that, indeed, there can be consciousness without an ego. Further, he claims that 'consciousness is deemed capable of transcending its ego conditions' and that, to us, this would be a state of unconsciousness due to lack of a witness. He 'cannot imagine a conscious mental state that does not relate to a subject, that is to an ego'. He supports his view that the ego is necessary for consciousness by arguing that, even though the ego may lose, for example, 'its awareness of the body', where there is awareness, 'there must be somebody who is aware'. Then he argues that the 'unconscious is a mental condition of which no ego is aware' (Jung 1978: 774–776).

In this analysis, Jung's assertion that 'Eastern' and 'Western' conceptions of mind are different because of the role the ego plays is controversial. Jung's point is debated by commentators on spiritual experiences, practices and their content. The egoless state is difficult to achieve, but it is present in, for example, 'Western' spiritual practice in the mystical tradition, discussions of which can be found in the broad subcategory of mystical experience. In the

Western Christian tradition, stages of spiritual progress are named as the Way of Purgation, the Way of Illumination and the Way of Union, or what is also called the Unitive State. Corresponding stages or states are either compared or contrasted with Eastern meditative states (Dale 2009). Thus Jung's conflation of the egoless state, achieved through mystical experience, and the unconscious is contentious. Yet we can see links here with mystical theorising Western philosophical and religious traditions.

His claim that the existence of an ego[1] is a necessary condition of awareness faintly echoes Descartes' *cogito.* Awareness plays a pivotal role in either pre-reflective experience or in reflective experience. Such awareness becomes a condition of the existence of an I in self-interrogation. Descartes' 'I' is, as we have seen, an effect of immediate intuition: the thinking I is uncovered in the act of direct, immediate perception, an I that in, its own awareness of itself, performs and thus manifests, and infers, its existence. We may hold with Husserl and Merleau-Ponty that this I is secondary to pre-reflective awareness. This latter is not what Jung is arguing. As we have seen, the body/consciousness/mind involves a mutuality of inter-relation. So while Jung might hold that the existence of an ego is a necessary condition of awareness, the phenomenological debate that ensued from Husserl's phenomenology is contemporaneous with him. As we have also seen, it is not that for the philosophers under consideration the body does not matter, that the body does not exist – far from it. It is that *awareness of body* becomes secondary to the task at hand, the attaining of epistemological certainty, an intellectual exercise, together with the attaining of wisdom. I argue that the same is the case for Jung. And for Jung, following this thinking, awareness assumes a constitutive role in identity, awareness fluctuating between body and mind, mind and body.

There is an alternative, another way of looking at all of this, which reinforces the value of flesh. Suppose that we, instead of divesting the ego of its awareness of the body, direct the aware, conscious ego, considered as a centre of consciousness, towards the body, making of the body our complete focus? Is awareness of the body, a fusion of directedness and that towards which it is directed, little more than a focus on consciousness' awareness of itself? For example, suppose I were to say to you:

> Be alone. Sit quietly in a comfortable cross-legged position, with your back straight, breathing normally. Just sit, just breathe. Keep your back straight, make sure you don't have to fidget, so look at your body balance as you sit. Adjust yourself if necessary. Just become aware of the equilibrium you can attain, just sitting. Now take your awareness to the triangular area below your nostrils, above the area of your top lip. Observe the breath as it passes over that area. Just observe that area, nothing more. Focus totally on that area, nothing more. Take ten breaths in and out in a cycle of inhalation, and then exhalation, observing all the time. Now feel your breath, just feel your breath moving over that area. Don't think or

> observe or calculate, or wonder if you have focused on the right area. Just feel the breath over the triangular area at the base of your nostrils, on your top lip. Stay there, resting yourself in the feeling of the breath moving over the area. Don't move or twitch or itch or scratch. Remain like that until you hear my voice once more . . .

This might seem like a strange question, but where does your consciousness go if you practise this small exercise? Does it stay in the small area to which I have directed you? Do you detect the difference between *observing* that area and *feeling* the breath over the area? Is there a difference? How long can you rest in this position? Can you, indeed, stay with your position at all? Or do your ankles and knees and hips and shoulders and neck begin to ache and to protest? Do you drift off and begin to think about what you will have for dinner, or the cricket score? Do you start to have brilliant, colourful, phantasies that draw your consciousness away, to follow some entirely other adventure? Just how difficult is this for you, to concentrate on one small area of your body?

The above exercise is a possible set of directions for the meditational practice, which is called *Ānāpānasati,* a form of mindfulness of breathing in Buddhist meditation. Some proponents of *Ānāpānasati* argue that 'breath is a tool with which to explore the truth about oneself', that we know very little about our own bodies, and that observation of the breath is observation of the mind (Goenka 2007: 2–3). It is sometimes taught as a prelude to the practice of *vipassana* or direct insight into the nature of one's mind, of change, and thus of impermanence. *Vipassana* meditation teaches that one can feel, and become aware of, sensations all over the entire body. In observing the sensations one learns to note them and then to pass on, not thinking about, or analysing, them. One does this in a series of passings-over of the body with conscious awareness, from head to toe and then back again. This is a form of directed attention, with the 'object' of attention being one's very own body. Usually one meditates for about an hour. Through this practice, one can achieve a state of equanimity in which desire and aversion, the cause of suffering, are accepted and not clung to.

Now think about this. Hatha yoga is a series of practices of the body, postures or asanas, which discipline the flesh in motion and in stillness. The feel and sensations of the body – its tensions, its ease, its strength, its weakness, its posture, and its location within the horizon of being, its placement and the placement of its various parts – work to open, calm and transform not just the body itself or the mind, but the being of this flesh in-the-world, this conscious being which is so much more than a thinking mind in a body. That one's body is always with one (Merleau-Ponty 1962: 103) is consciously exemplified as one becomes totally absorbed in the bends and stretches, reaches and curls, inversions and rests, in the breathing, the breathing that raises flesh into consciousness. Of what? Stillness of the psyche, and yet the activity of being in-the-world in one's body. In a sense one becomes utterly conscious that in these moments one is fully one's body.

In hatha yoga, the body, the flesh as conscious bodiliness, slowly moves, moment by moment, in acceptance, as each of those moments exceed each other, producing not only bodily transformation, but transformation of the psyche, its ego and non-ego. 'Don't think about how difficult it is, just do it.' Don't think, do . . . let the ego go[2]; let it, with its pernicious whisperings, fall over the precipice of bodily failure and disbelief; let the ego be depotentiated by bodily awareness where focus is not on conscious mind at all, but on this living flesh *now* as it moves, remains still, and moves again. Let the ego be depotentiated: there can be no transcendence without this permission but this is essentially a body-oriented depotentiation; focus is on the body in deep, egoless awareness. Consciousness is secured, not by an ego, but by a succession of disciplined, focused movements of flesh, the *telos* of which is, precisely, to depotentiate the ego. What seems to follow from this is that the necessity of an ego for consciousness is existentially compromised.

If this is the case, bodily awareness is primitive – it cannot be reduced to anything other than what it is *because* the cognitive process is itself parenthesised. Yet the states achieved in these fully immanent activities are profound states of consciousness which can be interrupted by the insertion of an ego that tells one that one is aware. I shall argue shortly that becoming aware that one is aware, and then to interrogate that awareness, is to be present to oneself in transcendental subjectivity. We could describe the difference manifested in suspension of cognition and intellection and the resulting awareness; and the interrogation, the asking, 'What is it, if anything that is enacting such awareness?' as the difference between immanence and transcendence.

For now, take these two practices back to Jung, and consider his claims above. We can see the emergence of a potential tension between the points I listed earlier when we locate the body as a site of awareness that circumvents the ego, when we conceive of the body as conscious flesh. The existence of mental states transcending consciousness does not entail what Jung asserts, that 'such states lose their consciousness to exactly the degree that they transcend consciousness'. Consciousness or awareness is enhanced without a correlated heightening of ego. Indeed, the opposite seems to be the case. In both *vipassana* and hatha yoga it is arguable that the body/consciousness dyad collapses. For the adept, there is a radical change in sensibility, in ongoing awareness, and in moral orientation towards the world. By focusing on the immediacy of the body, by localising and limiting one's experience, one is able to effect a transformation and emancipation, which is not an effect of intellectual pursuit or cognitive thinking. To that extent, these are quite different spiritual practices from what we have seen in Hadot's analysis. Yet many of the same processes are involved: learning, discipline, ethical disposition. What is important to us, though, is that attention or *prosoche* is central to both, the fulcrum around which consciousness turns.

But there is another important twist here. Above, I described reflection as a turn of consciousness away from the world. In the two practices under consideration, the turn is not *towards* consciousness, but the *use* of consciousness to turn towards one's own body. One's consciousness is effectively decentred into the body. The upshot of this decentring is that consciousness becomes hyperdirected as it becomes more and more highly refined. And an effect of this aspect of the process is the dissolution of the ego. Now, if we think of what is being described here, and if we think of these two forms of meditation as phenomenology, as a turn to things themselves, we are in a position to examine Jung's claims, firstly that 'if there is no ego there is nobody to be conscious of anything' and secondly, that 'the ego is therefore indispensable to the conscious process'. These interrelated claims are contrary to the evidence we find in accounts of *vipassana* and hatha yoga of highly experienced and highly evolved practitioners (Iyengar 2001, 2006; Goenka 2007). Interestingly, in these practices, the dissolution of the ego does not entail a dissolution of consciousness, but an expansion of conscious awareness and of one's place in the world, indeed the cosmos. Such practices are both consciousness and corporeally transformative. Involved in them is a mastery of the self that arises through a confrontation with oneself, and with how one has taken the world to be, always. As an agent in the world, the very assumptions that one makes, which underpin one's actions, one's beliefs, one's desires, are called into question.

So a question like, 'Is there somebody who is aware?' can be answered in the following way: 'Yes some body, but *not* somebody. Not a subject moving through the union of mind and body, but sensations existing in flesh.' The 'somebody' becomes translated into some conscious body where subjectivity in terms of an ego is erased. The suspension of cognition and intellection leads to different ends, through a differently articulated and practised existentially appropriate methodological approach.

It is not that consciousness and body become metaphysically disengaged, that there is an ultimate and final severance between consciousness and its corporeality. Rather, in these kinds of processes, we are able to discover the importance of making distinctions of various kinds, beyond an intellectual and practical boundary. These distinctions have an ontological impact depending on the level at which we engage with them. So that when I or you sit in *vipassana* or practise hatha yoga or enact any other mode of consciousness/corporeal mastery, we become aware of the range of possibilities simultaneously open to us, and us to them.

And the upshot of this conclusion? The body, the flesh, attains its rightful place in an ontology of the psyche where ego becomes *an* aspect of bodily and fleshly being and not an entity separable from the living being of flesh, and where consciousness has a possible existence outside an intentional regime available to our whole being, of which we become aware through varying levels of consciousness. Descartes' *cogito* is one example of this, and the insight achieved through *vipassana* is another. This is not to make a direct comparison between the *cogito* and psychomoral consciousness transformation achieved through 'Eastern' meditational practices. Nor is it to equate the process of individuation and any confrontation with oneself that occurs during that process. Rather, it is to suggest two things: that psychocorporeal transformation can take a number of forms; and that those forms need to be seen within the context of their occurrence. While this might seem obvious, Jung's claim that the 'fact that the East can dispose so easily of the ego seems to point to a mind that is not to be identified with "our mind"' can be evaluated against this background.

Descartes' view that there is no consciousness without an ego is in keeping with his *cogito* as it is standardly interpreted. Yet the debate that surrounds Descartes' *cogito* suggests that he accepts that there must be a doubting subject that actually does the doubting. The general principle here, which we can extrapolate to Jung, is that there must be a subject of any mental activity, what Gaukroger refers to, in the case of doubt, as a 'unified locus of subjectivity, a self, which is the origin or bearer of the particular doubt'. The ego about which Jung speaks can be seen as such a locus. Gaukroger argues that an alternative view, of which Descartes would have been aware, was that developed by the Averroists who held that 'there can only be one intellect in the universe, which precludes the intellect being identified with an individual self as Descartes maintains'. Gaukroger remarks that, although the point about the single-intellect universe was made to Descartes, he ignored it, perhaps because he assumed its falsity (Gaukroger 1995: 346–347).

Of course there is a rider to all of this. Without the complexity of flesh, as inter-relational and as intersubjective, none of this is possible. As I see it, it is only because of these elements that any of this can occur. Just as the body is suspended or bracketed in the *epochē,* so the cognitive, intellectual aspect of consciousness is suspended in *vipassana* and hatha yoga. I am proposing, then, that these two forms of meditation involve an *epochē* that brackets the natural attitude we have to our own consciousness.

Natural, and other, attitudes

I argued above that awareness is central to pre-reflective and reflective experience. The former is what we have seen articulated as natural attitude in Husserl's work. In my discussion of intersubjectivity, and also in my treatment of various spiritual practices, I have been arguing that the natural attitude is parenthesised. I now want, as I end this chapter, to explore these claims more fully because they have a direct bearing on our understanding of the work of analytical psychology. Husserl's distinguishes between attitudes that are available within an object field constituted by those objects. I quote at length since the text is very clear:

> I always find myself as someone who is perceiving, objectivating in memory or in phantasy, thinking, feeling, desiring, etc.; and I find myself actively related in these activities *for the most part* to the actuality continually surrounding me. For I am not always so related; not every cogito in which

> I live has as its cogitatum physical things, human beings, objects or affair-complexes of some kind or other that belong to my surrounding world. I busy myself, let us say, with pure numbers and their laws: Nothing like that is present in the surrounding world, this world of 'real actuality.' The world of numbers is likewise there for me precisely as Object-field of arithmetical busiedness; during such busiedness single numbers of numerical formations will be at the focus of my regard, surrounded by a partly determinate, partly indeterminate arithmetical horizon; but obviously this factual being-there-for-me, like the factually existent itself, is of a different sort. *The arithmetical world is there for me only if, and as long as, I am in the arithmetical attitude.* The *natural* world, however, the world in the usual sense of the word is, and has been, *there for me continuously* as long as I go on living naturally. As long as I am '*in the natural attitude*,' indeed both signify the same thing. That need not be altered in any respect whatever if, at the same time, I appropriate to myself the arithmetical world and other similar 'worlds' by effecting the suitable attitudes. In that case the natural world *remains 'on hand:'* afterwards, as well as before, I am in the natural attitude, *undisturbed* in it *by the new attitudes.* If my cogito is moving *only* in the worlds pertaining to these new attitudes, the natural world remains outside consideration; it is a background for my act-consciousness, but it is *not a horizon within which an arithmetical world finds a place.* The two worlds simultaneously present are *not connected,* disregarding their Ego-relation by virtue of which I can freely direct my regard and my acts into one another.
>
> (Husserl 1982: 54–55; italics in the original)

This is a very informative discussion of differing and existentially distinct mental attitudes. It is informative because it gives to us an idea of the psychic possibilities of enacting a multiplicity of worlds. So perhaps we can identify our own selves in what Husserl argues, even as he argues from his own case. The focus entailed by your reading my text, and by the practitioners of both *vipassana* and hatha yoga and, indeed, for anyone engaged in a highly directed activity such as Husserl describes here, for example, takes you from the natural attitude, where you live naturally, into a world not of your own making, yet available to you through the construct of a book. In that world, words, concepts, language constitute a new world that you can occupy. Likewise, through bodily movement and concentration on breath and corporeal position, a world of psychophysical presence is constituted. In either case, the natural world remains as it is, there for one's return.

The thereness of the natural world is important as a constituent of intersubjectivity and of inter-relatedness. What Husserl outlines here is not an idealist world of nature, but a rich conception of how we are to understand 'world'. Husserl remarks that his return to the natural attitude and to the natural world is undisturbed by the other worlds constituted by the objects on which focus is directed. As I see it, this might not be so. Sometimes, one deliberately parenthesises the natural attitude in order to transform and perhaps to relocate oneself in the natural world on one's return. But once one begins to reflect on the natural attitude, and the natural world in which one is, one has already performed an *epochē*. Consider the following.

If one is in the natural attitude, one does not know or realise that one is in that attitude. To become aware and to describe one's being in the natural attitude is to dislocate one from the natural world, and from that attitude. A phenomenological analysis of the natural attitude entails that one has to move outside that attitude. As Sebastian Luft puts it:

> A phenomenological analysis of the natural attitude will have to make the difference . . . between an object-level and a meta-level . . . The object level will give a description of the natural attitude itself, whereas the meta-level will clarify that which makes this attitude 'natural.' Myself, my surroundings and the people I deal with are all just common and natural. To call this 'situation' natural would be absurd for someone living in the natural attitude, yet making this mode of daily life explicit and thematic requires that we are no longer in it. The term 'natural' thus gives a thematic description of our life as it is carried out 'naturally,' but the fact that this is so can only become explicit in another attitude;
>
> (Luft 1998: 154–155)

The spatial metaphors deployed in both Husserl's text and Luft's commentary, the language of 'movement' and 'worlds' and 'thereness', 'living-in', 'meta', are suggestive of the importance of spatial tropes to discussions of consciousness and of psyche more generally. In other words, the narrativisation of the natural attitude makes of it an object that can be clarified. This is a kind of distancing or disentangling process. Outside the natural attitude, we can see a similar or parallel process operating when one describes what one is doing now, speaks of one's dreams or of one's psychic happenings. Thus, as I see it, we can extrapolate these considerations to other psychological attitudes. Before doing that, we need to think about Husserl's term 'attitude'.

We saw that Husserl uses the world of numbers, the arithmetical attitude, as his example of a non-natural attitude. For Husserl, who also speaks of the personalistic and naturalistic attitudes, an attitude is related to intentionality, interest and situation, and, as I understand it, is a form of interested directedness or stand or position in relation to an object and its world, either unthematised (e.g. nature as in the natural attitude) or thematised (e.g. arithmetic (numbers), Beethoven's Seventh Symphony (music), or one's great uncle Jack (relatives/family) (Husserl 1989: 183ff; Luft 1998: 156)). Note that he also speaks of appropriating to himself those worlds by 'effecting the suitable attitudes'.

The notion of suitable attitudes is echoed in the notion of existential appropriateness that we encountered earlier. Spiritual practice and method come together, you will recall, to achieve or bring about a *telos*. While Husserl is dealing with attitudes, it is easy to see that there is a connection between ends and means in each case: an arithmetical world would not be achieved by effecting an attitude that bears little resemblance to a world that has no transparent connection with numbers. If we extrapolate this model of attitude and world to the contexts we have been building in this book, we can see that it can enhance existential appropriateness.

In the case of Descartes, an indubitable belief world is effected by his appropriating to himself a hyperbolic doubt, that as he sees it, is entirely suitable to his ends. One of the reasons a Heideggerian reading of Jung does not make the grade with me as a scholarly and rigorous reading of Jung is that *poiesis*, as Brooke invokes it, does not effect attitudes suitable to achieving a comprehensive understanding of the philosophical underpinnings of Jung's work.

This analysis of attitude, natural or other, brings into sharp focus the idea that consciousness is capable of, and does move around itself, adopting various attitudes to suit particular situations. The taken-for-granted nature of the subject/object distinction can be seen as a result of the natural attitude. Without reflection, in the pre-reflective domain, we see a world to which we are joined, and enmeshed. Only upon reflection, only upon positing of questions does its (logical) object status emerge, and only in our attempts to clarify that does it begin to exist as a meta-object. This entails, though, that there is a shift in consciousness, a move from immanence *towards* transcendence which, I believe is the basis of the transcendental subject. Such a subject, then, is not postulated *before* the natural attitude but as a result of recognising that attitude. Merleau-Ponty argues this. But that does not result in transcendental subjectivity. This comes only when one interrogates the already reflecting subject. Thus Descartes' 'But what then am I'? is the question that moves him to the transcendental domain. This is also the case with Husserl.

On this view, one of the reasons that psychotherapy and analysis can be so effective, then, is that, rather than remaining stuck in a world of immanent images, for example, one is able to move to a meta-position from which to explore what can be the frightening domain of oneself. We see this demonstrated in Jung's *Red Book* and in his patients' journey to individuation. In the final chapter, I explore where an investigation of the transcendental subject might take us.

Interestingly, in *vipassana* and hatha yoga, the achievement of transcendental subjectivity is problematic. I am arguing that the interrogative is fundamental to transcendental subjectivity. The suspension of cognitive, intellectual processes in the performance of corporeally attentive practices erases temporarily the interrogating ego. Let us see where this takes us.

Chapter 7

Flesh issues

Elemental mattering

> Despite our evolutionary progress of rational transcendence (including the technological advancements that some regard as rendering us posthuman cyborgs), we still essentially and dependently belong to a much wider natural and social world that continues to shape the individuals we are (including our reasoning consciousness) in ways beyond the control of our will and consciousness. As oxygen is necessary for consciousness in the brain, so the practices, norms, and language of society are necessary materials for our processes of reasoning and evaluation. It is not moral perfectionism but blind arrogance to think otherwise.
>
> (Shusterman 2008: 213–214)

> Transhumanism is a philosophical, cultural, and political movement that holds that the human species is now in a comparatively early phase and that its very evolution will be altered by developing technologies. Future humans will be very like their present-day incarnation in both physical and mental respects, and will in fact resemble certain persons depicted in science fiction stories.
>
> (Schneider 2009: 242)

> No matter how beautiful and perfect man may believe his reason to be, he can always be certain that it is only one of the possible mental functions, and covers only that one side of the phenomenal world which corresponds to it.
>
> (Jung 1966: 110)

We saw that it is not simply the move to a conscious awareness of one's being in the natural attitude that constitutes transcendental subjectivity. The further move to asking, consciously, '*What it is that is consciously aware*, that has an attitude?' or cognate question, is the moment of such constitution. One remains *in fact* embodied throughout this process – that goes without saying. I have been arguing that the parenthesising or bracketing of the body, suspension, that is, of conscious corporeal awareness is an aspect of transcendental subjectivity. To remain conscious and to be aware that one is conscious is *already* to take a step towards transcendence, but only after one's focus turns *entirely* to one's consciousness. It is to engage in spiritual practice with close attention and meditation at its core. Hence the transcendental subject that emerges from enacting the *epochē* is embodied.

There is a trail from the immanence of corporeality or total immersion, that does not yield conscious awareness, to an awareness of body, that engages consciousness which may or may not lead to self-reflexivity. Transcendental subjectivity is ensured only with a self-interrogating question, and an awareness that the question is being asked about one's essence, and one's mode of being. Thus the transcendental subject is not a floating presence in the world: flesh anchors it and plants it firmly on the Earth; conscious awareness is what is at stake, not the fact of embodiment. I argue that this is the case with Descartes: and it has been the case with Jung, with you as reader: once your attention is drawn to your mental activities in a cognitive interrogation, the path to transcendental subjectivity is begun. With a hatha yoga or a *vipassana* practitioner this is less clear. Suspension of cognition and intellection is a necessary step into their practices: hence the transcendental move is not necessarily exhibited in deliberate practices of the body such as we have been discussing.

Nor is transcendental subjectivity a 'thing' that exists inside our psyches. Rather, it is a position we take up with respect to ourselves and to our worlds, that gives us both perspective and orientation. The ability and capacity to engage with oneself at a psychically conscious level are exercises of transcendental subjectivity. The 'having of a phantasy', for example, is one thing: to become aware that it is phantasy, to note it, and to take steps to find out what it is all about is another, and that is the work of approaching one's transcendental subjectivity. To ask who or what is doing all of this represents the arrival at the transcendental subjective position. I engage with my own psyche, with who I am in that psyche in all its dimensions that it makes available to me. I can interrogate 'what is going on in there', and I can do it in a way that no one else can, although I can get assistance from someone who is skilled in matters of the psyche, such as a therapist.

The I that reflects on all of this can move around within itself in a manner that is not possible for anyone else. That I is both separate from, and continuous with the whole of my psyche, a perspective which can give me a different point of view on myself and my world. Transcendental subjectivity names itself, and becomes aware of its own reflexivity and thus that it is caught in a circle that consistently turns back on itself, perhaps encapsulated in Merleau-Ponty's enfoldment. This is an inescapable fact of its own being, and what makes certain the impossibility of the Archimedean point to which we earlier saw Jung refer. Indeed, the multidimensionality of its complex being is revealed to the psyche through the exercise of its reflexive character. Jung's use of active imagination, of archetypal theory, and his treatment of aspects of one's dreams and phantasies is an expression of what I am talking about here.

In the *Red Book*, for example, Jung does not only describe his dreams and phantasies. The voice that steps in as a commentator is a voice distanced, a voice reflective and thoughtful about his psychic life, yet simultaneously a voice engaged and seeking understanding. It provides him with a perspective on both himself and on the collective unconscious. Jung's phantasy, 'The Red One' is a dialogue between himself and his own devil. Jung remarks:

> I earnestly confronted my devil and behaved with him as with a real person. This I learned in the Mysterium: to take seriously every unknown wanderer who personally inhabits the inner world, since they are real because they are effectual.
>
> (Jung 2009: 260)

I cannot, and do not intend to, pretend intimacy with the *Red Book*; my remarks here are only illustrative of my more general point: that the appearance of a perspective within the psyche is indicative of the activation of transcendental subjectivity and an orientation towards the material of the psyche that manifests itself through its own imaginative processes. We can detect in Jung's analysis that subjectivity has different manifestations, depending on the posing of questions, of conscious self-interrogating movement of psychic processes. The dialogical form is an existentially appropriate method of uncovering meanings relevant to one's own self.

The important point for us is that the asking of questions that engage the psyche and its personified manifestations is fundamental to forms of psychotherapy that take one's whole being as its subject. And this is what Jung's work does. Thus the embodied subject in all of its layers and dimensions is the centre for psychotherapeutic activity.

We recall, at this moment, Merleau-Ponty's use of the term 'flesh' as elemental; we note that, under the current view, the transcendental subject is existentially dependent on flesh, and is the condition on which flesh is perceived as flesh. It is that which shows that 'flesh is an ultimate notion, that it is not the union or compound of two substances, but thinkable by itself, if there is a relation to the visible' (Merleau-Ponty 1968: 140). Thought is always pushed back against itself to uncover itself and its ideas, its conceptions of itself. Thus the limit of Merleau-Ponty's 'flesh', I maintain, is always the question of how we come to conceive of the case in the first place, and where it takes us from there.

We also recall that such a process does not entail denying either the importance or the existence of one's very own flesh. In a way, it is a question of emphasis: one directs oneself to the existentially appropriate moment of being in which one is now residing. Hence the transcendental subject does a lot of work for us as psychic beings in the world, and as fleshy beings at that, in a world enveloped by, and enveloping, the psyche. The natural world is always what subtends this whole process of categorisation.

We might acknowledge all, or some, of this; but there are implications we need to examine. There are three, at least. Firstly, as flesh, sex/gender – or colour, or age, or genetic inheritance for that matter – must be appreciated as constituent in the possibility of interrogation and of self-conception. For now, I focus on sex/gender. We have not spoken of this small fact in this book. No whisper of the importance of sex/gender has escaped the lips of its author, a woman. It has been a silent presence. Our theorists have been predominantly men, for whom sex/gender does not count because . . . well, because why? Their assumption, and the default position, perhaps, is that when they speak they speak for themselves, and as theoreticians, they speak for everyone else – they are sex/gender theory-neutral, even as they inhabit their own masculine flesh. 'It is like this for me, and, therefore, for everyone.' On this reading, theory is more than biographical, more than a simple exploration of their own psychic states and beliefs, more than descriptive phenomenology. It is generalisable from the particular to the universal. Or else what is the point of even saying or making the theory in the first place? An operative assumption must be that, even if what they say is based on their assessment of the world, on their own experience, they in some way are capable of representing what is the case beyond themselves.

This brings us to the second point. In my view, we need to examine ourselves and our fundamental assumptions, as did Descartes. We need to enact the phenomenological *epochē*. And this we *have to do* if we are to see the point beyond a theoretical level. Phenomenology is not just description: it is, in the very first place, psychological activity. I have said, often, 'Go away and do this for yourself, and you will see . . . enact Descartes' doubt, enact the *epochē*, write, explore, illustrate your dreams and visions'. The 'doing it for yourself' makes of what I have been talking about a method that is deeply personal. That is the psychological activity required to make sense of, and to understand, phenomenology, not only as psychology, but as philosophy as well. We need to take this seriously, just once in our lives, as Descartes recommends. To engage only at the level of appreciating what is there on the page before us, to bracket or parenthesise the possibility of making an experience for ourselves, is to reinforce our forgetting of ourselves in the making of theory. The first-person perspective is elemental in how I have been reading Descartes, and Husserl. It is fundamental to the *Red Book,* and to Heidegger's exploration of *poiesis*. And it is part of what makes Abram's *The Spell of the Sensuous* so powerful.

The notion of sex/gendered fleshiness does not broach the question of where we are now, as human, possibly even as the posthuman cyborgs as suggested by Shusterman.

This brings us to our third point. We modify our bodies: prostheses, transplants, chemical intrusions of Botox. Does this have an effect, on our notions of sex/gendered flesh, on first-person sensibility and psyches? If body is *living body*, and if the living body is the whole psychism, what account are we to give to technologised human being in terms of psyche and world? Is the focus on *living* body a self-limiting conception of human being? Can we manufacture emotion as we have been able to manufacture reasoning and problem solving in machines, in early robots and complex computers? And how important is emotion to our survival? What are the consequences for our moral lives and our social values of any of these thoughts, questions and their consideration?

In my view, the second point more or less speaks for itself. But points 1 and 3 require rather more elaboration. Before I draw the threads of my argument together, I therefore take some time to explore those points a little more.

Sex/gendered flesh

One of the persisting problems of metaphysical dualism, whether it has its origins in Descartes or not, is that it is not taken seriously enough at a phenomenological level. OK, there is a problem with how physical and non-physical matter or substance or properties can affect each other. OK, we do not know how to explain consciousness, and we do not know if mental events are really chemical or electrical events in the brain. These are questions that can be dealt with scientifically, in the research lab as it were, as well as philosophically. But, at the level of explication, Husserl's insistence on intersubjectivity and interrelationality is ignored. That means (and he, himself, never makes this plain or even suggests that he has thought about it) that the *kind* of embodied subject that interacts and is embroiled in intersubjective relations is totally ignored. This is not really a question of suspension or parenthesising of sex/gender. It is that it never is considered. One might argue that sex/gender is part of the natural world, so part of the natural attitude, where there is no judgement or value. That may be so, but that is not quite the point I am making.

If there is a path to be traced from corporality, to reflection, to self-reflection, which I have been arguing there is, one might wonder how the body has not, even after Descartes, been considerable as a site of existential importance. On Plumwood's account of dualism, for example, we saw that the body and mind are in unequal relations with each other: the mind is superior to, and rules, the body – an idea, according to her, found in Plato and Descartes. If we take a very brief look at the history of the body, we can see that it has not enjoyed good press. In philosophical traditions, especially European, we can see this if we think about theological attitudes to corporeality in its relation to the Divine. So let us do that for a few minutes.

In many world religions, the body has enjoyed very little consideration as a mode of experiencing the Divine. It is often the case that quite the opposite holds. The body, for example in the writings of Augustine, is seen as a site of sin and excess, the origin of base desires that should be overcome in order to attain intimacy with and knowledge of the Divine (Augustine 1961). Although some religious traditions, in theory, claim the body as wonderful and Divine, a holy temple no less, in practice some of those very same religions abhor the body.[1] It might be, for example, that the body is the means by which a saving presence is brought into the world (as in the case of Jesus of Nazareth); but traditions develop differently according to indigenous cultural circumstances and the assumptions of prevailing theologies, mythologies and philosophies. No religion is ever 'pure', ever pristine and neutral. Each religion is an interpreted religion, understood and developed in a frequently unstable, changeable context.

Hence messages about the body, its importance in religion and, in particular, in spirituality (thought of in a theological or religious sense and not in Hadot's sense) can be vastly different even within a single tradition (say within Islam or within Christianity) and can change over time. Not only messages about the body, but how the body is theorised should be understood, then, trans-historically, intraculturally and transculturally. In my view, an important role is played by a conception of a transcendent Divine or God on the one hand, and humans (and other animals) as immanent, embodied creatures on the other.

There are several ways of conceiving of this distinction: God is a Creator, the cause, first principal or origin of all that there is. Thus the created (creatures and non-creatures) are ontologically dependent (the being of the created is dependent) on God. Without God there would be no creation. One might think of this as a causal argument: God causes the universe to come into being and thus the universe is an effect of divine utterance, such as we find, for example, in Genesis in the case of the Hebrew religions. As the Creator and the created are ontologically different (their being is different), that which is created is of less value than that which creates. Hence the body, as created, is always already of a lower value than God. We can detect here an instance of a full-blown dualism that falls under Plumwood's description.

On this story, the body is mortal and frail and full of desire. As a material being, it interacts in the world with other material beings which are equally mortal and frail and full of desire. Looking back, this is the kind of issue with which Descartes was dealing in *The Passions*. The therapeutic nature of Stoic spiritual exercises also addresses concerns that arise out of this picture – desire and uncontrolled passion cause pain and suffering and do not promote a good life. Desiring bodies interact with each other, desire each other, particularly sexually. They become attached to each other and are a distraction away from their home, God. Hence the desiring body is to be overcome so that it will not stand in the way of 'getting to God'. The more one is involved with one's body and the bodies of others, and with other created, material beings in the world, the less likelihood there is that one will be concerned with God. One, therefore, needs to overcome the body and its desires in order to attain closeness with God.

In some religious traditions, ascetic practices have been undertaken to scourge the body of its desires and its wayward passions, and bring the individual soul closer to God. The more abject in the Divine one becomes, the closer one is to the Divine. Grace Jantzen argues that, for women, this is a process of masculinisation in so far as women must abandon their feminine embodiment in order to become more Christ-like (Jantzen 1995). There are obvious questions to be raised here about women's autonomy and identity.

In the above argument, there is an underlying assumption that one is not identical with one's body, that one's body and one's 'true self', if you like, are substantially different, a position which is manifest in Descartes' *cogito* at *Meditation II*. What is mortal and frail and full of desire is not the essential self, the soul, but a bodily self that is weak precisely because it is body with its desires and unruliness. The essential or real self is more properly thought of as spirit or soul, as a kind of metaphysical matter or substance very different from the physical matter comprising the body. We see this spelt out fully in, for example, Descartes' *The World*, *Treatise on Man* and *Description of the Human Body* (Descartes 1985). In this view, the spirit or soul is most like the divine: it will survive bodily death, live forever in another heavenly mode (or be condemned to hell) and maybe even be reincarnated.

In the Aristotelian/Thomist view, the soul animates the body. The actions and desires of the body mark the soul. Thus the body can affect the soul and its destiny. As we saw with Descartes, the soul can also affect the body. This is not a European perspective alone. We can also find this view in various forms of Eastern religions, for example in Hinduism where the life one lives in one's body and the kind of *karma* which that life attracts determine the sort of embodiment one will have in the next incarnation (unless one attains *moksha*). Reciprocally, the soul affects the body and is seen as the seat of deliberation and grace. In Platonic philosophy, the soul has three different aspects, of which reason is the most noble. Reason's job is to overcome the appetites, to be a kind of moral and intellectual arbiter (Gray 2008). This view has been appropriated by some theologies and is found, for example, in much Christian theology.

The idea of the Christian God's personhood unquestionably is derivative of its Hebrew origins, from which emerged Yahweh, the monotheistic Divine. A god of the Semitic religions, Yahweh was a fertility god who was male as well as being a sky god (compared with the fertility goddess, Ishtar (Ashtaroth/Astarte), who was female and queen of Heaven). This male god has now become the God of the Jews and subsequently Christians and Muslims. This Divine has been conceived of as transcendent rather than immanent, just as the soul is transcendent and the body immanent.

This brief survey of theological attitudes to the body, especially in the domain of the mystical, is matched by the Christian belief that the body is the temple of God that will be resurrected at the final judgement. There is a paradox here, however. Gaukroger points out that in Reformation and post-Reformation Europe there was a 'widespread sense' of the necessity of reform in the Christian church. An aspect of the reform mentality was the gradual internalisation of religious practices that was inspired by mediaeval monasticism and which became a more general social phenomenon. Gaukroger say that 'the key ingredient in this process is a *contemptus mundi* . . . which has three components – hatred of the body and the world, the pervasiveness of sin, and a sharp sense of the fleetingness of time' (Gaukroger 1995: 25). Hatred of the *corpora-mundane* is arguably an underlying theme in the body/mind split at a metaphysical level. Feminists have argued, however, that the female body *in particular* has always been an object of both desire and contempt. The reformist attitude to the body, *any* body, thus masks, to some degree, a latent problem with the female body: that it is a site of sin and corruption, and that women are less capable of rational thought and dominated by their desires and by nature.

As we have seen, the spiritual exercises were therapeutic: it was held that they assisted in overcoming desire, positively assisted in disciplining the body and contributed to moral self-improvement. A generalised conception of the moral failure expressed in bodily desire and its expression overlooks the second-order social status of women who, it might be argued, epitomised the failure of flesh. Given the social order, it was men who continued to take the moral high ground at most levels of society where power mattered. Their 'natural ascendency' saw them ordain themselves as the embodiment of moral, political and social aspiration. To some degree, then, the model of reason presented as a social desideratum both excluded women from, and reinforced women's inability in, the sociopolitical sphere. Only exceptional women could ever hope to attain anything like the prestige seen as a birthright by many men. Princess Elizabeth and Queen Christina, Descartes' correspondent and patron, as royalty, were truly fortunate women by virtue of their births.

'What has this to do with transcendental subjectivity?' I hear you ask. This is my response: If we think of the movement to transcendental subjectivity as a manifestation of the place where one is at a particular moment in time, as a methodological effect constrained by opportunity, then one's spatiotemporal and one's existential situation counts. Richard Shusterman points out that Simone de Beauvoir, Judith Butler and Iris Marion Young have reservations about women's attending to their somatic experience because such attention confines one to passivity and immanence (de Beauvoir 1949; Butler 1990; Young 1990b; Shusterman 2008). As a contrast to the argument I have been attending to in this book, this gives us pause for thought: a return to the body or minimally, an acknowledgement of the body and of nature, is demanded by, for example, Brooke, Romanyshyn and Abram. The feminist critique requires a response.

But the return to the body consortium, which by no means consists in positions that mirror each other, highlights something else: this is a male quest for immanence in the body that is suggested by the phenomenological turn of Husserl and others. It is almost as if the 'discovery' of the body and of intersubjectivity and inter-relatedness has been a revelation – to male theorists – over the past hundred years or so. Menstruating, birth-giving, shit-cleaning-up women have always known about the possibilities of the body, defined as they are, and 'stuck' in its immanence. Why would women want to attend to the commonplace, the already known, when that is precisely how they have always been characterised? The 'discovery' of embodiment is thus of limited value to women: de Beauvoir, for example, argues that the subject of woman is irritating, that woman is defined by her uterus and her ovaries, that she is the Other: 'La femme? c'est bien simple, disent les amateurs de formules simple: elle est une matrice, un ovaire; elle est une femelle; ce mot suffit à la definer' (de Beauvoir 1949: 14, 32). If an aspect of phenomenology is a 'turn to the body' (which I think it is) and part of the objection to Husserl's phenomenology is his treatment of transcendent subjectivity which seems to bypass the body according to some, what could women gain from such a turn?

Further, if there is a therapeutically necessary engagement with corporeal immanence that helps to achieve a pragmatic and momentary transcendence of the body into a potentially ongoing subjectivity that opens oneself to deep exploration, how can women, defined by their immanence, ever hope to achieve wholeness? As I have argued elsewhere, Jung is less than respectful and honouring of the feminine (Gray 2008). On the one hand, he argues for a separateness of the masculine and the feminine that needs to be appreciated and acted upon, if individuation is to occur; on the other, his descriptions of the sex/gender categories are troublesome in just the terms of Plumwood's analysis of dualism.

The resurrection of the body into recent theory, seen in the foundational work of the phenomenologists, takes seriously the notion not only of the metaphysical importance of mind and body as a living unity – a living entity – the wholeness of human being. In psychology there is a related, and reiterated after Descartes, emphasis on the causal or, in the case of Jung, possibly synchronistic, relationship between mind and body (Jung 1972: 505ff). If a body is female or male, and if we follow the causal and/or synchronistic reasoning, it is clear that kind or type is affective in relation to the psyche. An important question, though, is how we are to conceive of that kindness or type when difference is under consideration. For if it is the case that power relations will always be at play, permeating and informing conceptions of difference, the truth of Plumwood's thesis is evident. A disruption of that power is possible, and a way to go about ensuring it is through spiritual practice that is therapeutically oriented; and which we saw instantiated in Jung's *Red Book*. Careful attention to oneself, to who one is and how that affects others in the intersubjectivity in which we are all agents, is necessary in the dismembering of debilitating power relations.

How the issues raised by questions around women's corporeal immanence can be addressed remains undecided. Luce Irigaray's notion of the sensible transcendental, the divinisation of corporeal immanence and the corporealisation of the divine, is instructive here.[2] Luce Irigaray's recent work, for example, *The Way of Love* (Irigaray 2004) and *Sharing the World* (Irigaray 2008), picks up and elaborates the themes of the transcendental sensible. What is made possible in all of this is an opportunity for women to reframe their confinement to immanence as symbolically conceived – and as reinforced by, for example, Jung's conception of female embodiment and the *anima*. What is certainly *not* the case is that women are not capable either of achieving transcendental subjectivity or of becoming adept at *vipassana* or hatha yoga (Iyengar 1998).[3]

This focus on sex/gendered corporeality brings us to another important question around the body, spiritual practice and individuation. This is not to do with what we might think of as natural or innate properties of bodies. Rather it is to do with the effect that recent technologies have had on our conception of what it is to be human, what might be called the cyborg body (Balsamo 1996; Bell and Kennedy 2000).

Cyborg body, transhuman being

> The ship wherein Theseus and the youth of Athens returned had thirty oars, and was preserved by the Athenians down even to the time of Demetrius Phalereus, for they took away the old planks as they decayed, putting in new and stronger timber in their place, insomuch that this ship became a standing example among the philosophers, for the logical question of things that grow; one side holding that the ship remained the same, and the other contending that it was not the same.
>
> (Plutarch 75 CE)

> If . . . that ship of Theseus [were continually repaired by] taking out the old planks and putting in new . . . and if some man had kept the old planks as they were taken out, and by putting them afterwards together in the same order, had again made a ship of them, [which ship would be the original one?].
>
> (Hobbes 1962: 128)

What is it that makes us human? A philosophical question for sure but one which subtends any consideration of human psyche. We have been looking at body, mind/psyche/consciousness and how they 'fit together'. An assumption is that the body is living, that it is, as Merleau-Ponty proposes the term, 'flesh'. Descartes imagined the human body as a machine; Jung sees human being as a whole living organism; Mary Shelley imagined Frankenstein's creature as animated, desiring love, capable of poetry, and possessing a sensibility of nature, yet this creature had no natural birth, no infancy, no genesis but at the hand of his creator, Frankenstein (Shelley 1818). As Andrew Martin in the film *Bicentennial Man* (1999), Robin Williams desires to be accepted as a human being in terms of law and freedoms, and finally, in his permitted 'mortality'; Haley Joel Osment as David in *Artificial Intelligence* desires to be a real boy so his human mother will love him. These imaginary characters who populate fictional worlds are from authors, all of whom are engaged in pondering what it is to be human. We can all name many, many more. Now consider the following:

> Dr C develops a disease which slowly and progressively affects each part of his body. As each part is affected, it is removed and replaced by a bionic part which easily integrates with the rest of his body. Eventually, all of Dr C's parts, including his brain and his reproductive organs, are replaced. As a result of this, Dr C attains extraordinary longevity. Dr C, when he was a young and virile man, donated his sperm to a sperm bank (the practice for all fertile males in that time) which has used the sperm to produce embryos, some of which have been successfully transplanted and eventually been born.
>
> Unbeknown to Dr C or his carers, a cryogenicist, Dr G, and her colleagues collect all of Dr C's body parts, freeze them and carefully reassemble them. Eventually, the team has all of the parts. Science and technology have developed to such an extent by this stage that they are able to reanimate the body. The resulting body looks just like Dr C as he originally looked before he developed his debilitating disease and as he now looks as a bionic being. Not only that, the reassembled body talks and acts like Dr C and seems to have Dr C's memory, his likes and dislikes, attitudes and values, his psychological makeup: each part of the cryogenic body seems to have 'remembered' the lived experience of the body from which it came. One cannot tell the replaced-body-part body and the cryogenic-reassembled body apart.

There are some fairly standard philosophical questions about identity that, following the ship of Theseus story, can now be raised: given that parts are replaced, when does the original Dr C cease to be himself? Does he? Who is the real Dr C, the 'replaced-body-part' individual, or the cryogenic-reassembled individual? Assuming both will count as Dr C, is either Dr C a human being? Is there a real Dr C? To whom can the moral life of Dr C be attributed? If there were decisions to be made about either the embryo of Dr C or his children who have been born, who would make those decisions, the replaced-body-part Dr C or the cryogenic Dr C? These are interesting questions, but not those with which we need be concerned here.

We should be concerned with these questions, though. Suppose that cryogenic Dr C begins to suffer from what appears to be depression, or hallucinations, or paranoia: how should he be treated? What is the ontological status of Dr C? Is he a *human person*? What would we say about his psychological life? The reassembled-body-part Dr C sounds as if he is very like Frankenstein's creature. Roy, the character in *Blade Runner* is a replicant: yet he makes that beautiful, evocative, poignant speech about what he has seen that fall outside human credulity, and the ephemeral nature of time and tears and rain and death (see Roy Batty's speech at the end of *Blade Runner*: Scott 1982). He is not human. But what would make him human? If I were to have my heart replaced, then my kidneys, then my joints, with artificial organs and prostheses, what is my status *vis-à-vis* human being? Indeed, in some sense, would I be transhuman, a being beyond what we currently take to be human? Are we witnessing a transformation of our basic concepts of 'human being' and its implications?

These questions are all important because not only has this book raised issues about our phenomenological standpoint on the world, our imaginations, the relationship between body and mind; it has courted an interrogation of what it means to be human. Our 'accepted' views usually include some idea of flesh, some idea of mind and body, some idea of imagination, reasoned thinking, intersubjectivity, desire. Importantly, they include ideas of natality and death. More and more, they have begun to include ideas of bodily modification and transformation. Primitive human life can now begin *in vitro*; we can keep people alive using all kinds of technologies. We can donate our organs to those who need them – kidneys, heart, liver, lungs. In a real sense we can become the physical other and they, us. Cosmetic surgery opens up the possibility of the 'outer me' matching the 'inner me' (not unproblematically from a theoretical perspective); sexual organs – breasts, labia, vagina and penis – can be made bigger or smaller depending on one's desires or the social pressures under which one finds oneself. Thus the concept of the 'normalised' body is challenged as a product of internalised social practice (Heyes 2007). With that challenge to the normalised body comes a challenge to what it means to be human.

It is very difficult to see how Husserl's and Jung's insights could have anything to offer these issues. Equally, it is difficult to see what impact such practices would have on how we think about these thinkers of the past. Heidegger advanced views on technology (Heidegger 1977). Potentially, Heidegger's views are of limited use to analytical and depth psychology: Don Ihde points out that Heidegger's views are now outdated (Ihde 2010). Heidegger's relationship with National Socialism has informed some of the discussion around his views (Farias *et al.* 1991; Feenberg and Hannay 1995; Pattison 2005). Further, does the notion of self-improvement through spiritual practice take on an entirely different complexion if the human status of the practitioner is under question? Could Roy or David or Andrew produce the *Red Book* with its stunning art, reflections, analyses and meditations?

I have no idea how to answer any of these questions. But they seem to me to be very big questions, and perhaps questions that will have a valuable contribution to make to many of the problems we have encountered throughout this book. In the end, perhaps it will be Descartes whose understanding of the body, mind and passions has more to offer given his conception of the human body as a machine.

So the questions, 'What are we doing to ourselves with technology?' 'What is technology doing to us?' are not simply the product of science fiction. They are serious questions deserving of serious answers; they raise more questions and more problems. We are in a time of transformation, and none of us really knows the answers – the answer may lie in developing our ideas around existential appropriateness, its possibilities and application. Who knows?

Some penultimate words about existential appropriateness. This notion is essentially descriptive. Existential appropriateness cannot be used, nor is it intended to be used, as justification which has to do with argument, as we have seen in Descartes' hyperbolic doubt and its answers. And justification is not to be conflated with description. *Telos* indicates its own means, and that is why when I describe what I do (I go to my room to think about what I can indubitably believe) I do not have to come up with some justification or other. Jung did not do that. He had his time when he created the *Red Book*, his time when he was a colleague and acquaintance of Freud, his time when he wrote, was a husband, father and lover. Descartes had his time for the *Meditations* and his time for the *Passions of the Soul.* They did what they needed to do to suit their ends; what happened out of their work has been up to us.

Some final words about distinction making. We all make distinctions. They help us to operate in the world. They can also be detrimental to ourselves and to others if they engage power structures that are repressive, colonising, demeaning. They can also empower us. The distinction between engaging the body as a site in which consciousness expresses itself, as I have described in the meditational techniques of the Eastern worlds, and the movement to transcendental subjectivity, as I have described in the meditational technique of Descartes and the practice of Jung, is not hierarchical. They each serve different purposes. In my view, Descartes was limited by the *cogito*; I do not know if Jung was limited by his own meditational practices and techniques that we see in active imagination, for example. To move beyond critical logical engagement with one's own mind, and to move beyond images is possible, and sometimes desirable. Correspondingly, to notice that one is indeed engaged, to become aware that one is aware, and to ask the existential questions – Who is thinking here? Is it me? What then am I? – are of utmost importance to us all. Pure spatiality, timelessness and imagelessness can affect our intersubjective relationships adversely, as well as enhance our being in the world with and without others. We need to make decisions on how to be, who to be, and whom to admire and with whom commune. We are fortunate that history provides us with the magnificence of Descartes and Jung; and we are indeed fortunate to be challenged by them, and to challenge them. That is our intellectual privilege, and our faithfulness to our passion.

Notes

Introduction

1 The primary and secondary literature supporting this claim is vast. See the pre-Socratic philosophers, Plato, Aristotle, *The Annals of Confucius*, *The Mahābhārata*, and then their commentators. See Barnes (2001).

1 Analytical psychologists read the philosophy of René Descartes

1 There were also two letters to Mersenne (June and July 1641) and another to Hyperaspistes (August 1641) which were published later.
2 *Discourse on the Method*, which had been published anonymously, anticipates the detailed treatment of the themes in *Meditations.*
3 Shamdasani argues that Jung's *Collected Works* are only a small part of his overall output. He says that a full catalogue was not produced until 1993. See Shamdasani (2005: 54). The C. G. Jung archives are at Eidegenössische Technische Hochschule (the Swiss Federal Institute of Technology) in Zurich. According to their website, they boast more than 1,000 manuscripts and over 3,000 letters to and from Jung. See: http://www.library.ethz.ch/en/Resources/Archival-holdings-documentations/C.G.-Jung-Papers-Collection. A catalogue of Jung's Manuscripts is available as a pdf download. See http://e-collection.library.ethz.ch/view/eth:22067?lang=en.
4 'The gland' to which Descartes is referring is the pineal gland, where he located the soul.
5 Daston and Galison distinguish between the ethical and the moral, maintaining that '*ethical* refers to normative codes of conduct that are bound up with a way of being in the world, an ethos in the sense of the habitual disposition of an individual or group, while *moral* refers to specific normative rules that may be upheld or transgressed and to which one may be held account' (Daston and Galison 2010: 40). We might say, then, that a code of conduct is something to which one subscribes as a member of, say, a professional group, while the rules to which one subscribes as an individual ('thou shalt not kill' or 'thou shalt not commit adultery') are rules that bind one to a specific set of personal practices and beliefs, the breaking of which may result in regimes of guilt, reparation, forgiveness. This distinction is tangential to my concerns in this book. I clarify it mainly for the purposes of understanding their thesis.

6 See the literature, for example, around the mind–body problem, the abortion debate, meaning, game theory or feminist theory.
7 The interpretational thesis maintains that all of our knowledge, beliefs and experiences is interpreted according to our preceding experiences, our beliefs and knowledge, and our sociocultural conditioning (our sex/gender, 'race', class, ability, and so on). This makes interpretation both the context and the effect of our being in the world. I shall be discussing this in greater detail later.
8 See, for example, *Principles 20–25,* in *Principles of Philosophy* (Descartes 1985).
9 For a full discussion of the dispute between Descartes and Voetius, mediated in part by Regius, see Gaukroger (1995: 357–361).
10 See Daston and Galison (2010) for a historical approach to the question of objectivity and its development and implications.
11 See Hegel (1977).

2 Spiritual exercises and Descartes' *Meditations*

1 Hadot believes this is the case. See Hadot (1995: 72).
2 See Becker (2001) for a full treatment of Jung's lectures.
3 See Becker's notes to each chapter.
4 His use of the term 'sciences', is, as many commentators note, not 'sciences' as it is today understood. It means, more generally, 'knowledge'. Check out general references here (Cottingham, Wilson *et al.*).
5 There is a debate about the possibility of direct knowledge which encompasses the idea of direct or immediate apprehension. I discuss this later. Direct or immediate apprehension of a meditator's own thinking becomes important later in considering different types of meditational practice in relation to the body.
6 Gaukroger also argues that there 'is a widespread view that Descartes thought that awareness of one's own mental states was in fact constitutive of the uniqueness of human cognition, and this view has been reinforced by an interpretation of the *cogito* whereby my grasp of my own existence is an instantaneous act of self-consciousness, rather than an inference or judgement. We have seen that such an interpretation is mistaken: the *cogito* does involve inference or judgement' (Gaukroger 1995: 349). I hold a hybrid view of the status of the *cogito* in that I think it involves both immediate apprehension and inference.
7 For a discussion of the controversial biography, *Memories, Dreams, Reflections,* see Shamdasani (2005). The *'Protocols'* refer to Aniela Jaffé's original German transcripts of interviews with Jung for *Memories, Dreams, Reflections* and are in the Library of Congress, Washington, DC, USA.
8 The paintings in the *Red Book* are not amateurish and show a strong painterly talent. Jung encouraged his patients to use visual imagery to explore their own psychic existences. Visual expression was obviously a legitimate form of exploring the contents of the unconscious. See, for example, *The Archetypes and the Collective Unconscious,* vol. 9 of the Collected Works, 'A Study in the Process of Individuation', where a series of paintings is reproduced with commentary (Jung 1968).

3 Descartes and the making of distinctions

1 See, for example, the writings of the early Greeks of remnants from Thales, Pythagoras, Heraclitus; or early Vedic and Brahminical texts: *The Rġ veda, The Mahābhārata.*
2 I detect a sentimental appreciation of such a world in Brooke's and Romanyshyn's texts. In my view, it can also be found in Bordo (1987) and Abram (1996)..
3 *A Clockwork Orange, The Minority Report* and *The Matrix* are fictional dealings with these topics.
4 For an excellent discussion of Jung's importance as a writer, see Rowland (2005).
5 The 'what it is like' characteristic is seen as a fundamental notion for some phenomenological understandings of experience and the mind. See Nagel (1974).
6 See, for example, Gaukroger (2006).
7 For a thorough discussion of the modal arguments in Descartes, see Cunning (2011).
8 See Chapter 2 for a brief discussion of this point.
9 This is a problem for Descartes since, as Gaukroger notes, a 'notoriously problematic part of Meditation 3 is the establishment of the existence of God, for Descartes must use the doctrine of clear and distinct ideas to prove the existence of God, and then use God to provide a divine guarantee for these clear and distinct ideas' (Gaukroger 1995). I am deliberately not focusing on this issue here, as it will take us too far away from our principal concerns.
10 By 'primitive notion' I take Descartes to be meaning that such a notion is not reducible to anything else.
11 See Chapters 5 and 6 for an elaboration of 'natural attitude'.

4 Inner and outer troubles

1 'The house I see is not in my mind – it is an object in the world, yet I see and represent it to myself: how is this possible?' See the Descartes references above and also Lagerlund (2011).
2 I am using Jung's terminology; he obviously saw 'man' as inclusive of man and woman in a way that today would not be acceptable by many scholars.
3 For differing views and also for elucidation of the ethical implications of such a view, see Plumwood (1993, 2002), Naess (1985), Abram (1996) and Sylvan (1985).

5 Jung and the phenomenological standpoint

1 Sonu Shamdasani says that in the Countway manuscript (named for the Medical School Library at Harvard), that is the manuscript on which editors based *Memories, Dreams, Reflections,* there is a chapter on Jung's very warm and empathic meeting with William James. This chapter does not appear in the published version of *Memories, Dream, Reflections.* See Shamdasani (2005).
2 See also Jung (1968: 126).
3 For a discussion of Brentano's influence on Freud, see Domenjo (2000).
4 Was Jung concerned with the Kantian distinction between noumena and phenomena? Certainly, he is concerned with phenomena as appearances, viz.

what appears to consciousness, but their ontological status is not examined. However, the idea of an appearance as a thing, as distinct from what is an appearance *of*, is a persistent and ubiquitous ontological dangler, wherever it is used, and it is a feature of Husserl's elucidation of phenomenology. Kant's influence on Jung is well known. The Fog Argument is Kantian.

5 If we consider Descartes' distinction between thinking substance and material substance, where, fundamentally, mental substance is not defined against material substance's extension, we can see that intentional inexistence as the mark of the mental, controversial though it is, is a big step from defining mental substance in terms of absence of extension.

6 Oskar Kraus' expression: p. 89 fn 11: (Brentano 1995). Kraus edited the 1924 second German edition of *Psychologie vom empirischen Standpunkt.* I use Linda L. McAlister's English translation (second edition) which retains Kraus' notes. In his 'Introduction to the Second Edition' Peter Simons remarks that Kraus' notes are 'frequently shrill and intrusive' and suggests that it is better to read the text proper (xv–xvi).

7 In this, he follows Plato.

8 His work in *Psychological Types* (1971) is a good example of this. See his discussion of Freud and Adler, where he does not interrogate his own assumptions.

9 Anglophone literature refers to this as the *cogito*, as I have been doing. I follow Husserl's use in my discussions of his work.

10 For a further and more comprehensive discussion of these issues, see Heidegger (1962) and Shamdasani (2003).

11 See Heinämaa (2003a).

12 Or '*poiesis*'. See above

13 For a comprehensive discussion of Heidegger's treatment of thinking and *poiesis*, see Di Pippo (2000) and Abram (1996).

6 Flesh, reflection and transcendence

1 This is Jung's meaning of 'ego'.

2 I am using *ego* more in the sense of the Freudian ego/superego/id sense here.

7 Flesh issues: elemental mattering

1 Such religions, and Christianity is an example, are often underpinned by appropriated philosophies that have an ambiguous relation with the body that is carried over.

2 I have argued this at length (Gray 2008).

3 There are similar issues here with body colour and 'race'. Penelope Deutscher finds Luce Irigaray lacking on this point. See Deutscher (2003).

Bibliography

Abram, D. (1996). *The Spell of the Sensuous*. New York, Vintage Books.

Annas, J. and J. Barnes (eds) (2000). *Sextus Empiricus Outlines of Scepticism*. Texts in the History of Philosophy. Cambridge, Cambridge University Press.

Aquinas, T. (1947). *Summa Theologica*. Available at: http://www.newadvent.org/summa/index.html.

Aristotle (1991). *The Metaphysics*. Buffalo, NY, Prometheus Books.

Augustine, S. (1961). *Confessions*. London, Penguin Books.

Augustine, S. (2000). *Soliloquies: Augustine's Inner Dialogue*. New York, New City Press.

Balsamo, A. M. (1996). *Technologies of the Gendered Body: Reading Cyborg Women*. Durham, NC, Duke University Press.

Bardon, A. (2005). 'Performative Transcendental Arguments.' *Philosophia* 33(1): 69–95.

Barnes, J. (2001). *Early Greek Philosophy*. London, Penguin Books.

Becker, K. L. (2001). *Unlikely Companions: C. G. Jung on the Spiritual Exercises of Ignatius of Loyola*. Leominster, Gracewing/Inigo Enterprises.

Bell, D. and B. M. Kennedy (2000). *The Cybercultures Reader*. London, Routledge.

Berger, P. L. and T. Luckmann (1967). *The Social Construction of Reality: A Treatise in the Sociology of Knowledge.* London, Penguin.

Beyer, C. (2011). 'Edmund Husserl.' In: E. N. Zalta (ed.) *The Stanford Encyclopedia of Philosophy (winter)*. Available at: http://plato.stanford.edu/archives/win2011/entries/husserl/.

Black, M. (1954). 'Metaphor.' *Proceedings of the Aristotelian Society* 55: 273–294.

Blackmore, S. J. (2005). *Consciousness: A Very Short Introduction*. Oxford, Oxford University Press.

Blackmore, S. J. (2006). *Conversations on Consciousness: What the Best Minds Think About the Brain, Free Will, and What It Means to Be Human*. Oxford, Oxford University Press.

Boghossian, P. (2006). *Fear of Knowledge*. Oxford, Oxford University Press.

Bordo, S. (1986). 'The Cartesian Masculinization of Thought.' *Signs* 11(3): 439–456.

Bordo, S. (1987). *The Flight to Objectivity: Essays on Cartesianism and Culture*. Albany, NY, State University of New York Press.

Brentano, F. C. (1995). *Psychology from an Empirical Standpoint*. London, Routledge.

Brooke, R. (1991). *Jung and Phenomenology*. London, Routledge.

Brooke, R. (2000). 'Jung's Recollection of the Life World.' In: R. Brooke (ed.) *Pathways into the Jungian World*. London, Routledge.

Brown, D. J. (2006). *Descartes and the Passionate Mind.* Cambridge, Cambridge University Press.

Butler, J. (1990). *Gender Trouble: Feminism and the Subversion of Identity.* New York, Routledge.

Carman, T. (1999). 'The Body in Husserl and Merleau-Ponty.' *Philosophical Topics* 27(2): 205–226.

Carriero, J. (2009). *Between Two Worlds: A Reading of Descartes's Meditations.* Princeton, NJ, Princeton University Press.

Casey, E. S. (2000). *Imagining: A Phenomenological Study.* Bloomington, IN, Indiana University Press.

Cottingham, J. (1985). 'Cartesian Trialism.' *Mind* 94(374): 218–230.

Cottingham, J. (2005). *The Spiritual Dimension: Religion, Philosophy, and Human Value.* Cambridge, Cambridge University Press.

Cottingham, J. (2006). 'Spiritual *Askesis* in Cartesian Philosophy.' In: C. Condren, S. Gaukroger and I. Hunet (eds) *The Philosopher in Early Modern Europe: The Nature of a Contested Identity.* Cambridge, Cambridge University Press.

Crowell, S. G. (2005). 'Heidegger and Husserl: The Matter and Method of Philosophy.' In: H. L. Dreyfus and M. A. Wrathall (eds) *A Companion to Heidegger.* Oxford, Blackwell.

Cunning, D. (2011). 'Descartes' Modal Metaphysics.' In: E. N. Zalta (ed.) *The Stanford Encyclopedia of Philosophy (summer).* Available at: http://plato.stanford.edu/archives/sum2011/entries/descartes-modal/.

Dale, E. (2009). 'An Introduction to the Horizon Model: An Alternative to Universalist Frameworks of Mystical Development.' *Sophia* 48(3): 281–298.

Daston, L. and P. Galison (2010). *Objectivity.* New York, Zone Books.

de Beauvoir, S. (1949). *Le Deuxième Sexe: Les faits et les mythes.* Paris, Gallimard.

Derrida, J. (1981). *Writing and Difference.* London, Routledge & Kegan Paul.

Descartes, R. (1701). 'Recherche de la vérité par les lumières naturelles.' Texte de l'édition V. Cousin. Available at: http://disparates.org/lun/2011/05/recherche-de-la-verite-par-les-lumieres-naturelles/.

Descartes, R. (1984). *The Philosophical Writings of Descartes,* vol. II. New York, Cambridge University Press.

Descartes, R. (1985). *The Philosophical Writings of Descartes,* vol. I. New York, Cambridge University Press.

Descartes, R. (1991). *The Philosophical Writings of Descartes,* vol. III. *The Correspondence.* Cambridge, Cambridge University Press.

Deutscher, P. (2003). 'Between East and West and the Politics of "Cultural Ingénuité".' *Theory, Culture and Society* 20(3): 65–75.

Di Pippo, A. F. (2000). 'The Concept of Poiesis in Heidegger's An Introduction to Metaphysics.' In: *Thinking Fundamentals, IWM Junior Visiting Fellows Conferences* vol. 9, Vienna.

Domenjo, B. A. (2000). 'Thoughts on the Influence of Brentano and Comte on Freud's Work.' *Psychoanalysis and History* 2: 110–118.

Farias, V., J. Margolis, T. Rockmore (1991). *Heidegger and Nazism.* Philadelphia, Temple University Press.

Feenberg, A. and A. Hannay (1995). *Technology and the Politics of Knowledge.* Bloomington, IN, Indiana University Press.

Flynn, B. (2011). 'Maurice Merleau-Ponty.' In: E. N. Zalta (ed.) *The Stanford Encyclopedia of Philosophy (fall)*. Available at: http://plato.stanford.edu/archives/fall2011/entries/merleau-ponty/.

Foster, J. (1991). *The Immaterial Self: A Defence of the Cartesian Dualist Conception of the Mind*. London, Routledge.

Galdston, I. (1944). 'Descartes and Modern Psychiatric Thought.' *Isis* 35(2): 118–128.

Gaukroger, S. (1995). *Descartes: An Intellectual Biography*. Oxford, Oxford University Press.

Gaukroger, S. (2006). *The Emergence of Scientific Culture: Science and the Shaping of Modernity 1210–1685*. Oxford, Oxford University Press.

Gay, V. 2009. *Neuroscience and Religion: Brain, Mind, Self, and Soul.* Lantham, MD, Lexington Books.

Goenka, S. N. (2007). *The Discourse Summary*. Maharashtra, Vipassana Research Institute.

Gray, F. (2008). *Jung, Irigaray, Individuation*. London, Routledge.

Hadot, P. (1995). *Philosophy as a Way of Life*. Malden, MA, Blackwell Publishing.

Hatfield, G. (1986). 'The Senses and the Fleshless Eye: The *Meditations* as Cognitive Exercises.' In: A. O. Rorty (ed.) *Essays on Descartes' Meditations*. Berkeley, CA, University of California Press.

Hegel, G. W. F. (1977). *Phenomenology of Spirit*. Oxford, Oxford University Press.

Heidegger, M. (1962). *Being and Time*. Oxford, Blackwell.

Heidegger, M. (1977). *Questions Concerning Technology.* New York, HarperCollins.

Heidegger, M. (1982). *The Basic Problems of Phenomenology*. Bloomington, IN, Indiana University Press.

Heidegger, M. (2001). *Poetry, Language, Thought*. New York, Perennial Classics.

Heinämaa, S. (2003a). *Toward a Phenomenology of Sexual Difference: Husserl, Merleau-Ponty, Beauvoir*. Lanham, MD, Rowman & Littlefield.

Heinämaa, S. (2003b). 'The Living Body and its Position in Metaphysics: Merleau-Ponty's Dialogue with Descartes.' In: D. H. Zahavi, S. Ruin, and H. Dordrecht (eds) *Metaphysics, Facticity, Interpretation: Phenomenology in the Nordic countries*. Dordrecht, Kluwer Academic Publishers.

Heyes, C. J. (2007). *Self-Transformations: Foucault, Ethics, and Normalised Bodies*. Oxford, Oxford University Press.

Hills, D. (2011). 'Metaphor.' In: E. N. Zalta (ed.) *The Stanford Encyclopedia of Philosophy (winter)*. In: E. N. Zalta (Ed.). http://plato.stanford.edu/archives/win2011/entries/metaphor/

Hintikka, J. (1962). 'Cogito, Ergo Sum: Inference or Performance?' *The Philosophical Review* 71(1): 3–32.

Hobbes, T. (1962). De Corpore, Part 2, Chapter 11, 'Of Identity and Difference.' In: R. S. Peters (ed.) *Thomas Hobbes. Body, Man, and Citizen*. New York, Collier Books.

Husserl, E. (1931). *Ideas: General Introduction to Pure Phenomenology*. London, Allen and Unwin.

Husserl, E. (1964). *The Idea of Phenomenology*. Dordrecht, Kluwer Academic Publishers.

Husserl, E. (1970). *The Crisis of European Sciences and Transcendental Phenomenology: An Introduction to Phenomenological Philosophy*. Evanston, IL, Northwestern University Press.

Husserl, E. (1982). *Ideas Pertaining to a Pure Phenomenology and to a Phenomenological Philosophy. First Book: General Introduction to a Pure Phenomenology*. The Hague, Martinus Nijhoff.

Husserl, E. (1989). *Ideas Pertaining to a Pure Phenomenology and to a Phenomenological Philosophy. Second Book: Studies in the Phenomenology of Constitution*. Dordrecht, Kluwer Academic.

Husserl, E. (1999). *Cartesian Meditations: An Introduction to Phenomenology*. Dordrecht, Kluwer Academic Publishers

Husserl, E. (2001 (1901)). *The Shorter Logical Investigations*. London, Routledge.

Ignatius of Loyola (1522–1523 (1914)). *The Spiritual Exercises*. New York, PJ Kennedy.

Ihde, D. (2010). *Heidegger's Technologies: Postphenomenological Perspectives*. New York, Fordham University Press.

Irigaray, L. (1985). *Speculum of the Other Woman*. Ithaca, NY, Cornell University Press.

Irigaray, L. (2004). *The Way of Love*. New York, Continuum.

Irigaray, L. (2008). *Sharing the World*. New York, Continuum.

Iyengar, G. (1998). *Yoga: A Gem for Women*. New Delhi, Allied Publishers.

Iyengar, B. K. S. (2001). *Light on Yoga*. London, Thorsons.

Iyengar, B. K. S. (2006). *Light on Life*. PA, Rodale.

James, W. (1916; originally published in 1902). *The Varieties of Religious Experience*. New York, Longmans, Green.

Jantzen, G. (1995). *Power, Gender, and Christian Mysticism*. Cambridge, Cambridge University Press.

Johansson, I. (2003). 'Performatives and Antiperformatives.' *Linguistics and Philosophy* 26(6): 661–702.

Jung, C. G. (1938). *Psychology and Religion*. New Haven, CT, Yale University Press.

Jung, C. G. (1954). *The Practice of Psychotherapy*. London, Routledge and Kegan Paul.

Jung, C. G. (1966). *Two Essays on Analytical Psychology*. London, Routledge and Princeton, Princeton University Press.

Jung, C. G. (1967). *Symbols of Transformation*. London, Routledge and Princeton, Princeton University Press.

Jung, C. G. (1968). *The Archetypes of the Collective Unconscious*. Princeton, NJ, Princeton University Press.

Jung, C. G. (1971). *Psychological Types*. London, Routledge and Princeton, Princeton University Press.

Jung, C. G. (1972). *The Structure and Dynamics of the Psyche*. London, Routledge & Kegan Paul.

Jung, C. G. (1976). *C. G. Jung Letters 1951–1961*. London, Routledge & Kegan Paul.

Jung, C. G. (1978). *Psychology and the East*. Princeton, NJ, Princeton University Press.

Jung, C. G. (2009). *The Red Book: Liber Novus*. New York, W. W. Norton.

Kittay, E. F. (1984). 'The Identification of Metaphor.' *Synthese* 58(2): 153–202.

Lagerlund, H. (2011). 'Mental Representation in Medieval Philosophy.' In: E. N. Zalta (ed.) *The Stanford Encyclopedia of Philosophy (spring)*. Available at: http://plato.stanford.edu/archives/spr2011/entries/representation-medieval/.

Lang, B. (1988). 'Descartes and the Art of Meditation.' *Philosophy and Rhetoric* 21(1): 19–37.

Lau, J. and M. Deutsch (2010). 'Externalism About Mental Content.' In: E. N. Zalta (ed.) *The Stanford Encyclopedia of Philosophy (fall)*. Available at: http://plato.stanford.edu/archives/fall2010/entries/content-externalism/.

Lavery, J. (2007). "Philosophical Genres and Literary Forms: A Mildly Polemical Introduction." *Poetics Today* 28(2): 171–189.

Lewis, D. (1970). 'General Semantics.' *Synthese* 22(1): 18–67.

Luft, S. (1998). 'Husserl's Phenomenological Discovery of the Natural Attitude.' *Continental Philosophy Review* 31(2): 153–170.

Machamer, P. and J. E. McGuire (2009). *Descartes's Changing Mind*. Princeton, NJ, Princeton University Press.

Markie, P. (1992). 'The Cogito and its Importance.' In: J. Cottingham (ed.) *The Cambridge Companion to Descartes*. Cambridge, Cambridge University Press.

Martin, R. and J. Barresi (2008). *The Rise and Fall of Soul and Self: An intellectual History of Personal Identity*. New York, Columbia University Press.

Merchant, C. (1989). *The Death of Nature: Women, Ecology, and the Scientific Revolution*. New York, Harper & Row.

Merleau-Ponty, M. (1962). *Phenomenology of Perception*. London, Routledge.

Merleau-Ponty, M. (1968). *The Visible and the Invisible*. Evanston, IL, Northwestern University Press.

Mohanty, J. N. (1995). 'The Development of Husserl's Thought.' In: B. Smith and D. Woodruff Smith (eds) *The Cambridge Companion to Husserl*. Cambridge, Cambridge University Press.

Molles, M. C. (2010). *Ecology: Concepts and Applications*. Boston, MA, McGraw-Hill.

Mook, B. (2000). 'Phenomenology, Analytical Psychology, and Play Therapy.' In: R. Brooke (ed.) *Pathways into the Jungian World*. London, Routledge.

Moran, D. V. (1966). '"The Inaugural Address: Brentano's Thesis." Inaugural Address to the Joint Session of the Aristotelian Society and the Mind Association.' *Proceedings of the Aristotelian Society Supplementary* LXX: 1–27.

Moran, D. (2005). *Edmund Husserl: Founder of Phenomenology*. Cambridge, Polity.

Naess, A. (1985). 'The World of Concrete Contents.' *Inquiry* 28(1–4): 417–428.

Nagel, T. (1974). 'What is it like to be a bat?.' *Philosophical Review* 83, 435–450.

Nagy, M. (1991). *Philosophical Issues in the Psychology of C. G. Jung*. Albany, NY, State University of New York Press.

Nietzsche, F. W. (1999). *Thus Spake Zarathustra* (trans. Hollingdale). London, Penguin Books.

Pattison, G. (2005). *Thinking about God in an Age of Technology*. Oxford, Oxford University Press.

Pietersma, H. (1979). 'Husserl and Heidegger.' *Philosophy and Phenomenological Research* 40(2): 194–211.

Plumwood, V. (1993). *Feminism and the Mastery of Nature*. London, Routledge.

Plumwood, V. (2002). *Environmental Culture: The Ecological Crisis of Reason*. London, Routledge.

Plutarch. (75 CE). 'Theseus.' Available at: http://classics.mit.edu/Plutarch/theseus.html.

Ricklefs, R. E. and G. L. Miller (2000). *Ecology*. New York, W. H. Freeman.

Robinson, H. (2009). 'Dualism.' In: E. N. Zalta (ed.) *The Stanford Encylopedia of Philosophy (winter)*. Available at: http://plato.stanford.edu/archives/win2011/entries/dualism/.

Romanyshyn, R. (2000). 'Alchemy and the Subtle Body of Metaphor.' In: R. Brooke (ed.) *Pathways into the Jungian World*. London, Routledge.

Rorty, A. O. (1983). 'Experiments in Philosophic Genre: Descartes' "Meditations".' *Critical Inquiry* 9(3): 545–564.

Rowland, S. (2005). *Jung as a Writer*. London, Routledge.

Rozemond, M. (1998). *Descartes' Dualism.* Oxford, Oxford University Press.

Rubidge, B. (1990). 'Descartes's Meditations and Devotional Meditations.' *Journal of the History of Ideas* 51(1), 27–49.

Said, E. W. (2003). *Orientalism.* London, Penguin.

Schneider, S. (2009). '*Mindscan:* Transcending the Human Brain.' In: S. Schneider. (ed.) *Science Fiction and Philosophy.* Malden, MA, Wiley-Blackwell.

Searle, J. R. (2008). 'Language and Social Ontology.' *Theory and Society* 37(5): 443–459.

Shamdasani, S. (2003). *Jung and the Making of Modern Psychology.* Cambridge, Cambridge University Press.

Shamdasani, S. (2005). *Jung Stripped Bare by his Biographers, Even.* London, Karnac.

Shelley, M. (1818). *Frankenstein.* New York, Bantam Books.

Shusterman, R. (2008). *Body Consciousness: A Philosophy of Mindfulness and Somaesthetics.* Cambridge, Cambridge University Press.

Soskice, J. M. (1985). *Metaphor and Religious Language.* Oxford, Clarendon Oxford University Press.

Speaks, J. (2011). 'Theories of Meaning.' In: E. N. Zalta (ed.) *The Stanford Encyclopedia of Philosophy (summer).* Available at: http://plato.stanford.edu/archives/sum2011/entries/meaning/.

Stohrer, W. J. (1979). 'Descartes and Ignatius Loyola: La Flèche and Manresa Revisited.' *Journal of the History of Philosophy* 17(1): 11.

Sylvan, R. (1985). *A Critique of Deep Ecology.* Canberra, Australian National University, Department of Philosophy.

Toadvine, T. and L. E. Embree (Eds) (2002). *Merleau-Ponty's Reading of Husserl.* Dordrecht, Kluwer Academic Publishers.

Tomhave, A. (2010). 'Cartesian Intuitions, Humean Puzzles, and the Buddhist Conception of the Self.' *Philosophy East and West* 60(4): 443–457.

Vendler, Z. (1989). 'Descartes' Exercises.' *Canadian Journal of Philosophy* 19(2): 193–224.

Walker, M. B. (2011). 'Becoming Slow: Philosophy, Reading, and the Essay.' In: G. R. Oppy and N. Trakakis (eds) *The Antipodean Philosopher.* Lanham, MD, Lexington Books.

Young, I. M. (1990a). *Justice and the Politics of Difference.* Princeton, NJ, Princeton University Press.

Young, I. M. (1990b). *Throwing Like a Girl and Other Essays in Feminist Philosophy and Social Theory.* Bloomington, IN, Indiana University Press.

Zahavi, D. (2002). 'Merleau Ponty on Husserl: A Reappraisal.' In: T. Toadvine and L. E. Embree (Eds) *Merleau-Ponty's Reading of Husserl.* Dordrecht, Kluwer Academic Publishers.

Zahavi, D. (2003). *Husserl's Phenomenology.* Stanford, CA, Stanford University Press.

Zahavi, D. (Ed.) (2010). 'The "Absolute" in Husserl's Transcendental Project: A Question of Method, Metaphysics or Manifestation?' In: C. Ierna, H. Jacobs and F. Mattens (Eds) *Philosophy, Phenomenology, Sciences: Essays in Commemoration of Husserl.* Dordrecht, Phaenomenologica Springer.

Zahavi, D., S. Heinämaa, H. Ruin. (2003). *Metaphysics, Facticity, Interpretation: Phenomenology in the Nordic Countries.* Dordrecht, Kluwer Academic Publishers.

Zaldivar, E. E. (2011). 'Descartes's Theory of Substance: Why He was Not a Trialist.' *British Journal for the History of Philosophy* 19(3): 395–418.

Index